REINVESTING IN FAMILIES

Strengthening Child Welfare Practice for a Brighter Future

Voices from the Prairies

REINVESTING IN FAMILIES

Strengthening Child Welfare Practice for a Brighter Future

Voices from the Prairies

edited by

Dorothy Badry, Don Fuchs,
H. Monty Montgomery, and Sharon McKay

University of Regina Press

Production of *Reinvesting in Families: Strengthening Child Welfare Practice for a Brighter Future: Voices from the Prairies* has been made possible through funding the Alberta Centre for Child, Family & Community Research (ACCFCR). The views expressed herein do not necessarily represent the views of ACCFCR or those of the editors. Every reasonable effort has been made to secure necessary permissions, but errors or omissions should be brought to the attention of Dorothy Badry at badry@ucalgary.ca.

Suggested Citation: Badry, D., Fuchs, D., Montgomery, H., & McKay, S. (Eds.). (2014). *Reinvesting in Families: Strengthening Child Welfare Practice for a Brighter Future: Voices from the Prairies.* Regina, SK: University of Regina Press.

Cover Illustration: "Happy Family" by Paci77/iStockPhoto
Cover Design: Duncan Campbell
Text Design: John van der Woude Designs
Editor for the Press: Donna Grant
Index: Patricia Furdek, Ottawa

Printed and bound in Canada by Friesens. This book is printed on 100% post-consumer recycled paper.

Library and Archives Canada Cataloguing in Publication
Cataloguing in Publication (CIP) data available at the Library and Archives Canada web site: www.collectionscanada.gc.ca and at http://www.uofrpress.ca/publications/Reinvesting-in-Families

The University of Regina Press acknowledges the support of the Creative Industry Growth and Sustainability program, made possible through funding provided to the Saskatchewan Arts Board by the Government of Saskatchewan through the Ministry of Parks, Culture, and Sport. We acknowledge the financial support of the Government of Canada through the Canada Book Fund for our publishing activities. We acknowledge the support of the Canada Council for the Arts for our publishing program. This publication was made possible through a Creative Saskatchewan Production Grant.

*This book is dedicated to those whose voices cry out for families,
communities, and human rights in a world with many hurts. To
those who seek a path for children grounded in care, community,
compassion, and belief in the resilience of the human spirit.*

Contents

ix   Foreword · *Margaret Kovach*

xiii   From the Editors

xvii   Acknowledgements

xix   INTRODUCTION: Offering Hope for Families · *Dorothy Badry*

1   CHAPTER 1: The PCWC Story: A Remarkable Collaborative Effort across Provincial, Jurisdictional, and Cultural Boundaries · *Sharon McKay*

21   CHAPTER 2: The FASD Community of Practice Project: Promising Practices for Children in Care with Fetal Alcohol Spectrum Disorder: A Model for Casework Practice · *Dorothy Badry, William Pelech, and Denise Milne*

45   CHAPTER 3: The Edmonton Model for Improving Delivery of Health-care Services for Children and Families in Care through Pediatric Case Management · *Tami Masterson*

63   CHAPTER 4: Hearing their Voices: The Experiences of Women with High-risk Substance Misuse Involved with Mentoring Programs to Prevent FASD · *Linda Burnside*

87   CHAPTER 5: Determinants of Mental Health Difficulties among Young Aboriginal Children Living Off-reserve · *Christine Werk, Xinjie Cui, and Suzanne Tough*

111   CHAPTER 6: Research *with*, not *on*: Community-based Aboriginal Health Research through the "Voices and PHACES" Study · *Amrita Roy, Wilfreda Thurston, Lynden (Lindsay) Crowshoe, David Turner, and Bonnie Healy*

133   CHAPTER 7: The Youth Restorative Action Project: Evaluating Effectiveness as a Youth-run Program · *Elly Park, Katie Gutteridge, Auralia Brooke, and Erik Bisanz*

155   CHAPTER 8: Outcomes-based Service Delivery (OBSD): The Process and Outcomes of Collaboration · *Susan Gardiner, Bruce MacLaurin, and Jon Reeves*

183   CHAPTER 9: The Voices of Youth with Fetal Alcohol Spectrum Disorder Transitioning from Care: What Child Welfare Agencies and Youth Practitioners Need to Know · *Don Fuchs and Linda Burnside*

201   CHAPTER 10: Community Networking for Social Change: A Promising Practice for Aboriginal Child Welfare · *Judy Gillespie, Georgina Supernault, and Miriam Abel*

221   CHAPTER 11: What Albertan Adults Know aboutFetal Alcohol Spectrum Disorders (FASD) · *Cecilia Bukutu, Tara Hanson, and Suzanne Tough*

243   CHAPTER 12: Collaboration or Competition? Generalist or Specialized? Challenges Facing Social Work Education and Child Welfare · *William Pelech, Rick Enns, and Don Fuchs*

263   Epilogue · *H. Monty Montgomery*

267   Abstracts
277   Contributors
287   Subject Index
295   Author Index

Foreword

It was on one of those sleepy afternoons during a mid-term university class that Bertha Capen Reynolds, that radical, strength-based social worker, orbited into my consciousness. It was through a reading in an undergraduate social work class at the University of Regina. I remember little of the lecture, the conversations, nor the topic of the day—in fact, much is hazy. What I do remember is a perceptual shift followed by an awakening, the aha, the click, the connection. In her social work voice and from her quite different place than mine—she an American radical social worker in the red-baiting era of 1950s McCarthyism—Bertha Capen Reynolds (1963) specifically named social work and inexorably bound it with social justice. She wrote, "In such a titanic world struggle for human welfare, it is vastly important how we do our work, ministering to individuals and groups while the battle for social justice goes on" (p. 293). She went on to accentuate the significance of the daily practice choices we make. "It is in seemingly small things that we learn how to serve democracy and the good life through our profession. We are defeated and rise again to fight the harder" (p. 293).

After that class, I sought out more writings by Capen Reynolds, purchasing her 1963 published book, *An Uncharted Journey*—a capstone memoir charting her 50 years in social work. Non-temporal and soulful, but perfectly concrete, she put words to my unarticulated hopes. As a young, Aboriginal, prairie social work student in the 1980s I hungered for a kind of social work that through the promise of practice and "the passion for action" (McKay, Fuchs, & Brown, 2009, p. xi) was restorative, not remedial. I held my breath for a social work vocation that served societal justice in its philosophy and served justly in its practice. I had expectations. I didn't think it would be that hard.

Twenty-five (or so) years later I find myself with a weariness that has come with watching social work grow weary itself from persevering within a society that rewards those who power the economic engine and pays much less attention to those attending to the marginalized. At the same time I have watched social work, as a profession, burdened by its own complicity, participating in actions that further compromise those it seeks to serve. As it applies to Aboriginal children and families, this statement is confirmed time and again. According to Cindy Blackstock (2003), an advocate on behalf of First Nations children, there are currently three times more Aboriginal children in state care than at the height of residential schools. In the November 2013 Special Report of the British Columbia Representative for Children and Youth, Mary Ellen Turpel-Lafond could not be more declarative regarding provincial ministry of child and family service expenditures on Aboriginal child welfare: "More than $66 million has been spent without any functional public policy framework, no meaningful financial or performance accountability, and without any actual children receiving additional services because of these expenditures" (p. 5). Increasingly, Aboriginal parenting has been outsourced to foster care while monies being allocated to support Aboriginal families are usurped within a labyrinth of bureaucracy. Questions resound: "How did this happen?" "Who is being served?"

With stark evidence of a complicated present before me, I reflected upon the contributions in this book and thought about the possibilities for social work practice and why it is, as Capen Reynolds writes, "vastly important how we do our work" (1963, p. 293). *Reinvesting in Families: Strengthening Child Welfare Practice for a Brighter Future: Voices from the Prairies* showcases social workers actively involved in a range of social work capacities. Titles in this collection lift off the page—"Community Networking," "Promising Practice," "Hearing their Voices"—and evoke the varied landscape of social work practice with children and families. Researchers, practitioners, educators, community developers, and individual authors in this collection share their stories of what it means not only to serve, but to serve *collaboratively*, representing social work in relational action.

Collaborative approaches that nurture supportive relationships hold the potential to shift social work from an hierarchical, individualistic enterprise to a more lateral, collective endeavour. In doing so, "power *over*" lessens and "power *with*" is animated. Collaborative practices interrupt isolation and create potential for mutuality. How social workers go about the "small" acts of daily practice influences the profession and says much about how social work is perceived. If social workers so choose there can be a pause to remember that, when practiced in the spirit of Dr. Martin Luther King's call to conscience and a "dangerous unselfishness" (2001, p. 217), social work has the potential to serve justly. In seeing practice through the minds and hearts of those who are being served and finding time for comforting and discomforting conversations, social work can collaboratively, and radically, reimagine itself. The contributions in the fourth volume of the Prairie Child Welfare Consortium Series offer readers an opportunity to think about collaborative, relational practice, to remember who it is that social workers serve, and to find the way back to a Bertha Capen Reynolds kind of social work. It is worth the read.

Margaret Kovach, Department of Educational Foundations
College of Education, University of Saskatchewan

References

Blackstock, C. (2003). First Nations child and family services: Restoring peace and harmony in First Nations communities. In K. Kufeldt & B. McKenzie (Eds.), *Child welfare: Connecting research, policy and practice* (331–342). Waterloo, ON: Wilfred Laurier Press.

Capen Reynolds, B. (1963). *An Uncharted Journey*. New York: Citadel Press.

King, Martin Luther, Jr. (2001). I've been to the mountaintop. In C. Clayborne & K. Shepard (Eds.), *A call to conscience: The landmark speeches of Dr. Martin Luther King, Jr.* (pp. 207–223). New York: Warner Books.

McKay, S., Fuchs, D., & Brown, I. (Eds.). (2009). *Passion for action in child and family services: Voices from the prairies.* Regina, SK: Canadian Plains Research Center.

Turpel-Lafond, M. (2013). *When talk trumped service: A decade of lost opportunity for Aboriginal children and youth in B.C.* (Special Report). Victoria: Representative for Children and Youth.

From the Editors

We are very pleased to bring you this book, *Reinvesting in Families: Strengthening Child Welfare Practice for a Brighter Future: Voices from the Prairies*. The book is the fourth publication of the Prairie Child Welfare Consortium (PCWC) and is strongly supported by the Faculties of Social Work at the University of Calgary, University of Manitoba, University of Regina, and the Alberta Centre for Child, Family and Community Research (ACCFCR).

The chapters in the book represent a selection of some of the outstanding presentations made at the Prairie Child Welfare Consortium's sixth biennial symposium, "Reinvesting in Families: Strengthening Child Welfare Practice for a Brighter Future," held May 28–30, 2012, in Edmonton, Alberta. Individuals attending previous PCWC symposia (Saskatoon, 2001; Winnipeg, 2003; Edmonton, 2005; Regina, 2007; and Winnipeg, 2009) emphasized the great importance of sharing information about programs, policies, and initiatives found to be supportive and effective when working with at-risk children and families. Also, individuals attending previous symposia have emphasized the urgent need to reawaken the passion for action to reduce the growing rates of child maltreatment and increased number of children coming into care. The

past symposia have highlighted the need for the development of innovative programs based on Indigenous knowledge and methods. In addition, they have pointed to the need to develop evidence-based practice
to ensure that well-intentioned policy, programs, and intervention do no
harm, but continue to evolve to provide effective services to children and
families at risk for child maltreatment.

The 2012 symposium highlighted strengths-based, preventative, and
early intervention approaches to support at-risk children and families.
Research and innovative programs, projects, and practices that are making a difference were featured. Special emphasis was placed on supporting vulnerable families due to the overrepresentation of poor and
marginalized children and families in Canada's child welfare system.
Many presenters emphasized that family stability has positive effects on
child health, behaviour, academic achievement, social skill development,
and emotional functioning. Children experience stability when they have
mentally healthy caregivers who engage in appropriate parenting practices and provide supportive, nurturing, and consistent home environments. In addition, the symposium emphasized the point that protective
factors that reduce risk to vulnerable children and families also include
parental employment, adequate housing, and access to health care and
social services. Many presenters emphasized that reinvesting in families
requires increasing access to these resources.

Resources need to be invested or reallocated to support and strengthen
families. Securing a brighter future requires co-operation and collaborative planning between child welfare and other systems to better serve and
support families. Major efforts must be undertaken to bring creative collaborations across disciplines and sectors to address family stress issues.
The "Reinvesting in Families" event appealed to cross-sectoral, multidisciplinary service providers, educators, health-care providers, social
workers, government and agency staff, policy-makers, and researchers
concerned about child and family well-being.

Holding to the conference theme, and the PCWC desire to provide
educational resources to practitioners, conference planners incorporated a day of training workshops for participants, an event widely
appreciated. Significantly, the planners also provided a pre-conference
day for Indigenous scholars and allies that drew about 100 participants. This meeting brought together academics, Elders, government

representatives, and practitioners involved in child welfare research and practice to share their ideas for moving child welfare forward, with a particular emphasis on Alberta. In their report on this meeting, the participants indicated that the presence of Indigenous scholars reaffirmed the perspective that "children are seen as gifts from the Creator, gifts to be cherished and cared for" by and within communities. Together the three conference days stimulated numerous informative, enthusiastic, and passionate exchanges between and among participants and presenters. This book has attempted to capture the spirit of innovation and sharing that would prompt an awareness of the need to reinvest in and provide support for families through the conference presentations and activities.

Consistent with the mandates of both the PCWC and ACCFCR, this book is intended to convey the work of presenters who were able to dedicate time and energy to the difficult task of presenting their experiences, ideas, and research in print form for publication purposes. The outstanding contributions that have resulted reflect the dedication, commitment, and passion of the authors. The first chapter of this book highlights the history of the PCWC and our efforts to bring together child welfare ministries from Alberta, Saskatchewan, and Manitoba and the respective universities in these provinces in a collaboration to develop and guide a child welfare focus in social work education. The need for training and courses focused on child welfare within social work education is a major focus of the PCWC. Our contention in this book is that respectful inquiry, action-based research, and innovative, community-based, culturally anchored approaches are necessary for bringing about transformative change in child and family serving systems. Such change is essential if Canada's children, youth, and families are to thrive and truly enjoy well-being.

The PCWC is a tri-provincial and northern multi-sector, cross-cultural child and family services network representing university educators, government, First Nations, and Métis in-service training and service delivery administrators. Members of the consortium and its network are dedicated to working together collaboratively for the purpose of strengthening and advancing education and training, policy, service delivery, and research in aid of children and families in need across the Prairie provinces. The development of the PCWC has been powerfully and fundamentally influenced by the urgent voices of Aboriginal people deeply concerned with the escalating numbers of their children and youth in the care of the state. This influence permeates the PCWC's vision, mission, and goals, which are directed towards ensuring that child and family services in the Prairie provinces and the North meet the needs of the children, families, and communities they support. Working together across many levels and sectors, PCWC partners seek to influence, advocate for, and change education, training, research, policy, and practice/service delivery through collaboration, innovation, and partnering. Ensuring respect for the needs of Aboriginal communities in the delivery of child welfare services is fundamental. In this quest, the PCWC seeks affiliation with other national child welfare bodies for joint initiatives that would further the PCWC mission and present a Prairie/Northern perspective at the national level.

It is the intention of the editors and the authors of this book to help strengthen the child welfare community in Canada by adding to its distinctive body of child welfare knowledge. Further, it is our hope that the perspectives contained within this book will help foster a renewed investment in providing research, policy, programs, and community resources that work to strengthen families and to provide safe and healthy environments for children to grow and thrive, free from the risks of maltreatment, in supportive cultural and community contexts.

Dorothy Badry, Faculty of Social Work, University of Calgary
Don Fuchs, Faculty of Social Work, University of Manitoba
H. Monty Montgomery, Faculty of Social Work, University of Regina
Sharon McKay, Faculty of Social Work, University of Regina (Emerita)

Acknowledgements

This book is a product of the effective collaboration amongst the Prairie Child Welfare Consortium partners. It would not have been possible without the contribution of many people and, as editors, we would like to thank each of them for their hard work and support. We must begin by acknowledging the outstanding contributions of the chapter authors, whose expertise, wisdom, and patience with the editing process have created a manuscript that will benefit the field of child welfare research and practice. The chapters reflect the breadth of the authors' considerable experiences as practitioners, program planners, and academics. Readers can learn more about the chapter authors in the "Contributors" section of the book.

The following persons served as peer reviewers and provided feedback and suggestions on the chapters. Their comments helped to sharpen the focus and the messages in each chapter, and we are sincerely grateful for their input: Jason Albert, Marlyn Bennett, Ivan Brown, Keith Brownlee, Linda Burnside, Peter Choate, Deborah Goodman, Therese Grant, Les Jerome, Bruce MacLaurin, Audrey MacFarlane, Pat Mackenzie, Gordon Martel, Pam Miller, Jay Rodgers, Cathy Rocke, Deb Rutman, Amy Salmon, Rebecca Stotzer, Caroline Tait, and Christine Walsh.

We are grateful to Bruce Walsh, director and publisher at University of Regina Press, who agreed to publish and distribute the hard copies of the book. We are greatly indebted to Donna Grant, senior editor at the press, for her wonderful support, encouragement, and amazing efforts and endless patience, and to Duncan Campbell, art director at the press, for the cover design, which complements the work he has done for the second and third books of the PCWC series. Copy editor Anne James meticulously corrected all the inconsistencies across chapter formats and contributed substantially to the overall quality of the book.

We wish to acknowledge the time and commitment of the planning committee members of the PCWC's Sixth Biennial Symposium held in Edmonton, Alberta, May 28–30, 2012. Particularly, we would like to acknowledge Tara Hanson and Aimee Caster of the Alberta Centre for Child, Family and Community Research (ACCFCR), Jean Lafrance, Faculty of Social Work, and Joanne Woloshyniuk, Métis Association of Alberta, for their work in organizing the Edmonton symposium. The presentations of the Edmonton symposium have formed the basis of the chapters contained in this book. We also acknowledge Maggie Kovach for writing the foreword to this fourth book in the PCWC series.

We wish to thank the Faculties of Social Work at the University of Calgary, University of Manitoba, and University of Regina for providing us with the encouragement and administrative infrastructure support to carry out much of the work of this book. The editors had valuable assistance from a number of people within their universities.

Finally, we would like to thank the Alberta Centre for Child, Family and Community Research for their contribution to the conference and the publication of this book. As well, we would like to thank the core partners of the Prairie Child Welfare Consortium and the Centre of Excellence for Child Welfare, listed below, for their cooperation and support.

Prairie Child Welfare Consortium
University of Manitoba, Faculty of Social Work
University of Calgary, Faculty of Social Work
University of Regina, Faculty of Social Work
Manitoba Family Services
Alberta Human Services
Saskatchewan Child and Family Services
Federation of Saskatchewan Indian Nations
Métis Association Alberta

Offering Hope for Families

Dorothy Badry

In the report *Reconciliation in Child Welfare: Touchstones of Hope for Indigenous Children, Youth and Families*, Cindy Blackstock and colleagues identified these guiding statements:

> *Build a united and mutually respectful system of child welfare capable of responding to the needs of all children and youth.... Affirm that all Indigenous children and youth have the right to family (nuclear and extended), safety, and well-being, and to be able to identify with, and thrive as, a member of their culture of origin....Respect the intrinsic right of Indigenous children, youth, and families to define their own cultural identity. (2006, p. 4)*

The Sixth Biennial Prairie Child Welfare Consortium Conference, "Reinvesting in Families: Strengthening Child Welfare Practice for a Brighter Future: Voices from the Prairies," was held in Edmonton,

Suggested Citation: Badry, D. (2014). Introduction: Offering hope for families. In D. Badry, D. Fuchs, H. Montgomery, & S. McKay (Eds.), *Reinvesting in Families: Strengthening Child Welfare Practice for a Brighter Future: Voices from the Prairies* (pp. xix–xxiv). Regina, SK: University of Regina Press.

Alberta, in 2012. Current trends in child welfare practice are shifting to recognize that the needs for family and cultural connectedness are crucial and have a lifelong impact. Engaging in child welfare work is one of the most daunting and challenging professions a social worker or allied health professional can undertake. The Prairie Child Welfare Consortium (PCWC) has collaborated to produce this fourth book emerging from the Edmonton conference.

The focus of the biennial PCWC symposium is to bring together child welfare professionals, allies, and scholars and provide a venue for engagement in critical dialogue on the complexities and collaborations involved in change. These symposia provide an opportunity to consider and appreciate the vulnerability of children in care, and to recognize the historical impact of colonization. The intergenerational aspect of this work is an important consideration in child welfare practice. Many children who come into care are there due to challenges their parents have with mental health, addictions, homelessness, and parenting skills. The challenges faced by families who for many reasons cannot care for their children or meet their basic needs often reflect their own impoverishment and struggles. The increasing prevalence of children in care with fetal alcohol spectrum disorder (FASD) is a direct result of ever-increasing rates of parental alcohol addiction and is a major concern for the child welfare system. Substance abuse remains a vexing problem that is not easily ameliorated.

As patterns in child welfare practice shift to consider the needs of children in care across the lifespan and to recognize that decisions made for children early in life have implications for the future, reinvesting in families is critical. One of the roles of the PCWC is to support culturally informed practice as a way of connecting to families and communities. The call for cultural connections to community remains clear, and it is hoped that the benefit of child welfare work today can contribute to the next generation growing up without the experience of being in care. Today, child welfare work is often complex, and the need for research on best practice has increased in an era when evidence-based practice is a factor shaping both policy and practice. One goal of *Reinvesting in Families* is to give voice to that important research.

The first chapter by Sharon McKay, a founding member of the PCWC, offers a critical history of the roots and growth of the PCWC and its role in bringing together mainstream and Aboriginal child welfare directors, practitioners, policy-makers, social work researchers, and educators to critically consider the state of child welfare practice in the Prairie provinces. McKay traces the complex historical context of Canadian child welfare, noting some of the factors leading to the somewhat fragile beginnings of the PCWC, which has since developed into a unique tri-provincial, multi-sector, and cross-cultural child welfare network in Canada dedicated to working together across the Prairie provinces to influence and promote best practice. Fundamental to the structure and processes of the consortium is respect for the needs of Aboriginal communities in the delivery of child welfare services. The chapter illustrates the remarkable development of the consortium given inherent tensions existing between and among the member organizations. Through tracing the history and present-day activities, and emphasizing the critical importance of respectful relationships and thoughtful communications, McKay sets the tone for this book and the role of the PCWC in supporting and influencing change in child welfare practice in the Prairie provinces.

In Chapter Two, Dorothy Badry, William Pelech, and Denise Milne report on "The FASD Community of Practice Project: Promising Practices for Children in Care with Fetal Alcohol Spectrum Disorder: A Model for Casework Practice." The Child and Family Service Authorities of Alberta Human Services in Alberta have been engaged in specialized supports for children and youth with FASD in care. The efforts made in Alberta to offer FASD specific training and intensive casework practice have shown positive benefit as voiced by caseworkers and foster parents through qualitative research on the FASD Community of Practice (2009–2011).

In Chapter Three, building on the theme of "reinvesting in families," Tami Masterson profiles the Edmonton–Pediatrics for Kids in Care (E-PKIC) program. This unique program ensures that children in care receive pediatric medical and dental assessments and follow-up care through a multidisciplinary team that includes a child and family services worker, a hospital social worker, a nurse, and a pediatrician—allowing them to make a remarkable difference by ensuring that children whose families often lack the capacity for follow-up due to social/emotional and financial barriers receive medical care that is sensitive to their vulnerabilities and protection needs.

In the fourth chapter, Linda Burnside reports on the experiences of women with a high risk for substance misuse who completed a three-year program aimed at preventing FASD. Burnside includes excerpts from the interviewees and she identifies various phases—Engagement, Discoveries through Mentoring, Change and Transformation, and Life after the Program—to show how these long-term programs support critical change for these women in their social/emotional health, in relationships, and in the reduction of substance abuse.

In Chapter Five, Christine Werk, Xinjie Cui, and Suzanne Tough report on a research-based study that examined the mental health determinants of young Aboriginal children living off-reserve through analysis of the findings of the Aboriginal Children's Survey (2006). The study makes possible a deeper understanding of the complex factors associated with mental health, including sleep, screen time (playing video games and television watching), and placement stability.

In the sixth chapter, the community-based approach and academic-community partnerships involved in the "Voices and PHACES" (Prenatal Health in Aboriginal Communities and EnvironmentS) project are highlighted in this report on a study of the phenomenon of prenatal depression and the contributing determinants for pregnant Aboriginal women. In this chapter, Amrita Roy, Wilfreda Thurston, Lindsay Crowshoe, David Turner, and Bonnie Healy reflect upon the importance and value of research that takes into consideration the First Nations principles of OCAP (ownership, control, access, and possession) and the need for respectful, meaningful research dissemination.

In Chapter Seven, Elly Park, Katie Gutteridge, Auralia Brooke, and Erik Bisanzon evaluate the effectiveness of Edmonton's Youth Restorative Action Project (YRAP). This project is youth-led and offers supports to vulnerable youth who engage in criminal activity and have harmed others. YRAP supports youth aged 15–25 who are involved in the criminal justice system through providing mentors in the community.

In Chapter Eight, Susan Gardiner, Bruce MacLaurin, and Jon Reeves examine outcomes-based service delivery (OBSD) as an important approach to child welfare protection work. A brief historical review of social policy and child welfare legislation provides the background to examine shifting child welfare practice and the development of the Alberta Response Model. This chapter highlights research on child welfare outcomes and identifies the need for ongoing reviews and re-evaluation of child welfare practice and OBSD that seeks to support children remaining in or returning to the community wherever possible.

In Chapter Nine, Don Fuchs and Linda Burnside note the increasing number of children in care with disabilities and highlight the challenges faced by youth with fetal alcohol spectrum disorder who have been in care. They are often unprepared for the transition to adulthood due to their cognitive disability, a transition made more difficult because they now lack the supports they received while in care. This chapter highlights strategies to support such transitions and clearly recommends the need for further research on the life trajectory of this young population.

In Chapter Ten, Judy Gillespie, Georgina Supernault, and Miriam Abel identify the values of multi-sector community networking — an approach that supports social change in similar fashion to the work of the Prairie Child Welfare Consortium. Respect for the Aboriginal life world and tradition is a foundation of this chapter. The Aboriginal Interagency Committee, established in Northwestern Alberta, and the Sisters in Spirit annual gatherings are profiled as examples of community networking.

In Chapter Eleven, Cecilia Bukutu, Tara Hanson, and Suzanne Tough report on research commissioned to the Alberta Centre for Child, Family and Community Research (ACCFCR) to assess the knowledge of fetal alcohol spectrum disorder (FASD) amongst Albertans. The survey indicated that 85% of Albertans over 18 had some awareness of FASD when asked, and an even higher proportion had basic knowledge that alcohol use in pregnancy can cause harm. The need to conduct similar surveys for those under age 18 was identified as an important future direction.

In the final chapter, William Pelech, Rick Enns, and Don Fuchs explore the need for schools of social work on the prairies to prepare social work practitioners with both generalist foundational and specialized knowledge and skills. The authors identify the work of the PCWC E-Learning Committee to illustrate how the online delivery of specialized courses is breaking down geographic and institutional barriers to assist in better preparing social workers with the knowledge and skills necessary for the challenges of today's complex child welfare settings.

A guiding theme throughout these chapters is a focus on reinvesting in families. It is now widely recognized that children raised in care often return in adulthood to their families and communities. Children return to their families out of a need to connect with culture and identity. Several chapters highlight the importance of family-focused work and consider the value of tradition and culture and the need to engage in respectful research. Concerns about the needs of children in care with fetal alcohol spectrum disorder were identified in three chapters, and best practices continue to develop. A focus on women's health is one of the most important aspects of prevention. Child welfare practice has become increasingly complex, and the need for training and learning for practitioners should begin while attending post-secondary education.

An ongoing emphasis of the consortium's biennial symposia and in the three publications prior to this book has been to identify and value the work of Aboriginal child welfare practice and to support and strengthen community-based work and research. This book highlights issues relevant to policy and practice that consider the needs of children and families while recognizing the often difficult balance between child protection needs and family autonomy. While an uneasy tension between children, families, and the child welfare system will always exist, the efforts of the PCWC in presenting research that is focused on promising practices and interventions is intended to offer hope and promote collaboration. The need to "reinvest in families" offers a critical imperative that moves us in a direction that is grounded in both culture and change going forward.

References

Blackstock, C., Cross, T., George, J., Brown, I., & Formsma, J. (2006). *Reconciliation in child welfare: Touchstones of hope for Indigenous children, youth and families.* Ottawa, ON: First Nations Child & Family Caring Society of Canada / Portland, OR: National Indian Child Welfare Association.

CHAPTER 1

The PCWC Story: A Remarkable Collaborative Effort across Provincial, Jurisdictional, and Cultural Boundaries

Sharon McKay

Introduction

The publication of this book occurs in the 13th year of collaborative activities taking place under the rubric of the Prairie Child Welfare Consortium (PCWC), a unique tri-provincial, multi-jurisdictional, multi-level, cross-cultural Aboriginal and mainstream voluntary network dedicated to the field of child welfare. One of the primary goals of the PCWC has been to establish a framework for communication, sharing knowledge, and best practice in child welfare in this part of Canada. The partnership that has emerged is a collective effort to share information, conduct research, and consult, collaborate, and partner with one another to enhance and strengthen child welfare service delivery, education and training, and research and policy development in the Prairie provinces. This chapter outlines the factors that spurred interest

Suggested Citation: McKay, S. (2014). The PCWC story: A remarkable collaborative effort across provincial, jurisdictional, and cultural boundaries. In D. Badry, D. Fuchs, H. Montgomery, & S. McKay (Eds.), *Reinvesting in Families: Strengthening Child Welfare Practice for a Brighter Future: Voices from the Prairies* (pp. 1–19). Regina, SK: University of Regina Press.

in bringing practitioners, service delivery agents, and university teachers and researchers together to talk about the potential for a collaborative child welfare initiative in the Prairie provinces.

This chapter traces the history, shaky beginning, steady development, and ongoing challenges of the PCWC over more than a decade. It is written from a personal perspective, my role in this initiative being that of a founding member and steering committee chair from late 1999 to the fall of 2011. The chapter is intended to provide a history and context for individuals and organizations that are taking part, or will take part, in the consortium's ongoing growth and development. It celebrates the accomplishments of the PCWC, while at the same time acknowledging the inherent frailty of an informal network dependent largely on goodwill, respectful relationships, and a shared vision. The work of the PCWC is shared between provincial child welfare leaders (Alberta, Saskatchewan, and Manitoba); the University of Manitoba, University of Regina, and University of Calgary Faculties of Social Work; the School of Indian Social Work, First Nations University of Canada; and Aboriginal partners represented by the Saskatchewan Federation of Indian Nations and the Métis Nation of Alberta.[1] The feature that stands out most prominently respecting the PCWC is the decades-long partnership across provincial, jurisdictional, and cultural boundaries.

Context: 'Setting the stage' for a Prairie Initiative

The UN Declaration of the Rights of the Child (1989) to which Canada was a signatory (1991) prompted several responses across the country such as provincial children's advocate appointments; development of the Centre of Excellence for Child Welfare; development of specialized bachelor of social work programs in British Columbia; and establishment of the Canadian Child Welfare League and the First Nations Child and Family Caring Society. Each of these initiatives drew attention to the number of children and youth deemed "at risk" of physical, emotional, or spiritual harm for reasons of social conditions such as poverty, addictions, and

---

1   The School of Indian Social Work at the First Nations University of Canada and
     the Métis Nation of Alberta are currently inactive.

health concerns (including poor health, poor nutrition, lack of access to services, and mental illness), all factors affecting their families and/or communities. The history of Aboriginal child welfare in Canada including jurisdictional, cultural, and professional issues further "set the stage" for the development of the PCWC and other bodies. This history reaches back to the 1867 Constitution Act, which divided federal and provincial responsibilities respecting Indian children and families: provincial governments were deemed responsible for child welfare except for children on reserves, who would be cared for by the federal government under the Department of Indian Affairs.

The tragic history of Aboriginal children forcibly removed from their families and communities to attend federally established residential schools and the ongoing legacy of residential schools, which operated from 1874 to 1996, is well-known and will not be repeated here. Patrick Johnston (1983) traces this history, including the role of provincial governments following a 1951 amendment to the Indian Act allowing provincial authorities the legal authority to enter reserve communities on matters of child welfare. This amendment led to a startling increase in the numbers of children being placed in foster care across Canada. More often than not, children were placed with non-Aboriginal foster parent families, far from the children's home community. Johnston notes that the phenomenon known as the "Sixties Scoop," whereby Indian children were adopted by non-Aboriginal families across Canada and internationally, had its genesis in the 1951 amendment. Federal/provincial jurisdictional disputes having to do with which jurisdiction will be responsible for the cost of various interventions continue to create barriers to delivering urgently needed services for children and families caught in the middle of arguments that are beyond their capacity to understand or do anything about. The heart of the joint declaration of support for "Jordan's Principle," adopted unanimously by the federal House of Commons in 2007, stems directly from recognition that jurisdictional disputes have seriously, and, in the case of young Jordan Rivers Anderson, tragically, impeded the delivery of urgently needed health services to Aboriginal children (First Nations Child and Family Caring Society). By the time of Johnston's study, escalating numbers of children were in the care of the state, the great majority of these being Aboriginal children and youth. These numbers have continued to grow and have been major factors influencing child welfare in the Prairie provinces.

Social Work and Preparation for Child Welfare Work

Related to the foregoing history, and also influential to the development of the PCWC, were concerns amongst social work educators that the profession, long held to be the lead profession in the child welfare field, was being questioned as to the readiness and competence of social work graduates to undertake front-line protection work. Several well-publicized deaths of children either in foster care or living in families in contact with child welfare agencies led to searing reports highly critical of the social work practitioners and agencies involved and of government policies that were viewed as faulty or inadequate. Media attention on these incidents was unrelentingly eviscerating (Callahan & Callahan, 2001).

Alongside of these reports, government and agency employers, worried about recruitment and retention challenges in the face of anticipated retirements and looming cutbacks, questioned whether social work education adequately prepares students for the field. Social work degree programs were criticized for what is viewed as the "lack of fit" between their curriculum and the needs of the agencies engaged in child protection work. Some administrators argued that bachelor's degree graduates in general Arts or other majors are equally qualified for front-line positions. Deans and directors of schools of social work across Canada discussed these issues, including options for strengthening child welfare curriculum within BSW degree programs. An informal survey of schools across the country, conducted by the deans and directors group, led to prairie-based discussions about the possibility of collaborative efforts to strengthen each school's child welfare curriculum.

At the same time as these discussions were being held, claims were made that the social work profession had participated actively in the removal of thousands of Aboriginal children from their families and communities, failing to acknowledge or understand systemic oppression of Aboriginal families and communities and failing to act with cultural sensitivity (Blackstock, Brown, & Bennett, 2007). These claims were moderated somewhat by Timpson (1995) based upon her extensive search of four decades of professional literature respecting child welfare and Native children. Regardless, all parties agree that the historical roots of colonialism and oppression of Canada's Aboriginal population had, in Timpson's words, created conditions that reflect "generations of cultural and spiritual destruction" (Timpson, 1995, p. 540). The generational impact of colonialism continues today, notably complicated by jurisdictional/cultural/political issues between provincial and federal authorities and First Nations governments and Aboriginal communities (Turpel-Lafond, 2013).

Hearing the Voices: The Spark that Launched the PCWC

The PCWC partnership grew from an invitational meeting held in late 2001 for the purpose of exploring ways and means to work together across the Prairie provinces on child welfare practice, policy, and research. The meeting, located in the Saskatchewan Indian Federated College in Saskatoon, Saskatchewan, was organized by representatives of the four university programs in social work education and the Alberta, Manitoba, and Saskatchewan provincial government departments delivering child welfare services. Documented in the first PCWC book, the meeting, dubbed as an occasion to "hear the voices," did not go as planned (McKay, 2007). Participants objected strongly to the tight agenda, leading to a quick decision to abandon plans for the second day, replacing these by a traditional Aboriginal sharing circle.

Over 100 participants spoke that day, many telling poignant, compassionate stories of first-hand experiences with the child welfare system, residential schools, and the phenomenon known as the "Sixties Scoop." Frustrations with government policies on child welfare, agency practices, and the ever-increasing numbers of children, primarily Aboriginal children, in foster and/or residential care were expressed. Many participants in the circle expressed despair. The event ended when all had spoken. There was no time for a proper wrap-up—people had to return to their homes and offices. There was no opportunity to develop a plan for working together. Organizers quickly agreed to hold a follow-up meeting, as each felt an urgent need to move forward together in some positive way on the ideas conveyed and challenges identified through the talking circle.

The energies stimulated by the unanticipated turn of events and the sharing circle that followed can be viewed as the spark needed to strengthen individual and organizational commitment to work together across jurisdictional, cultural, and professional boundaries towards the goal of ensuring that child welfare services in the Prairie provinces meet the needs of the children and families they support. Organizers believed that promoting education and training opportunities on child welfare practice and working collaboratively across provinces would support the vision of the PCWC to influence and promote best practice.

What has the PCWC Accomplished?

To date, the PCWC has held six biennial symposia, each featuring keynote speakers who have spoken passionately about the needs of troubled children, families, and communities. The focus of the biennial symposium has been to offer and disseminate a range of practice and/or research-based presentations pertinent to the field, with special emphasis on Aboriginal children and youth and their families, as this is central to our work. New additions to the conference structure in the 2009 and 2012 symposia include pre-conference training workshops and pre-conference meetings of Indigenous scholars and allies, focused on education and research pertinent to Aboriginal child welfare. The symposia have been attended by a broad sector of Aboriginal and mainstream practitioners, administrators, policy-makers, and researchers.

Also included in the list of accomplishments has been the successful delivery of web-based courses to social work students based in the three participating universities. Each course is focused on specialized topics not found on the regular curricula. The first of these, a University of Calgary course titled Residential Schools and Child Welfare, was offered in 2011 and served as a pilot project, informing the organizers of institutional needs and mechanisms for such matters as course outline approvals (via separate committees at each institution), course registration, calendar listing, electronic delivery mechanism, payment of student fees, record keeping, and registration of grades, among other matters. The successful delivery of this course, which has now been taught several times, has provided a template for the development of additional courses across the three universities.

A second University of Calgary course, Fetal Alcohol Spectrum Disorder (FASD) and Child Welfare Practice, was successfully delivered to 28 students from four provinces attending either the University of Calgary or the University of Manitoba. At the University of Manitoba, Addictions and

Child and Family Services Practice was offered in the Fall 2013 semester, and Crisis Intervention and Child Welfare was offered in Winter 2014. The FASD and Child Welfare Practice course was again offered in Summer 2014 across the three universities. To date, course enrollments have been approximately 30 students, 10 from each institution. Future course offerings will include space for a limited number of government and/or agency personnel in addition to university students. A draft agreement between participating universities is currently being reviewed, as is the possibility of developing a cross-university child welfare specialty within the regular bachelor of social work degree programs that would be based upon courses initiated and developed by the PCWC.

An important goal of the PCWC from its inception has been to conduct research pertinent to the field of child welfare practice. Research principles have been established, ideas have been shared, proposals have been written, and, thanks to the support of the Public Health Agency of Canada through the now defunct Centre of Excellence for Child Welfare, three major research projects have been conducted: Making Our Hearts Sing, a partnership project of the Alberta Ministry of Children's Services, the University of Calgary Faculty of Social Work, the Blood Reserve, the Sturgeon Lake Cree Nation, and Region 10 (Métis Settlements) Child and Family Services Authority (Lafrance & Bastien, 2007); The Transmission of Values project, developed and guided by Elders, community and agency representatives, and researchers from the First Nations University of Canada, School of Indian Social Work, and the Faculty of Social Work, University of Regina (McKay & Thomas Prokop, 2007); and Children with Disabilities Involved with the Child Welfare System in Manitoba, a research initiative led by University of Manitoba Faculty of Social Work researchers based upon data received from both Aboriginal and non-Aboriginal child welfare agencies in the province (Fuchs, Burnside, Marchenski, & Mudry, 2007). All three projects were featured as part of a national Research and Policy Forum co-sponsored by the PCWC and the Centre of Excellence for Child Welfare. A group of key researchers and policy-makers from across Canada attended this invitational event, held in Regina, Saskatchewan, in February 2006.

Two important tri-provincial meetings have been held. A meeting of lead training staff from the three government partners held in Winnipeg in 2007 led to the development of a charter for the purpose of sharing training materials and information. A similar meeting of faculty members teaching and/or conducting research in the field was held in Calgary in 2008. This meeting established the e-learning committee that has overseen the development and delivery of the web-based courses noted above.

Finally, this book represents the fourth major publication of the consortium. Each subtitled *Voices from the Prairies*, a title that echoes the intent of the 2001 symposium, the books bring together prairie voices concerned about and actively involved as practitioners, researchers, and policy analysts in the field of child welfare. Of the 34 chapters written for the first three published books (Brown, Chaze, et al., 2007; McKay, Fuchs, & Brown, 2009; Fuchs, McKay, & Brown, 2012), 16 chapters are specific to Aboriginal child welfare.

Table 1 provides an overview of PCWC accomplishments.

Table 1. Prairie Child Welfare Consortium History (1999-2013)

Year	Activities	Location
1999	Prairie-based Deans and Directors meeting to discuss ways to work together on child welfare curriculum and research.	Saskatchewan Indian Federated College (SIFC), Saskatoon, SK
2000	Expanded meeting with provincial and Aboriginal child welfare representatives to consider the potential for collaboration. Ideas for the first symposium were generated here. *Memorandum of Understanding (PCWC)* signed by the University of Manitoba, University of Regina, University of Calgary, Saskatchewan Indian Federated College, School of Indian Social Work (now First Nations University of Canada)	SIFC, Saskatoon, SK
2001	*Invitational Symposium (Honoring the Voices) 1st Biennial PCWC Symposium* at the Saskatchewan Indian Federated College	SIFC, Saskatoon, SK
2002	Face-to-Face Steering Committee Meeting leading to formalizing the Consortium as the PCWC	University of Calgary, Calgary, AB
	Ceremony at the Saskatchewan Indian Federated College celebrating the signing of an addendum to the MOU with the Federation of Saskatchewan Indian Nations	SIFC, Saskatoon, SK

2003	*2nd Biennial PCWC Symposium: Child & Family Services Transformation: Research, Policy and Best Practices*	Winnipeg, MB
2005– 2007	Funding received by the Public Health Agency of Canada (PHAC) and Centre of Excellence for Child Welfare (CECW) supported hiring a part-time coordinator for two years	Saskatoon, SK
2005	*3rd Biennial Symposium: Putting a Human Face on Child Welfare.* New PCWC members include: The Government of the Northwest Territories, Department of Health and Social Services; The Métis Nation of Alberta	Edmonton, AB
2006	National (Invitational) Child Welfare Research and Policy Forum	Regina, SK
2007	*4th Biennial Symposium: Passion for Action in Child and Family Services.* Pre-conference training workshops added to program	Regina, SK
	Tri-provincial meeting of provincial staff trainers. Charter for sharing information and material developed	Winnipeg, MB
	Book Publication Brown, I., Chaze, F., Fuchs, D., Lafrance, J., McKay, S., & Prokop, S. (2007). *Putting a human face on child welfare: Voices from the Prairies.* Prairie Child Welfare Consortium / Centre of Excellence for Child Welfare.	
	Research Projects (Funded by the Public Health Agency of Canada through the Centre of Excellence for Child Welfare) • Making Our Hearts Sing (Alberta). • Identity, Community and Resilience: The Transmission of Values (Saskatchewan). • Children with Disabilities in the Child Welfare System (Manitoba)	
2008	*Tri-provincial meeting* of faculty members teaching and/or conducting child welfare research held. *E-Learning Committee established*	Calgary, AB

2009	**5th Biennial Symposium: Awakening the Spirit: Moving Forward in Child Welfare.** Including pre-conference training workshops and Indigenous Scholars 1-Day Pre-Conference Meeting **Book Publication** McKay, S., Fuchs, D., & Brown, I. (2009). *Passion for action in child and family services: Voices from the Prairies*. Regina, SK.: Canadian Plains Research Center. **First course offering:** Residential Schools and Child Welfare	Winnipeg, MB
2012	**6th Biennial Symposium: Reinvesting in Families.** Including pre-conference training workshops and Indigenous Scholars and Allies 1-day Pre-Conference Meeting **Book Publication** Fuchs, D., S. McKay, Brown, I. (2012). *Awakening the spirit: Voices from the Prairies*. Regina, SK.: Canadian Plains Research Center Press. **New course offering:** FASD and Child Welfare Practice	Edmonton, AB
2013	**PCWC Face-to-Face Steering Committee Meeting** **Course offerings:** FASD and Child Welfare Practice, University of Calgary; Addictions and Child & Family Services Practice, University of Manitoba	Calgary, AB

The Structure of the PCWC: How it All Works

The consortium is organized in the following way. A central steering committee oversees the network, serving as the primary communication vehicle between and amongst member constituencies. Three subcommittees link to the steering committee: a biennial symposium planning committee, an e-learning committee (refers to the courses offered online by the University of Manitoba, University of Regina, and University of Calgary), and a book publication committee. Each of these committees is chaired by a volunteer and supported by his or her employing organization. Representatives from each of the participating organizations participate on the steering committee, currently the Faculties of Social Work at the University of Regina, the University of Manitoba, and the University of Calgary, the three government Ministries (Alberta Children's Services, Saskatchewan Social Services, and Manitoba Family Services and Labour), and the Federation of Saskatchewan Indian Nations. Two positions are kept open for organizations that have actively participated over the years but have not been able to do so recently for a variety of reasons: the First Nations University of Canada School of Indian Social Work and the Métis Nation of Alberta.

Table 2 provides a broad framework of the PCWC structure:

Table 2. PCWC Organizational Chart

Structure	Committees	Activities
Central Steering Committee (meets monthly) Governance, membership, communication, and information sharing	*E Learning Committee (meets monthly)*	Course Development and Offerings across the University of Manitoba, University of Regina, & University of Calgary
Membership University of Manitoba, University of Regina, & University of Calgary Alberta Children's Services, Saskatchewan Social Services, and Manitoba Family Services and Labour, and the Federation of Saskatchewan Indian Nations	*Book Publication and Editorial Committee (meets monthly)*	*Book Publications* This committee invites presenters from the biennial conference to submit proposals for a chapter in the edited PCWC book series. Each book focuses on the theme of the biennial conferences and the books are published within 2 years.
Steering Committee Members	*Biennial Symposium Committee*	The Biennial Symposium rotates within the Prairie provinces. The committee puts out a call for presentations, reviews and organizes the biennial conference.

"How it all works," of course, is highly dependent upon the solid commitment of each of the member organizations and each of their individual representatives. Early on in the consortium's development, a vision, mission, and goals statement was developed (McKay, 2007, pp. xxxiii–xxxvi and http://cat.uregina.ca/spr/pcwc-vision.html). The founders conceived of the PCWC as a collaborative, partnering effort to work together to influence, advocate for, and change child welfare education, training, research, policy, and practice/service delivery. The PCWC would seek affiliation with other national child welfare bodies for joint initiatives, which would further the PCWC mission and present a prairie perspective at the national level. The mission statement underscores as a fundamental value the importance of ensuring respect for the needs of Aboriginal communities in the delivery of child welfare services.

Given the inherent tensions between and among the partners, respectful relationships and thoughtful communications are a must. Committee chairs carry significant responsibility with limited infrastructure support. To date, academic faculty members, whose workloads, while demanding, are not subject to the daily demands of front-line practice, have chaired these committees. In reality, tenured senior professors with established careers have carried the major roles. Communication between and amongst committee members is predominantly by email and conference calls. Smaller meetings have been held online using Skype. E-learning meetings have been conducted using web-based technology and platforms. Government partners have had to find ways through existing firewalls in order to access these meetings. Individuals unfamiliar with the technology have had to learn how to use online programs that enable voice and written discussion.

Challenges: Funding, Institutional Membership and Support, Staff Turnover, Establishing and Maintaining Relationships and Continuity in a Challenging Field

Funding

The consortium does not have a central source of funds. All activities are dependent upon institutional contributions in the form of resources (for example, conference calls, web services), travel funds for representatives to attend occasional face-to-face meetings, and financial contributions to support planning for the biennial symposia. This said, it is important to note that the partnership between the consortium and the Centre of Excellence for Child Welfare (CECW), established early on in the network's history, has been a key factor to moving ahead on many of the accomplishments noted in this chapter. Funding from the Public Health Agency of Canada through the CECW enabled the hiring of a staff person between 2005 and 2007 to help coordinate the work of the network, helped fund and organize the 2005, 2007, and 2009 symposia, organized and administered the 2006 Policy Forum in Regina, and assisted with the organizing and funding of the two tri-provincial meetings involving academic staff and ministry in-service training staff. Publication of the first three consortium books was accomplished in collaboration with the CECW. Indeed, the network may not have survived during its early years were it not for the infrastructure support and administrative encouragement provided through the CECW. The loss of this support, due to the federal government closure of the CECW, placed the consortium in a vulnerable position vis-à-vis survival in the long term.

Staff Turnover, Institutional Membership and Support

Maintaining continuity despite the transiency and turnover of staff is a major problem for the consortium across all of its member organization. There is a great need for institutional commitment, transition planning, and strategies for membership representation renewal. Turnover in senior positions is ongoing, necessitating continued efforts by steering committee members to acquaint incoming administrators with the work of the network and the importance of maintaining institutional involvement. Deans and directors of schools of social work change regularly, deputy ministers come and go, government staff move on to other positions or are unable to continue as agency representatives due to pressures of their daily work. Aboriginal representatives and their agencies have had a very difficult time keeping in contact, in part because of structural changes within their own organizations. Membership in a network of this kind is not part of any of the participating organizations' own mandate. This means that newly appointed administrators may not be acquainted with the role their organization has played as part of the consortium. In order to gain the continued involvement of the organization with the network, a concerted effort must be made by institutional representatives and members of the PCWC steering committee to acquaint new administrators with the work of the consortium. The history of the consortium and its values of linking together the Prairie provinces' social work faculties and mainstream and Aboriginal child welfare directors, policy-makers, and practitioners need to be shared through regular meetings with designated representatives. For these reasons, the support of senior administration in each organization is critical to ensuring ongoing contact and participation within the consortium.

Relationships

Establishing and maintaining multiple relationships and continuity of purpose within and between members of a network of this kind is especially demanding due to inherent tensions across institutional, jurisdictional, and cultural boundaries. Sustaining relationships, maintaining communication, and responding to concerns from different stakeholders is important within and between the universities, within government, and within First Nations communities/organizations. The concern within academia generally revolves around autonomy, the worry that collaboration with government will unduly influence teaching and research. Within First Nations and government, the concerns are often expressed as distrust. First Nations experiences with residential schools and the child welfare system have been devastating and, as noted previously, are well-documented, giving rise to inherent tensions between First Nations people and government agencies (Johnston, 1983; Hepworth, 1980; Thomlison, 1984; Timpson, 1995; Trocmé, Knoke, & Blackstock, 2004; Blackstock, 2011). Government agencies operate under the close scrutiny of provincial child welfare advocates, Aboriginal leaders and communities, and, when things go wrong, the unrelenting surveillance of the public press.

Social services administrators periodically experience the scorn of outspoken faculty members and their students. Indeed, front-line practitioners responding to a survey conducted by the Canadian Association of Social Workers, as part of their project entitled Creating Conditions for Good Practice, reported that "schools and faculties of social work generally devalue the child protection setting as a career choice" and that "child welfare teaching in schools of social work is often not informed by the real and current experience of practitioners working on the frontline" (Herbert, 2007, p. 230).

Essential guiding values are imperative to supporting and maintaining PCWC relationships over the years: acknowledgment of and appreciation for institutional mandates and a strong and steady commitment to ensuring respect for the needs of Aboriginal communities in the delivery of child welfare services.

Moving Ahead in Light of Known Limitations and Criticisms

While the development and work of the PCWC has been lauded, there has also been criticism. One concern has been that individual members of the consortium steering committee and of various subcommittees have been predominately non-Aboriginal and have represented institutions and bodies that are viewed by some Aboriginal peoples as not to be trusted. Also criticized has been the lack of representation from service users and groups directly affected by social services, such as youth in care. While ongoing efforts have been made to balance participation from all stakeholders, a gap exists, and this "absence of representation" is painfully understood by many PCWC participants. On this point, there has been strong representation from First Nations researchers and communities at the six biennial PCWC symposia. The addition of the pre-conference meetings for Aboriginal scholars and allies has also helped to address these limitations and has supported developing and maintaining connections with Aboriginal communities and organizations.

As previously noted, staff turnover and other factors have affected institutional participation in the consortium. This has particularly been the case for representatives from the School of Indian Social Work, First Nations University of Canada (FNUC), a founding member of the consortium, and for the Métis Nation of Alberta Association (MNAA), an important participant at points in our history. Regrettably, intra-institutional changes and reorganizations have resulted in lack of participation by FNUC and MNAA in recent years. Two positions are being kept open for the two institutions on the understanding that they will return when participation is more feasible for them.

The reality, as with many volunteer bodies, is that the majority of committee work that has gone into organizing symposia, arranging meetings,

undertaking research, and editing the four publications has been undertaken by individuals who are essentially doing this work over and above
the responsibilities of the positions each holds within their own institution. Engaging other groups would entail a significant effort that is
currently beyond the scope of the small number of individuals that have
laboured to complete the work to date. Other than one paid position — the
coordinator hired between 2005 and 2007, the work of the PCWC has been
accomplished on a voluntary basis.

Another criticism has had to do with registration fees for the consortium's biennial symposia. Every effort has been made to keep these as
low as possible, and funds accruing from these events, once all the bills
have been paid, have been passed on to the next planning committee to
be used as seed funding for the symposia to follow. These funds have
been essential to ensure continuation of the biennial PCWC symposia.

The need exists to establish a new website to support communication
and highlight the profile of the PCWC, and this topic is currently being
addressed by the steering committee.

As partner organizations embark on planning the network's future,
the concerns noted will be part of the challenges to be addressed. Not
mentioned above is the essential fragility of a network dependent upon
volunteer commitment. The volunteers who have contributed the most
have been, as noted, senior administrators and professors holding significant responsibilities in their places of work. Over the course of the
past decade and more, a number of these individuals have retired or
moved on to other positions. In some instances — for example, in the
Department of Health and Social Services, Government of the Northwest
Territories; the School of Indian Social Work, First Nations University
of Canada; and the Métis Nation of Alberta Association — replacements
have not yet come forward. The need exists to keep partner institutions
engaged and informed about the work of the consortium. Time moves
on and relationships that once were well-established become distant
memories. This situation means that, to some extent, the viability of
the network over time cannot be guaranteed. There is a very clear and
critical need for infrastructure funding to support at least one staff
person holding responsibility for working with steering committee
and subcommittee chairs to ensure stability, maintenance, and continuing growth and development of the network. Formal or informal

agreements between the partners will assist greatly in ensuring commitment to the work. These may also alter in some way the essential "spirit" of working together voluntarily, a factor that will need to be recognized and discussed.

Concluding Remarks

In many respects, the story of the Prairie Child Welfare Consortium is quite marvelous. Meaningful collaboration across jurisdictional, cultural, and professional boundaries requires the commitment and support of partner organizations and the commitment, energies, and talents of individual representatives. The continued growth and development of the consortium over more than a decade is a testament to the power of the collaborative vision guiding the PCWC from the beginning. Financial support from the Center of Excellence for Child Welfare helped significantly in the beginning years. However, financial support has not been a key factor to ongoing progress and viability of the network. Indeed, considerable work has ensued since the loss of these funds. At the point of writing, members of the consortium are working on moving forward with the development of the interuniversity e-learning sub-agreement. Offering e-learning courses and the planned trajectory of course offerings are all signs of vibrancy. We are reconnecting with the School of Indian Social Work at the First Nations University of Canada and the First Nations Child and Family Research Centre in Saskatchewan. We have a strong 2014 conference-planning group, and we have renewed revitalized membership in all our collaborating partners. All three new deans from the Prairie provinces are supportive of the consortium.

The network has helped, and is helping, to "raise the voices" of child welfare practitioners, researchers, policy analysts, students and educators, and in-service trainers in the Prairie provinces. Much information has been shared, with special emphasis on strategies and programs that have "worked," a clear request of attendees at each of the symposia. The primary emphasis on hearing Aboriginal voices has hopefully helped to pave a better future for First Nations and Métis children, families, and communities.

References

Blackstock, C. (2011). Why if Canada wins, Canadians lose: The Canadian Human Rights Tribunal on First Nations Child Welfare. *Children and Youth Services Review, 33*(2), 187–194.

Blackstock, C., Brown, I., & Bennett, M. (2007). Reconciliation: Rebuilding the Canadian child welfare system to better serve Aboriginal children and youth. In I. Brown, F. Chaze, D. Fuchs, J. Lafrance, S. McKay, and S. Thomas-Prokop (Eds.), *Putting a human face on child welfare: Voices from the Prairies* (pp. 59–88). Toronto: Prairie Child Welfare Consortium / Centre of Excellence for Child Welfare. Retrieved from http://cwrp.ca/publications/1012

Brown, I., Chaze, F., et al. (2007). *Putting a human face on child welfare: Voices from the Prairies.* Toronto: Prairie Child Welfare Consortium / Centre of Excellence for Child Welfare. Retrieved from http://cwrp.ca/publications/907

Callahan, M. & Callahan, K. (1997). Victims and villains: Scandals, the press and policy making in child welfare. In J. Pulkingham and G. W. Ternowetsky (Eds.), *Child and family policies: Struggles, strategies and options* (pp. 40–57). Halifax: Fernwood Books Ltd.

Fuchs, D., Burnside, L., Marchenski, S., & Mudry, A. (2007). Children with disabilities involved with the child welfare system in Manitoba: Current and future challenges. In I. Brown, F. Chaze, D. Fuchs, J. Lafrance, S. McKay, & S. Thomas Prokop (Eds.), *Putting a human face on child welfare: Voices from the Prairies* (pp. 127–145). Toronto: Prairie Child Welfare Consortium / Centre of Excellence for Child Welfare. Retrieved from http://cwrp.ca/publications/1015

Fuchs, D., McKay, S., & Brown, I. (2012). *Awakening the spirit: Voices from the Prairies.* Regina, SK: Canadian Plains Research Center Press.

Hepworth, H. P. (1980). *Foster care and adoption in Canada.* Toronto: The Canadian Council on Social Development in association with James Lorimer & Company.

Herbert, M. (2007). Creating conditions for good practice: A child welfare project sponsored by the Canadian Association of Social Workers. In I. Brown, F. Chaze, D. Fuchs, J. Lafrance, S. McKay, & S. Thomas Prokop (Eds.), *Putting a human face on child welfare: Voices from the Prairies* (pp. 223–250). Prairie Child Welfare Consortium / Centre of Excellence for Child Welfare www.cecw-cepb.ca: 223-250. Retrieved from http://cwrp.ca/publications/1020

Johnston, P. (1983). *Native children and the child welfare system.* Toronto: The Canadian Council on Social Development in association with James Lorimer & Company.

Lafrance, J., and Bastien, B. (2007). Here be dragons: Breaking down the iron cage for Aboriginal children. In I. Brown, F. Chaze, D. Fuchs, J. Lafrance,

S. McKay, & S. Thomas Prokop (Eds.), *Putting a human face on child welfare: Voices from the Prairies* (pp. 89–113). Toronto: Prairie Child Welfare Consortium / Centre of Excellence for Child Welfare. Retrieved from http://cwrp.ca/publications/1013

McKay, S. (2007). Development of the Prairie Child Welfare Consortium and this book. In I. Brown, F. Chaze, D. Fuchs, J. Lafrance, S. McKay, & S. Thomas Prokop (Eds.), *Putting a human face on child welfare: Voices from the Prairies.* Toronto: Prairie Child Welfare Consortium / Centre of Excellence for Child Welfare. Retrieved from http://cwrp.ca/publications/1107

McKay, S., Fuchs, D., & Brown, I. (2009*). Passion for action in child and family Services: Voices from the Prairies.* Regina, SK: Canadian Plains Research Center.

McKay, S., & Thomas Prokop, S. (2007). Identity, community, resilience: The transmission of values project. In I. Brown, F. Chaze, D. Fuchs, J. Lafrance, S. McKay, & S. Thomas Prokop (Eds.), *Putting a human face on child welfare: Voices from the Prairies* (pp. 25–57). Toronto: Prairie Child Welfare Consortium / Centre of Excellence for Child Welfare. Retrieved from http://cwrp.ca/publications/1011

Thomlison, R. (1984). Case management review: A report submitted to the Alberta Department of Social Services and Community Health. Calgary, AB.

Timpson, J. (1995). Four decades of literature on native Canadian child welfare: Changing themes. *Child Welfare, 74*(3), 525–546.

Trocmé, N., Knoke, D., & Blackstock, C. (2004). Pathways to the overrepresentation of Aboriginal children in Canada's child welfare system. *Social Service Review, 78*(4), 577–601.

Turpel-Lafond, M. (2013). When talk trumped service: A decade of lost opportunity for Aboriginal children and youth in B.C. British Columbia Representative for Children and Youth Reports. Retrieved from http://www.rcybc.ca/content/publications/reports.asp

The FASD Community of Practice Project: Promising Practices for Children in Care with Fetal Alcohol Spectrum Disorder: A Model for Casework Practice

Dorothy Badry, William Pelech, and Denise Milne

Introduction: FASD and Child Welfare Practice

Casework practice for children in care who live with fetal alcohol spectrum disorder (FASD) requires complex case management tailored to their particular needs. It takes an inter-professional team to respond to the high needs of these children in care, as children and youth diagnosed with FASD have a lifelong disability. In Alberta, Canada, a project was launched in 2009 that offered basic and advanced training in FASD to caseworkers, casework supervisors, and foster and group care providers. The project focus was on developing core competencies in responding to concerns about FASD within the population of children and families involved with child welfare services. Supporting children in care with FASD requires specific training that addresses concerns such as behavioural challenges, learning and attention difficulties, use of

Suggested Citation: Badry, D., Pelech, W., & Milne, D. (2014). The FASD Community of Practice project: Promising practices for children in care with fetal alcohol spectrum disorder: A model for casework practice. In D. Badry, D. Fuchs, H. Montgomery, & S. McKay (Eds.), *Reinvesting in Families: Strengthening Child Welfare Practice for a Brighter Future: Voices from the Prairies* (pp. 21–43). Regina, SK: University of Regina Press.

respite, advocacy, and transitions. Individuals who receive a diagnosis along the FASD spectrum do best with early intervention and diagnosis before the age of six (Olson, Jirikowic, Kartin, & Astley, 2007; Paley & O'Connor, 2009; Koponen, Kalland, & Autti-Ramo, 2009; Coles, 2003; Streissguth, Barr, Kogan, & Bookstein, 1997; Streissguth & Kanter, 1997). That children will eventually age out of care needs to be kept in mind, as the transition to adulthood will require preparation and planning (Fuchs, Burnside, Marchenski, & Mudry, 2010). This chapter will provide a description and brief history of the FASD Community of Practice (FASD CoP) research project in the province of Alberta, with a specific focus on qualitative findings emerging from focus groups with caregivers, case-, workers, and foster parents about their experience with and the influence of the training.

In 1973 the first article on fetal alcohol syndrome (FAS) was published in North America (Jones & Smith, 1973). Today, we use the term fetal alcohol spectrum disorder (FASD) in order to describe a range of effects caused by prenatal alcohol exposure (Streissguth & O'Malley, 2000). Burd (2007) suggests that professionals and caregivers must be educated about FASD and further recommends that infrastructure for research and interventions to support those with FASD across different medical and social service institutions must be developed. Research specifically related to practice for children in care with FASD is limited. Ryan, Bohjanen, and Humphrey (2009) examined the literature for evidence-based practice on intervention and education for children with FASD and indicated finding only three studies. Fuchs, Burnside, Marchenski, and Mudry (2010) produced a hallmark study on children with FASD in care in Manitoba that offered insight into the need to respond to FASD from a disability-informed lens. A strong linkage between FASD and child welfare exists, as children suspected of having FASD, or with a diagnosis of FASD, often come from chaotic homes with concerns related to safety, neglect, and exposure to substance abuse (Badry, 2009; Badry & Pelech, 2005; Rutman, Callahan, Lundquist, Jackson, & Field, 2000).

The need to examine best practice for children in care who have an FASD diagnosis was the focus of the FASD Community of Practice (FASD CoP) research in Alberta. In order to understand the impact of the FASD CoP research, focus groups were held with caseworkers and foster parents in five regions. These focus groups provided an opportunity to engage in a conversation about the experiences associated with this approach; the voices of caseworkers and foster parents are included in this chapter. Additionally, this chapter provides an historical overview of the FASD CoP to contextualize the response to FASD and child welfare practice in Alberta with children primarily in care.

As well as providing a brief history of FASD CoP in Alberta, this chapter will discuss FASD and child protection: the importance of an FASD diagnosis, the contextualization of need, and the identification of a Community of Practice approach. Key literature on these topics will be included. The qualitative research findings based on focus groups with foster parents and caregivers will be presented including qualitative themes, key findings in relation to teamwork, communication, transition to adulthood and the impact of the project, conclusions, and acknowledgements.

Promising Practices and the Community of Practice Model

In 2002, regional staff (casework supervisors, managers, and caseworkers) prepared a document known as the *FASD Practice Standards*. These standards (now known as *Promising Practices*) identified key areas of practice and case management approaches in relation to intervention, assessment, and referral for diagnosis of FASD. The key practice areas defined in *Promising Practices* include screening for FASD, child assessment, referral for diagnosis, determining parenting ability, service plans and reviews, home visitation, caseworker contact with children or youth in care, caseworker contact with foster parents, permanency planning, transition to adulthood, and training and workload (caseload) standards. Additionally, program considerations related to kinship care, foster care, residential care, adoption, private guardianship, and family preservation were included.

The *Promising Practices* standards were specifically developed to address the needs of families who faced challenges such as substance abuse, alcoholism, and problems caring for their children who have FASD. There was a growing awareness that parents who themselves have FASD may have difficulty parenting their children. Additionally, there were concerns about the behavioural problems of children with

FASD, as well as their learning and attention problems. Foster parents and other substitute caregivers reported that the care needs of children with FASD were often challenging and difficult on a daily basis. Those delivering child welfare services became increasingly aware of the high needs of children with FASD and recognized that additional supports were required if they were to adequately provide care for these children and their families.

The FASD Community of Practice (FASD CoP) took place from 2009–2011 in five Child and Family Service Authorities (CFSA) regions in Alberta. The primary focus of the study was to examine the impact of a specific casework practice model, the FASD *Promising Practices*, which was designed to respond to the needs of children, families, and care providers. Both qualitative and quantitative methodologies were used in this research project, examining areas such as behavioural challenges, placement stability, use of respite, and number of training hours. In addition to these measures, qualitative research focused on the experiences and responses of caseworkers, casework supervisors, and care providers (foster and kinship care) in relation to their learning and experiences through this project.

The focus of the FASD CoP was to provide training in best practices in relation to meeting the needs of children and families who come into contact with the child welfare system. The key features of the FASD CoP were specific training on FASD to foster parents, caseworkers, and supervisors through seminars and workshops. Additionally, caseload reductions were supported through additional staffing in order to provide more time for caseworkers to work more intensively with FASD children and youth, as well as their caregivers and families. This dual approach of training and caseload reductions supported increased involvement with children and families for caseworkers and allowed for monthly versus quarterly contact with children/youth and foster parents or other caregivers. This approach resulted in improved placement stability, improved caregiver relationships, a reduction in risk behaviours, and a reduction in school absences (Pelech, Badry, & Daoust, 2013; Badry & Pelech, 2005). Foster parents indicated that FASD-specific training was highly valued and improved their ability to respond to social/emotional/behavioural issues for children in their care. Foster parents also reported stronger connections with caseworkers as a result of the FASD CoP.

Examining child welfare practice in response to FASD was important because it offered a pathway to understanding and appreciating challenges for children, youth, foster parents (caregivers), kinship care providers, caseworkers, casework supervisors, and regional management. The complexity of caring for children and youth with FASD has been largely underestimated, and a standard format for practice does not exist in Canada. Knowledge on child welfare practice approaches with children and youth diagnosed with FASD is developing, but is not yet uniformly applied in child welfare authorities. This research examined an applied model of casework practice that included specific training on FASD and decreased caseloads to support increased contact with children in care, their families, and foster parents.

A Brief History of the FASD Community of Practice in Alberta Human Services

In one of the Child and Family Services Authority (CFSA) regions in Alberta, concerns were raised that children born of mothers who heavily consumed alcohol during pregnancy had unique and demanding needs when placed in care. It was recognized that these children had some type of disability including developmental, behavioural, and physical concerns. Because there was no major research activity within the CFSA at the time, these concerns were raised primarily by caseworkers, casework supervisors, and experienced foster parents. Children were referred to physicians and psychologists for assessment, diagnosis, and recommendations for treatment. There was also a concern that many children could not return to their families of origin if substance abuse remained a problem.

As FASD became more widely known and recognized, knowledge about the complex psychosocial needs of families slowly increased. Training on FASD was developed, with the earliest training in Alberta occurring in the early 1990s through the efforts of Donna Debolt, a social worker and former casework supervisor with government. Training on FASD within the province has further developed over the past two decades and has become an important focus in professional development for caseworkers, casework supervisors, regional managers, and foster parents,

as well as other allied health professionals such as physicians, pediatricians, and psychologists. Training on FASD is important as it is not yet
embedded in post-secondary education consistently and there is a need
to understand that children in care with FASD have different needs than
children without FASD.

Developing Promising Practices—Defining a "Good Guardian"

The notion of being a "good guardian" for children in care with FASD
was raised as a critical factor in child protection casework for this population. The notion of guardianship and its responsibilities in relation
to vulnerable children and youth was a guidepost for this project. This
concept served as an underpinning of a pilot research project in 2005
on the *FASD Practice Standards* that showed children with FASD fared
better in care through more intensive case management (Badry, 2009;
Badry, Pelech, & Norman, 2005). Questions and discussions that guided
the initial research project (2003–2005) included: What does it mean to
be a good guardian to children with FASD? What supports are required to
effectively meet the needs of children with FASD, their caseworkers, and
foster parents/caregivers? Why is this important? What will be achieved
through this work? How do we convey what translates to best practice for
children and youth with FASD? Can we state that we have designed an
effective practice approach to help children and youth with FASD medi-
ate their own challenges of being in care with enhanced supports?

These questions are highlighted from the early discussions in the
province of Alberta around 2002–2003, as they represent core practical
and philosophical considerations of responding to children and youth
with complex needs and set the stage for later research on the FASD CoP
(2009–2011). The importance of these discussions amongst staff delivering child welfare supports to children with FASD is that they offer points
to review and reflect on practice. Reviewing practice offers an opportunity to change practice. The study indicated that practice-related questions must be asked, as it is the responsibility of child protection agencies
to recognize what works and what needs to change, and subsequently, to
apply the findings in striving for excellence in the care of children and
youth with FASD. Table 1 below provides a description and profile of the

work to date in developing an FASD-specific trained child protection workforce through an historical overview of the FASD CoP in Alberta.

Table 1. A History of the FASD Community of Practice in Alberta

Date	Activity
1988 – 2000	Initial contact made with Dr. Ann Streissguth and Dr. Sterling Clarren at the University of Washington in Seattle to ask for guidance in responding to the needs of children in care who were prenatally exposed to alcohol and living in foster care (1988).
	First Training on FASD in Lethbridge, Alberta – December, 1992.
	Second Training on FASD in Edmonton, Alberta – May, 1993.
	Development of additional training across the province leading to increased awareness of Fetal Alcohol Syndrome.
2001 – 2002	Round table of stakeholders in Region 1 held regarding the needs of children with fetal alcohol syndrome or other prenatal alcohol-related conditions. Region 1: Development of the Fetal Alcohol Practice Standards.
2003	Engagement with research partners at the Faculty of Social Work, University of Calgary. A demonstration project was funded for $10,000 by the FASD Initiatives with Children's Services. This work represented collaboration between the Children and Family Services Authority (CFSA) Region 1 and the Faculty of Social Work, University of Calgary (2003–2005).
2003 – 2005	*Fetal Alcohol Spectrum Disorder Practice Standards Evaluation Project Final Report* published.
	Key Findings from the 2003–2005 Study
	• Children in care had a significant decrease in placement changes over time.
	• Application of the new practice approach appeared to minimize life disruptions such as school absences and behaviour problems.
	• Caseworkers and foster parents expressed a great deal of satisfaction with the process and indicated that children and youth were doing better through increased contact with the foster homes and school.
	• A total of 1,932 hours of training occurred for foster parents and caseworkers during this project.

2008 – 2009	*Project proposal: A good guardian: Addressing the complex needs of children with fetal alcohol spectrum disorder in the care of Children's Services* prepared by Dr. Sandra Stoddard, Innovation and Improvement Unit, Research and Innovation Branch, and approved by the ministry. Stoddard recommends a Community of Practice approach modelled after similar work within the education system. This proposal led to the development of a full application for funding for $100,000 to the Alberta Centre for Child, Family & Community Research granted in 2009. Development of the FASD Community of Practice.
2009 – 2011	*Fetal Alcohol Spectrum Disorder Promising Practices for Children in the Care of Children's Services Final Report* for Alberta Centre for Child, Family & Community Research. Regions 1, 7, 9, & 10 with Region 6 included as the comparison group. Key qualitative findings from the 2009–2011 research project are included in this chapter.

FASD Diagnosis

The diagnosis of FASD in children and youth in care has been identified as a hallmark of sound practice, because assessment and diagnosis provide a pathway for organizing services and supports around identified needs (Astley & Clarren, 2000). Child welfare practice is often focused on return-ing children to their families of origin or relations if possible. However, it is important to consider that a diagnosis of FASD remains fraught with stigma because it is considered to be preventable through abstention from alcohol during pregnancy. The use of alcohol during pregnancy by child-bearing women is a complex problem, and practice wisdom sug-gests that the diagnosis of a child with FASD is a diagnosis for two; that is, research focused on the diagnosis of a child with FASD has consistently identified that both the mother and child should be perceived to be in need of supports (Astley, 2011; Astley, Bailey, Talbot, & Clarren, 2000).

While great strides have been made in social science research, includ-ing the development of service frameworks to respond to the psychoso-cial needs of children, youth, and families involved in the child welfare system, there remains a long road ahead. Astley (2011) states:

> *A diagnosis reflects the condition of a patient; however, because a diagnosis serves many purposes (e.g., treatment, prevention,*

communication among specialists, and qualification for services),
the process of rendering a diagnosis can sometimes be influenced
by those different purposes. The only diagnosis that serves all pur-
poses most effectively is a correct diagnosis. Access to services
should be based on an individual's disabilities and not on what
caused their disabilities. Therefore services should be available
for individuals across the full continuum of FASD and not just
those with FAS. (p. 25)

Framing diagnosis as a purposeful activity to guide interventions
along a continuum and over the lifespan is crucial. Foster parents and
caseworkers often speak of the need to have a diagnosis, as well as a
clear understanding of what the diagnosis means in day-to-day life for a
child and their caregiver. The purpose of diagnosis is to develop a plan
for intervention that will provide guidance to caregivers, caseworkers,
and the community supporting the child.

FASD and Child Protection: Contextualizing Need

The role of child welfare has featured heavily in the care of children with
FASD who have been removed from parental care and placed in the foster care system. Children with FASD are frequently brought into care due
to protection needs related to substance abuse and neglect at home. An
examination of young children in care with complex needs indicated that
up to 80% may have had prenatal alcohol exposure, while factors cited
in removal of children from parental (biological) care broadly included
"neglect and parental incapacity" (Vig, Chinitz, & Shulman, 2005, p.
147). Aronson (1997) suggested:

Even though early fostering did not appear to eliminate the harmful
effects of exposure to alcohol in utero, foster care seems to be the most
favorable alternative for children whose biological mothers, despite
vigorous attempts at psychological support, continue to abuse alcohol
and have severe personal psychological problems. Children prenatally
exposed to alcohol...remain at continued risk. (p. 24)

For children with FASD, stability and structure are crucial in mediating
against the neurological difficulties they encounter. Routine schedules

and predictability in all aspects of daily life are important to help children with FASD manage their days. Children with FASD are reliant on their caregivers to create this structure. The neurological impairment and disabilities associated with FASD are different from those of other children in care. Children with FASD often have significant behavioural problems that are known as neurobehavioural problems, as well as psychiatric conditions caused by the neurological injury from prenatal alcohol exposure (O'Connor & Paley, 2009). Common problems include challenges in linking behaviour and consequences, learning from previous experience, and sleep difficulties (O'Connor & Paley, 2009). While the needs of children with FASD may not be higher than those of children who have experienced abuse and trauma, their needs are different and exceedingly demanding/intensive because of their disability and poor adaptive functioning (Rasmussen, Andrew, Zwaigenbaum, & Tough, 2008). Rasmussen et al. (2008) have provided insight through research that suggests children and youth with FASD are prone to memory and behavioural problems and often have poor developmental outcomes due to the neurological problems associated with FASD. Children with FASD are often misunderstood because their disability is not always readily visible—FASD is often referred to as the invisible disability (Ory, 2007).

Children and youth with FASD in care are vulnerable and therefore dependent upon professionals such as social workers (caseworkers), educators, and caregivers (foster parents or residential care providers) to provide a structured, consistent, and cohesive environment. It is crucial that all professionals working with children and youth have a comprehensive and common understanding of FASD that is sensitive to the complexities of child protection. For example, besides basic information on the developmental disabilities associated with FASD, it is important for caseworkers and allied health professionals to have an understanding of addictions, challenges in treatment, effects of intergenerational trauma that can lead to addiction, and various oppressions such as socioeconomic factors and marginalization.

The implications for child protection casework practice directly relate to the need for training on FASD that is relevant to the child, their environment, and the community where they live. For children in care, training and supports for foster parents, adoptive parents, and kinship care placements are also required. If FASD is not well understood, the possibility for placement breakdown exists. Caley, Winkelman, and Mariano (2009) identified challenges faced by caregivers including discipline, behaviour management, and a lack of knowledge about mental health concerns due to a lack of training on FASD. A lack of knowledge about Prenatal Alcohol Exposure (PAE) and FASD can lead to challenges in effectively communicating the child's needs in multiple areas, including the education system, community supports, the mental health system, and within the child protection system.

Caley et al. (2009) also highlighted the travails of caring for children with FASD, including the stress associated with the high needs of children in care and caregivers not fully appreciating or understanding the implications of FASD in relation to day-to-day behavioural functioning. Further, Caley et al. described adverse effects on caregivers including marital discord, financial concerns, lack of adequate resources, and dissatisfaction that is somewhat related to a lack of training and knowledge on FASD and the day-to-day care needs of children affected by the disorder. The need for caregivers to receive ongoing training on FASD, particularly in relation to behaviour management, developmental issues, and challenges across the child's lifespan, is critical to supporting stability for children and youth in care, including maintaining their placements.

A Community of Practice Approach

Stoddard (2008) suggested that a Community of Practice (CoP) approach offered a framework of innovation and improvement that could influence decision-making, resource allocation, and policy development in response to the needs of children and youth in care. The FASD CoP research focused on outcomes of using the *Promising Practices* and discovered that such practices benefitted children in care, caseworkers, and foster parents. This work was grounded in its approach in several major areas: intensive training on FASD, increased hours for case management, increased contact with children and foster parents by caseworkers, and the provision of negotiated respite resources—all considered interventions. The value of the FASD CoP was in demonstrating through research that such interventions were successful. One of the strongest areas of benefit was shown to be placement stability, which showed a marked increase during the project period (Pelech, Badry, & Daoust, 2013; Badry, Pelech, & Stoddard, 2012). Additionally, it was discovered that structures around casework, supervision, training, and resource management were important features and functions in managing the needs of children and youth with FASD in care. The following sections detail key concepts that were seen as beneficial in responding to the needs of children with FASD in care.

The knowledge gained from the FASD CoP, in relation to what constitutes solid practice to support children, youth, and caregivers, is critical for the development of effective approaches to practice. With knowledge about FASD gained through training and a diagnosis, it was believed that case management would be organized in such a way that the challenges faced by children with this diagnosis would be mediated through structured supports. Expertise within the FASD CoP developed as caseworkers, supervisors, and management recognized that children and youth in care who were prenatally exposed to alcohol had special needs. Identifying care needs for children and youth in foster homes, schools, and community settings and then structuring case plans that offered support in different environments was a focus of this project.

Qualitative Research Findings

To address the experience of caseworkers, casework supervisors, and foster parents in the FASD CoP, focus groups were held in all five participating regions with a focus on examining the impact of participation in this research project. The primary question asked was: *What is the impact of the FASD Promising Practices for children in care, for those caseworkers implementing the practices, and for the caregiving network of foster parents providing care?* Qualitative research provides a means to elicit information from participants in research that attends to their voices and allows for the expression of different experiences over time and throughout the duration of the project (Denzin & Lincoln, 2003). The focus group interviews were recorded and transcribed for analysis in Atlas Ti, a qualitative research software program. Themes emerging from the FASD CoP from the different perspectives of caseworkers and foster parents are highlighted in Table 2 below. A discussion follows that offers interpretive meaning of the themes, subthemes, and quotations.

Table 2. The FASD CoP (2009–2011), Some Key Qualitative Findings

Theme	Sub-Theme	Illustrative Quotation *FP = Foster Parent, CW = Caseworker*
FASD training	Increased awareness of neurobehavioural problems; Knowledge development; Understanding FASD	*FP*: [Increased understanding of] the disability itself [as] more permanent. I inform people more around my kids and about why, rather than 'just do this and this,' and I didn't give explanations [before training] and, you know, if you explain it – lots of explanations help.
Teamwork	We are all on the same page (The same training on FASD was offered to caseworkers and foster parents across regions)	*CW*: I have found in terms of having a team to support foster parent has been helpful, instrumental, and vital; of course I have a caseload too. For instance, one girl was suicidal two weeks ago and [the] foster parent took [the] child to emergency and I couldn't get there and we needed someone to go and sit with child, and it was wonderful because we had extra people on the team to [provide support]. *CW* (supports foster parents): I think for me what's made the most difference is developing really good teams with my support workers and the foster parents....I feel that we're all as much on top of it as we can be. That we are all working together for the same outcome....We all have the same focus. That's very, very nice. I feel supported in my work by knowing that I have assistance from the support workers. I don't know if I make their job any easier, probably harder, but I know that the foster parents are feeling very supported and very cared for.

Communication	Communication between foster parent and caseworker	CW: If the foster parents have said 'too bad' about something that I think is completely silly and I reverse that or want to reverse that, you know, if I don't understand the reasoning behind it [and] we haven't already discussed the decision, then it would be pretty bad. But really, both of my homes have been wonderful in terms of, 'This is what we see coming down the pipe, what are we gonna do about it?' Then we can talk to the foster parent so we can develop a plan before we ever approach the child with it.
Support	Giving foster parents a voice	FP: As foster parents, we feel more confident to say to workers, "well things aren't going as smooth"....We feel more supported. CW: In the past when [name of trainer/consultant] were out here meeting [the foster parents] and are telling her stuff we don't know. Foster parents told her stuff we didn't know about – their burden, they felt they could finally tell somebody.
Transition to adulthood	Grief and loss; Worry; Commitment beyond age 18	CW: It's grief and loss for those caregivers too because they have invested so much in that child and have looked at [the] child as a member of their family.
Impact of the project on foster parents	New awareness of foster parent needs by caseworkers	FP: I think this kind of project is good where we have people who share their experiences, share their frustrations, to share the good and the bad and the ugly and are able to talk about it freely, openly, and just get the feedback and just, you know, it's kind of a purging in a way. CW: I think that the whole project has put a lot more emphasis on foster parents and their needs and just the fact that we recognize that this is a difficult job. That they need supports. That we're thinking about how much this is impacting them and so on. *continued...*

		CW: I found I learned a lot from the foster parents as experts. It's one thing to read about a disorder in a book and then completely another to have people who are experiencing it every day, come up with all sorts of strategies....I thought it was very important for them to remain a part of this project, to share that knowledge with other foster parents.
Increased contact with child and foster parents		*CW*: I think if you're having the monthly contact then you're far more in tune with everything that's going on, so then you're able to maybe pinpoint things that otherwise may have taken a few more visits or months to focus. *FP*: The home visits....Our social worker was able to appreciate that there's a lot more challenges with the kids than what she sees in her case file.

The key areas reported on from the focus groups include FASD training, teamwork, communication, support, transition to adulthood, impact of the project on foster parents, and increased contact with the child and foster parents. Following training on FASD, foster parents realized the importance of explaining expectations to the child, moving beyond saying "Just do this," as one foster parent reflected. Creating a shift in practice also involved developing new ways to support children and youth's needs for safety and congruency across different environments. It helped the foster parent to shift from perceiving the child as "defiant" to perceiving the child as needing an explanation regarding the task through better communication. Training was focused on some of the challenges and frustrations in caring for children with FASD day-to-day and explained a great deal about neurobehavioural challenges and understanding developmental delays. For caregivers, the recognition that certain behaviours were not purposeful or manipulative was important in helping to adjust their responses to the child, focusing instead on being consistent, maintaining routines, and offering reminders and cues on a daily basis.

Caseworkers and other allied professionals in child welfare casework also require specialized training in FASD. Why? The intensive needs of children with FASD and the nature of this disability are such that daily intervention and accommodations are required across environments for the child. While foster parent training increases stability and security in the home environment, it is also essential that caseworkers and other professionals are able to provide congruent interventions. Although one could state that this is true for all children, particularly those who have come into care in need of protection from abuse or neglect, exigent circumstances unique to those with FASD exist. Caseworkers, foster parents, and other professionals involved require advanced and practically focused training on FASD. Training was seen as highly valued by caseworkers, foster parents, and casework supervisors throughout this project.

Teamwork

In relation to *teamwork*, it was evident that training and increased contact through home visitations supported better communication between caseworkers and foster parents. Foster parents and caseworkers appeared to assign great importance to working together as members of a team, responding to the needs of the child in care. The "team" includes foster parents and caseworkers. In one example presented in Table 2, a suicidal youth had to be assessed in hospital, and the caseworker commented positively about the support provided by the foster parent in responding to this crisis. In the event of an emergency situation with a child in care, a team member, the foster parent in this instance, was able to step in and offer support during this crisis. Utilizing a collaborative case management approach in the FASD CoP project contributed to an enhanced sense of "team" among caseworkers, support workers, and caregivers. As a group formed around the needs of a child with FASD in care, the term "team" was used; this helped everyone in the group to feel included and actively engaged in case-planning for the child.

A number of participants emphasized that they are now "all on the same page" in planning for families and children and that they feel as though they are functioning as a team. Communication was enhanced as a result of the FASD CoP approach. Foster parents and caseworkers shared ideas with one another, and identified this activity as brainstorming, rather than working individually or independent of one another when planning or decision-making. Some foster parents stated that they were feeling more supported after participating in the project: "As foster parents, we feel more confident to say to workers 'well things aren't going as smooth'....We feel more supported." This quote suggests that communication was more open as a result of project participation, and that foster parents felt more supported and found it easier to contact the caseworker when struggles or conflict took place around the child's needs.

Communication

Focus group statements concerning *communication* typically fell into two categories: communication between foster parents and children, and communication between foster parents and caseworkers. Foster parents described various forms of communication between themselves and their children. For example, the use of a cellphone allowing children to freely contact the foster parent (particularly in the event of a concern or crisis) was considered key to a greater sense of security (which fosters stability) for both child and foster parents. Increased visits by caseworkers—on a monthly basis versus a quarterly basis—was viewed as a strategy for decreasing distance and establishing more effective, ongoing communication. It was also perceived as a means of *support* to both foster parents and the child or youth in care. Foster parents saw increased visits with the child as important and helpful, while caseworkers described the value of streamlined case-planning resulting from increased communication with foster parents.

Transition to Adulthood and Beyond Age 18

Focus group discussions also identified the challenges associated with *transition to adulthood (age 18)* for children with FASD. These discussions indicated that foster parents and caseworkers do not stop caring for, or worrying about, these young people when they transition out of their care. The need to acknowledge caregivers' emotional ties to the children and their concerns associated with a child's transition to adult-hood was emphasized.

According to one caseworker, "It's [about] grief and loss for those caregivers too because they have invested so much in that child and have looked at [the] child as a member of their family." This quote reflects the anticipatory worry and concern a foster parent may have with respect to the foster child's transition to adulthood and that young person's vulner-ability as they transition from the foster care system. Fuchs, Burnside, Reinink, and Marchenski (2010) identified that young adults with FASD transitioning from care are not developmentally ready for the tasks of adulthood, often have complicated relationships with their biological families, and often face challenges in accessing adult disability services. It is important, therefore, that developmental supports and readiness are assessed for youth with FASD transitioning out of care.

It was evident through focus groups with foster parents that *commitment to wards beyond age 18* was a crucial issue for foster parents dealing with transitions to adulthood and from care. Recognizing that foster parents experience grief and loss in these transitions is critical to developing sup-ports for the youth and the foster home. In some instances, caseworkers, with the support of supervisors and regional management, were able to provide extensions of care until age 21. Foster parent commitment beyond age 18 is grounded in care, compassion, and love for this young person despite the struggles, challenges, and worries. After many years of caring for this individual and protecting her/him from harm, foster parents know the young person's needs and, in the absence of other options, they often keep the young person in their care as an adult. The issue of transitioning to adulthood for children and youth with FASD requires further exploration.

Impact of the Project

Foster parents and caregivers described a variety of benefits associated with participation in the project. One caseworker felt that the primary contribution of the project was that it brought much-needed attention to the caregiving experience. As one foster parent stated, "[Through] the home visits...our social worker was able to appreciate that there's a lot more challenges with the kids than what she sees in her case file."

In addition, there was increased understanding by all parties of the roles of caseworker and foster parent. Caseworkers and foster parents began to identify more as part of a team, brought together to meet the needs of a child or youth in care. As a result, a sense of respect and appreciation of roles developed. This sense of the "team" was strengthened because caseworkers were required to visit the children and youth in their caseload on a monthly basis. These visits facilitated stronger connections between the child's caseworker and the child or youth.

Of course, regular caseworker contact with the child also meant regular caseworker contact with the foster parent. Foster parents felt that through this increased engagement the caseworker developed deeper connections with the child/youth and with the foster parent. This deeper connection between the child/youth, caseworker, and foster parents was, in fact, one of the major findings of the FASD CoP researchers, particularly as they listened to the focus groups with foster parents across regions. Creating this sense of "team" around a child/youth became a focal point of much of the discussion within focus groups and was clearly identified as a concept that was valued. Increased contact in the home with the child and foster parent was identified as a highlight of this project, in part because foster parents felt less isolated in caring for the child, and also because they got to know the caseworker better and because they appreciated that the caseworker was getting to know the child better in the home setting. Opportunities to increase and enhance contact and communication for children with FASD in care supports best practice.

Implications for Other Jurisdictions — Child Welfare Practice and Research on FASD in Canada

Although FAS was first identified in 1973 by Jones and Smith, the birth of children with prenatal alcohol exposure remains a significant social problem. The Institute of Health Economics has estimated that the total cost of the disorder in Canada in 2009 is conservatively estimated at CAD7.6 billion, based on a prevalence of nine cases per 1,000 births (Clarren, Salmon, & Jonsson, 2011). In the years following the identification of FAS in 1973, the focus on biomedical research has influenced the understanding of the effects of prenatal alcohol exposure, the importance of diagnosis, and the recognition of the complexity of families (Astley & Clarren, 2000). While significant financial costs are noted, the social/emotional cost of FASD within society is a huge burden. Another area of concern in terms of informing practice is the lack of child welfare intervention research on FASD. It is critical for child welfare ministries and agencies to begin to systematically document the numbers of children in care, compile statistics on diagnosis, and gather data both qualitative and quantitative to inform best practice.

Conclusion

Children with prenatal alcohol exposure have significant life challenges and often have traumatic experiences before coming into care. The need to develop best practice and interventions in response to FASD is critical in child welfare practice as this supports both intervention and prevention/mediation of the challenges children have with life skills, learning, and behaviour. The foundations of the FASD CoP model were training on FASD and increased contact/communication between children, caseworkers, and foster parents. While these foundations appear basic, when combined they support positive outcomes for children in care with FASD. Such training offers a framework for FASD-informed practice, supports stronger communication and consistency across environments, and provides hope for the future of children with FASD.

Acknowledgements

This research project was funded by the Alberta Centre for Child, Family and Community Research (ACCFCR) and their support is deeply appreciated. In particular the support of Tara Hanson is acknowledged. We acknowledge the caseworkers, casework supervisors, regional management, and foster parents/caregivers in Region 1 and the leadership of Brenda Burton, Darci Kotkas, Mark Weninger, and Donna Debolt (consultant and lead trainer). Other contributors from the regions and administration of Alberta Human Services and the Child and Family Service Authority offices included: Denise Milne, Larry Gazzola, Eoin Rouine,

Dude Johnson, Darla Yanchuk, Shawn Miller, Tiara Samson, and Julie Mann. Thanks to Jamie Hickey, research assistant, for her support in preparing the final manuscript.

References

Alberta Government. (2007). *FASD 10-Year Strategic Plan*. Retrieved from http://fasd.alberta.ca/documents/FASD-10-year-plan.pdf

Aronson, M. (1997). Children of alcoholic mothers: Results from Goteborg, Sweden. In A. Streissguth & J. Kanter (Eds.), *The challenge of fetal alcohol syndrome: Overcoming secondary disabilities* (pp. 15–24). Seattle, WA: University of Washington Press.

Astley, S. J. (2011). Diagnosing fetal alcohol spectrum disorders (FASD). In S. A. Adubato & D. E. Cohen (Eds.), *Prenatal alcohol use and fetal alcohol spectrum disorders: Diagnosis, assessment and new directions in research and multimodal treatment* (pp. 3–30). Retrieved from http://depts.washington.edu/fasdpn/pdfs/astley-FASD-chapter2011.pdf

Astley, S. J., & Clarren, S. K. (2000). Diagnosing the full spectrum of fetal alcohol exposed individuals: Introducing the 4-digit diagnostic code. *Alcohol, 35*(5), 400–410.

Astley S., Bailey D., Talbot T., & Clarren S. (2000). Fetal alcohol syndrome (FAS) primary prevention through FAS diagnosis: Identification of high-risk birth mothers through the diagnosis of their children. *Alcohol, 35*(5), 499–508.

Badry, D. (2009). Fetal alcohol spectrum disorder standards: Supporting children in the care of Children's Services. *First Peoples Child & Family Review, 4*(1), 47–56.

Badry, D., & Pelech, W. (2011). *The Fetal Alcohol Spectrum Disorder (FASD) Community of Practice: Promising Practices for children & youth in the care of Alberta Children & Youth Services final report*. Retrieved from http://fasd.alberta.ca/ documents/FASD-COP-Final-Report-2011.pdf

Badry, D., Pelech, W., & Norman, D. (2005). *Fetal alcohol spectrum disorder practice standards evaluation project – Region 1*. Retrieved from http://www.fasdconnections.ca /HTMLobj1652/FASDPracticeStndEvaluationProjectalbta.pdf

Badry, D., Pelech, W., & Stoddard, S. (2012). Fetal alcohol spectrum disorder communities of practice in Alberta. In S. McKay, D. Fuchs, & I. Brown (Eds.), *Awakening the spirit in child and family services: Voices from the Prairies* (pp. 179–212). Regina, SK: Canadian Plains Research Center Press.

Burd, L. (2007). Interventions in FASD: We must do better. *Child: Care, Health and Development, 33*(4), 398–400.

Caley, L. M., Winkelman, M. S., & Mariano, D. N. (2009). Problems expressed
    by caregivers of children with fetal alcohol spectrum disorder. *International
    Journal of Nursing Terminologies and Classifications, 20*(4), 181–188.
Clarren, S., Salmon, A., & Jonsson, E. (2011). *Prevention of fetal alcohol spectrum
    disorder – FASD: Who is responsible?* Edmonton, AB: Institute of Health
    Economics; Weinheim, Germany: Wiley-Blackwell.
Coles, C. D. (2003). Individuals affected by fetal alcohol spectrum disorder
    (FASD) and their families: Prevention, intervention and support. In R. E.
    Tremblay, R. G. Barr, & R. V. Peters (Eds.), *Encyclopedia on early childhood
    development* (pp. 1–6). Montreal: Centre of Excellence for Early Childhood
    Development and the Strategic Knowledge Cluster on Early Childhood
    Development.
Denzin, N., & Lincoln, Y. (2003). *The landscape of qualitative research: Theories
    and issues* (2nd ed.). London, UK: Sage Publications.
Fuchs, D., Burnside, L., Marchenski, S., & Mudry, A. (2010). Children with
    FASD related disabilities receiving services from child welfare agencies in
    Manitoba. *International Journal of Mental Health and Addiction, 8,* 232–244.
Fuchs, D., Burnside, L., Reinink, A., & Marchenski, S. (2010). *Bound by the clock:
    The voices of Manitoba youth with FASD leaving care.* Retrieved from http://
    cwrp.ca/publications/2138
Jones, K. L., & Smith, D. W. (1973). Recognition of the fetal alcohol syndrome in
    early infancy. *Lancet, 302*(7836), 999–1001.
Koponen, A. M., Kalland, M., & Autti-Ramo, I. (2009). Caregiving environment
    and socio-emotional development of foster-placed FASD-children. *Children
    and Youth Services Review, 31,* 1049–1056.
O'Connor, M. J., & Paley, B. (2009). Psychiatric conditions associated with
    prenatal alcohol exposure. *Developmental disabilities research reviews, 15*(3),
    225–234.
Olson, H. C., Jirikowic, T., Kartin, D., & Astley, S. (2007). Responding to the
    challenge of early intervention for fetal alcohol spectrum disorders. *Infants &
    Young Children, 20*(2), 172–189.
Ory, N. (2007). *Working with people with challenging behaviors: A guide for
    maintaining positive relationships* (2nd ed.). New Lenox, IL: High Tide Press.
Paley, B., & O'Connor, M. (2009). Interventions for children with fetal alcohol
    spectrum disorders: Treatment approaches and case management.
    Developmental Disabilities Research Reviews, 15, 258–267.
Pelech, W., Badry, D. E., & Daoust, G. (2013). It takes a team: Improving stability
    among children and youth with fetal alcohol spectrum disorder in care in
    Canada. *Children and Youth Services Review, 35*(1), 120–127.

Rasmussen, C., Andrew, G., Zwaigenbaum, L., & Tough, S. (2008). Neurobehavioral outcomes of children with fetal alcohol spectrum disorders: A Canadian perspective. *Journal of Paediatric and Child Health, 13*(3), 185–191.

Rutman, D., Callahan, M., Lundquist, A., Jackson, S., & Field, B. (2000). Substance use and pregnancy: Conceiving women in the policy-making process (Vol. 112). Ottawa: Status of Women Canada.

Ryan, S., Bohjanen, S., & Humphrey, M. (2009). Left behind: Lack of research based interventions for children with fetal alcohol spectrum disorders. *Rural Special Education Quarterly, 28*(2), 32–38.

Stoddard, S. (2008). A good guardian: Addressing the complex needs of children with fetal alcohol spectrum disorder in the care of Children's Services (Unpublished project proposal). Alberta, Canada.

Streissguth A. P., Barr H. M., Kogan J., & Bookstein, F. L. (1997). In A. Streissguth & J. Kanter (Eds.), *The challenge of fetal alcohol syndrome: Overcoming secondary disabilities* (pp. 25–39). Seattle, WA: University of Washington Press.

Streissguth, A., & Kanter, J. (Eds.). (1997). *The challenge of fetal alcohol syndrome: Overcoming secondary disabilities*. Seattle, WA: University of Washington Press.

Streissguth A. P., & O'Malley, K. (2000). Neuropsychiatric implications and long-term consequences of fetal alcohol spectrum disorders. *Seminars in Clinical Neuropsychiatry, 5*(3), 177–190.

Vig, S., Chinitz, S., & Shulman, L. (2005). Young children in foster care: Multiple vulnerabilities and complex service needs. *Infants & Young Children, 18*(2), 147–160.

CHAPTER 3

The Edmonton Model for Improving Delivery of Health-care Services for Children and Families in Care through Pediatric Case Management

Dr. Tami Masterson

Introduction

My interest in the topic of caring for vulnerable children and families is grounded in my experience working in the Alberta health-care system for over 20 years. My first job was in the capacity of an emergency room nurse, then as a medical student and resident in pediatrics, and finally as a pediatrician. I believe I received excellent medical education in both of my professional programs. However, my education rarely touched upon the health-care needs of socially vulnerable children. Details about the purpose, mandate, policies, and procedures of the foster care system were never discussed. Most significantly, the unique health-care needs of socially at-risk families were not addressed. Based on my personal experience, I believe that medical providers are trained in the social determinants of health, but that concrete, practical teaching regarding the

Suggested Citation: Masterson, T. (2014). The Edmonton model for improving delivery of health-care services for children and families in care through pediatric case management. In D. Badry, D. Fuchs, H. Montgomery, & S. McKay (Eds.), *Reinvesting in Families: Strengthening Child Welfare Practice for a Brighter Future: Voices from the Prairies* (pp. 45–61). Regina, SK: University of Regina Press.

health management of at-risk children and families is not provided (see Leslie et al., 2003).

In this chapter, I describe the health needs of vulnerable children and families and explore the association between emotional trauma and an individual's lifelong health and well-being. I briefly describe the Edmonton–Pediatrics for Kids in Care (E-PKIC) program, a health-care initiative with the goal of improving health-care delivery to vulnerable children, especially those children involved with the Child and Family Services Authority (CFSA). Furthermore, I identify barriers to health-care delivery and argue that systemic policy shifts must occur for the health-care needs of at-risk individuals to be adequately met. Lastly, I will discuss some potential research questions that may help health-care professionals deliver improved care. Additionally, these questions are aimed at assisting administrators and policy-makers with creating and supporting socially just and financially responsible health-care delivery.

At-Risk Children and the Health-care System

I began my pediatrics career in an inner-city hospital that delivered approximately 5,000 babies each year. As part of my pediatric duties at this hospital, I would examine newborn babies prior to their discharge home. I found it startling how many families lacked the basic resources and necessities that so many of us take for granted (Committee on Early Childhood, Adoption and Dependent Care, 2000). Some of these families had previous involvement with the CFSA. Many of the mothers and fathers had been children in need and in the care of the CFSA after suffering abuse and neglect. For similar reasons, many of the families' older children were in the temporary or permanent care of the CFSA. In their study of reactive attachment disorder (RAD) in infants and young children, Zeanah and Gleason (2010) noted its especially high prevalence in "maltreated, institutionalized, and formerly institutionalized children," who were raised in "inadequate caregiving environment[s]" (p. 1). RAD is just one of many mental and physical disorders suffered by this population of parents. The majority of mothers had used substances including alcohol, street drugs, and prescription drugs throughout their pregnancies, had mental health issues, lived in a violent home environment, and had limited, if any, social supports. Our hospital health-care team included social workers that met with socially at-risk families in the hospital and often consulted with the CFSA prior to discharging a child. The vast majority of these children left the hospital without the CFSA's involvement, their only discharge instructions being to make an appointment with the assigned pediatrician in two weeks' time.

In my hospital's general pediatrics clinic, I (like all pediatricians) provided medical care to foster children, many of whom were born at the hospital where I worked. Very few of these children saw the assigned pediatrician for follow-up; in fact, most had never seen a doctor. At the initial examination, the majority of foster children I assessed were physically unhealthy, developmentally delayed, and had academic, mental health, and behavioural issues. All had experienced significant emotional trauma related to neglect and abuse. Schore (2001) recognized the prevalence of this traumatic abuse on children. He explored the long-term effects of neglect and abuse on children, concluding that, "repetitive, sustained emotional abuse is at the core of childhood trauma...and that parental maltreatment or neglect compromises cognitive development" (Schore, 2001, p. 205; see also O'Hagan, 1995; Trickett & McBride-Chang, 1995). There is a great deal of research and literature on the effects of trauma on the well-being and health of children and adults. Prior to my work at E-PKIC, I was unfamiliar with the literature on the adverse health effects of emotional trauma. As such, I question whether there is widespread awareness of the health impacts of trauma among medical care providers.

Even if the health-care providers caring for the thousands of at-risk babies born each year are not familiar with the literature on the effects of trauma, common sense tells us that being exposed to some or all of the risk factors for CFSA involvement is unhealthy, to say the least. These risk factors include but are not limited to poverty; homelessness; parental addictions; capacity and mental health issues; and exposure to domestic violence, abuse, and neglect (Committee on Early Childhood, 2000). As doctors, we are also well aware that these families are unlikely to seek preventative health care after hospital discharge. Children in socially vulnerable families are much more likely to receive their medical care in medi-centres or emergency departments than from a family physician or pediatrician. If traumatized children are not receiving ongoing care in a medical home from a consistent long-term medical provider, their health needs are unlikely to be met (Garner et al., 2012).

After coming to this realization, I began to question my professional practice and wonder how I could increase my effectiveness as a physician working with socially at-risk patients. I also knew that unless I modified and improved my medical practice, I would continue to feel culpable regarding the numerous ways that these children and families *fall through the cracks* in the health-care system. This questioning marked a turning point in my career. My priorities as a pediatrician changed, and my primary goal became helping families *before* their children had health issues related to mental or physical trauma, and if possible prior to CFSA involvement. I also strove to be a better pediatrician to children in foster care. In order to achieve these goals it was clear to me that I had a great deal to learn, and that the best solution was to partner with the CFSA. Up to that point, I had very limited knowledge about how the CFSA worked. In order to better understand how the health-care and CFSA systems support these families, I have attempted to provide a medical home that offers specialized, comprehensive, and ongoing care to hundreds of at-risk children.

Barriers to Health-care Delivery

Over time, I began to identify specific barriers that impeded the effective delivery of health care to children and families who were at risk for involvement, or already involved, with the CFSA. It is my belief that most barriers to the delivery of adequate health care are a response to limited resources. In many cases, we have a "God helps those who help themselves" attitude toward the delivery of services. This attitude may be reasonable when we are working with families who are resourced and well supported. However, it is imperative that policy-makers and health-care professionals understand that a large number of people will be excluded from services because of their inability to follow the complicated processes necessary to access care. Many of the people excluded from services are those most in need of help. These families lack necessary support systems and often struggle with meeting their basic needs, such as transportation, adequate nutrition, and stable, secure housing. The caregivers in these families are often employed in work environments with managers who are intolerant of requests for time off to attend medical appointments. Without employment, overcoming poverty becomes a family's most immediate challenge, and meeting health needs is rendered secondary. I have seen many parents lose their jobs because of the health-care needs of their family members.

Certain families also lack access to a phone to facilitate communication regarding medical issues and appointments, and few have safe, skilled childcare for their children. Some parents are illiterate and/or cognitively impaired, and the majority live in a violent and impoverished home environment. Many of these parents also suffer from some type of addiction and/or mental health issue. I believe that many socially vulnerable families feel disconnected and distrustful of the very systems that are supposed to help them. This phenomenon occurs primarily because of an individual's or family's past experiences with medical providers who have been unable to help them. Some medical providers display frustration, indifference, and prejudice toward socially vulnerable families, creating yet another barrier to health care. I believe that most professionals wish to help vulnerable families, but we fail in this endeavour because we work within systems that by design do not adequately address the needs of at-risk families. This leaves those we are trying to help feeling defeated.

Another significant barrier to health-care delivery is the fact that health-care professionals are often unable to locate children, caregivers, or children services workers to arrange appointments for children in care. Because children move between placements and because caseworkers change frequently, contact information is often inaccurate. If the appointment is missed or the child cannot be located, his/her health needs will not be met. While the movement of children between different care situations within the CFSA system is unchangeable in the short term, there is a clear need to increase communication and collaboration between the CFSA and health professionals.

It is also necessary for all individuals involved in service delivery to socially vulnerable children to realize that these young patients are the most medically at-risk children in society. I believe that many professionals involved with at-risk children, regardless of their discipline (i.e., health, CFSA, education, justice, etc.), do not appreciate the critical fact that children in care have unique health needs that are exacerbated by frequent change and a lack of consistent caregiving relationships. Leslie et al. (2003) opened similarly, remarking that primary "providers need to be knowledgeable with respect to the unique circumstances of children in foster care, mental health, and developmental assessments" (p. 143). The authors stressed the fact that "pediatric literature is replete with research documenting the limited training of pediatricians with respect to behavioral and developmental problems and consequent limited identification of these types of problems in primary care in children in the general population" (Leslie et al., 2003, p. 143). The need for additional education and reform in medical practices is indeed apparent, yet 10 years after their study (Leslie et al., 2003) was published the same problem persists within the health-care community.

Breaking Down the Barriers

I believe the first and most important barrier to health-care delivery is many professionals' lack of understanding of the needs and challenges that at-risk families and children face when seeking appropriate health-care services (Leslie et al., 2003), and the practitioners' inability to dedicate the time necessary to arrive at that understanding. Those professionals that do consider the inadequate delivery of health care to at-risk individuals or families often conclude that it is a system-wide issue that is beyond their control, or that the problem is so big that there is nothing we as individuals can do. After years of witnessing ineffective service delivery because of missed phone calls and appointments, I decided to alter my approach to health-care delivery for socially vulnerable families. The Edmonton–Pediatrics for Kids in Care (E-PKIC) program is a result of the changes that I implemented in my pediatrics practice.

E-PKIC is a program that successfully delivers medical care to socially vulnerable families because of the ability of our health-care team—comprised of a children services worker, a hospital social worker, a nurse, and a pediatrician—to identify and overcome barriers to that care. Once the reasons for obstruction to care are identified and understood, it is often possible to work toward breaking down those barriers that stand in our way. Breaking down barriers requires proactive change, and many of the E-PKIC partners within health care, including the CFSA, foster care, education, and justice and government officials, seem unable to advo-cate for the positive transformation of the systems in which we currently work. Our partners experience constant changes to the delivery of ser-vices that they can offer individuals, and the majority of these changes result in fewer services being provided to socially vulnerable families.

The driving force behind E-PKIC is the strong belief that positive changes in service delivery must occur. Professionals need to see the health of the families they work with improving. If not, many of us experience compassion fatigue and burnout. Most of us care for socially vulnerable families because we want to help, but unfortunately our cur-rent model of care delivery leaves many of us feeling discouraged and overwhelmed by the enormity of the issues. While I still become over-whelmed, I am much less discouraged today due to the success of the E-PKIC program. Many of our families are healthier as a result of the care rendered by our clinic, which in turn motivates us to continue to be inno-vative in the ways we deliver health-care services.

E-PKIC works because we are a team of professionals coming together with a common goal: the improved health of socially vulnerable children and families. We share a collaborative attitude as well as the conviction that the manner in which services are delivered to socially vulnerable families must change (Committee on Early Childhood, 2000; Leslie et al., 2003; National Collaborating Centre for Mental Health, 2005). While Leslie et al. (2003) specifically recommend the establishment and enforcement of national guidelines to render more adequate care to foster children and those involved with the CFSA (p. 135), I have found that local pro-grams like E-PKIC also offer effective solutions. E-PKIC challenges barri-ers directly in order to achieve our goal.

How Does E-PKIC Help Families?

We understand that services will not be delivered to socially vulnerable families if adequate support is not offered. In sum, our clinic has a practical approach to care. Our specialized process of health-care delivery includes

- The organization and coordination of appointments for families, and assistance with money and transportation when necessary;

- The distribution of phone cards to patients, thus enabling care-givers to make the phone calls necessary to their family's health;
- Provisions of food, household supplies, and clothing for families in need;
- Assistance in filling out paperwork, and support by accompany-ing patients to conferences and meetings in person, in order to serve as immediate advocates for the well-being of these at-risk children and families; and
- Clarifying what we can and cannot do, thus maintaining the accountability of the E-PKIC program and in turn expecting accountability from the professionals and families with whom we work.

I firmly believe that accountability is absolutely necessary to build healthy and trusting relationships. As previously stated, many of these families have worked unsuccessfully with professionals in the past, and if E-PKIC is unable to gain the confidence of the families we serve, it is impossible for us to be effective in reaching our goals.

E-PKIC is also committed to challenging health-care policies that put children in care at a disadvantage. We ask our professional partners to be accountable to socially vulnerable families. For example, we noted that children in Edmonton were frequently denied mental health therapy and tertiary-level developmental pediatric services unless they had been in a "stable" placement for several months. Yet the idea of "stable" place-ment is fairly subjective, pointing to the ineffective nature of much of the policy surrounding at-risk children whose living conditions are subject to different types of interpretation by the numerous individuals involved in the process. This subjective, unreliable form of interpretation can have serious consequences for a child's health, depending on their short- or long-term medical care needs.

Any professional who works with at-risk families understands that often it is the children who are most in need that are moved frequently and are much less likely to live in stable, long-term placements (Sallnäs, Vinnerljung, & Kyhle Westermark, 2004). Many of these children live in group-care settings, which further complicates health-care delivery. In the past, early intervention services would only work with families, not individual children without a "parent." However, discussions with the administrators of early intervention services resulted in a change in health policy, and young children living in group-care placements are no longer excluded from their programs. This achievement marks an important step in our process of improving health-care delivery to at-risk children. Unfortunately, we have been less successful in effective partnering with mental health services (Leslie et al., 2003; Committee on Early Childhood, 2000).

Every child who is assessed at the E-PKIC receives a comprehensive and specialized medical assessment; regular follow-up appointments in the clinic initially occur at a minimum of every three months. All of the children have screening laboratory work, focused predominantly on detecting anemia — a condition that is present in many of our patients — and infectious diseases such as HIV, syphilis, and hepatitis C and B. All of the children are referred for hearing, vision, and dental screens, and we collaborate with the child's school program and/or refer the child for early intervention services.

The incidence of health issues in traumatized children is under-reported in the literature, based on our experiences in the E-PKIC program. As previously stated, all the children we see have health issues of varying degrees of severity. Each time a child moves placement, they will often have their eyes and teeth checked as well as have a medical exam, but because E-PKIC provides ongoing care we know the child and can maintain accurate health records for the child that we communicate to every new caregiver. Furthermore, we see the children when they are ill so there is less need to seek medical care in emergency rooms and medi-centres. Also, because pediatric medicine is dependent on the history provided by the child and caregiver — as well as ongoing medical assessments — the relationships we build with the children and caregivers allow us to provide improved medical care. For example, there is no medical test to detect asthma in small children; this diagnosis is based on the clinical presentation of the child over time and the child's response to medications. A positive family history also supports the diagnosis of asthma. Prior to working in the E-PKIC medical home model of care, I frequently provided medical care without a family and past medical history, and without the ongoing assessment of the child. I was also unable to provide the child with the comfort and support that comes from the long-term relationship that children and families build with their pediatrician.

Socially vulnerable children, especially those in the care of CFSA, often have unmet health needs, and many have never seen a doctor or had regular medical care. At E-PKIC, we believe that the concept of "health" encompasses an individual's spiritual, emotional, behavioural, mental, developmental, academic, and physical well-being. Children in care have compromised health because of lifelong trauma, often beginning at the prenatal stage and continuing through CFSA involvement (Schore, 2001). Most of the health issues children in care experience can be directly related to the trauma they endure.

Trauma's Adverse Effects on the Growth of Vulnerable Children

Children in care are frequently abused and neglected. They often live with impoverished parents who have come from families with intergenerational trauma caused by addictions and violence. A large proportion of the children we see have suspected or confirmed in-utero substance exposure. The National Scientific Council on the Developing Child (2006) reported that "recreational neurotoxins [like alcohol and recreational drugs] are most damaging during pregnancy because of the heightened susceptibility of the embryonic and fetal brain to developmental disruption," causing debilitating long-term disorders and developmental defects (p. 4). Many of our families have a high burden of mental illness as a consequence of family stress and trauma. Mental health issues can also contribute to and/or cause family trauma. This cycle of trauma demonstrates substantial growth with each generation.

Families involved with the CFSA in the Alberta, Canada, region are disproportionately of First Nations ethnicity. Aboriginal people constitute approximately 4% of the Canadian population and 8% of the Albertan population, but they represent nearly 75% of the children currently under the care of the CFSA (Garner et al., 2012). Cultural sensitivity and awareness surrounding the trauma experienced by First Nation people is essential in order to work effectively with these families. Trauma must be recognized as a significant cause of lifelong disability and dysfunction (Garner et al., 2012).

The health status of Aboriginal peoples is intimately associated with the historical trauma endured by Aboriginal populations. Since the

onset of Canadian colonialism, the subsequent creation of public policies like the Indian Act of 1867 and residential schooling have perpet-
uated Aboriginal trauma. Historical trauma is defined as a "collective
emotional and psychological injury over the lifespan and across generations" that results in adverse "psychological, behavioural, and medical"
consequences (Mitchell & Maracle, 2005). The enormous harm perpe-
trated upon Aboriginal peoples as a consequence of complex historical
trauma is appropriately conveyed through the use of terms like cultural
genocide and/or the Native holocaust (Morrissette, 1994; Stannard, 1992;
Churchill, 1997).

Aboriginal cultural genocide has created an environment of per-
sistent health inequality that the majority of medical professionals and
policy-makers have simplistically approached through the concept of
risk factor analysis. For example, science has proven that factors/deter-
minants such as underemployment or unemployment, food insecurity,
and inadequate housing can contribute to illness (Mikkonen & Raphael,
2010), but the poor health status of Aboriginal peoples is inadequately
explained by risk factor analysis and/or social determinism. I am sad-
dened to say that during my medical training I was taught uncountable
times that Aboriginal ethnicity was a risk factor for multiple medical
conditions, but not once was the concept of historical trauma discussed.
Common sense tells us that the effects of a genocide cannot be repaired
solely through wealth, food security, and housing.

Why do Aboriginal people continue to experience poverty, hunger, and
homelessness? Generations of medical professionals and government
policy-makers have been unable to positively impact the health status of
Aboriginal peoples. I believe this is because professionals and policies
have inadequately considered the complex social-political root cause of
health disparity between Aboriginal and non-Aboriginal Canadians. Non-
Aboriginal Canadians need to educate themselves about the history of
our government's public policies pertaining to Aboriginal people. In my
professional and personal life, this knowledge has changed my approach
to pediatric health care and has endowed me with immense compassion
and respect for my Aboriginal patients. Many academic and clinical professionals are creating models for health care built on the awareness of
the effects of intergenerational trauma (Menzies, 2010). Yet, these tools
for care are only available to health-care providers who understand the

effects of historical trauma. All Canadians need to advocate for changes to policies in order for the effects of trauma to be taken into account in the health-care system. If this does not occur, subsequent generations of Aboriginal children will, unfortunately, continue to experience health disparity and illness.

Recognizing Trauma

Regardless of the origins of trauma, its effects are the same. Traumatized children are at an increased risk for physical, developmental, behavioural, mental health, and academic issues (Perry, 2000; Schore, 2001). In the E-PKIC clinic, almost all the children we see have at least one developmental problem and generally present with multiple behavioural issues. Most of the children we see have severe global delays and behavioural issues that are extremely challenging for caregivers. Almost all of our children have difficulty with regulating their responses to stress and emotions, which is one of the key features of reactive attachment disorder (RAD), a condition that is much more prevalent in at-risk children (Zeanah & Gleason, 2010). Perry et al. (1995) documented that "children exposed to sudden, unexpected man-made violence appear to be more vulnerable—making the millions of children growing up with domestic violence or community violence at great risk for profound emotional, behavioral, physiological, cognitive, and social problems" (p. 273). This is especially true for newborns and children who were exposed to stress and substance abuse during pregnancy.

Trauma, whether from substance abuse in pregnancy, neglect, or physical or mental abuse, can impede the normal development of a child's brain (Perry, 1994; Perry, 2000; NSCDC, 2006; Schore, 2001). The cognitive effects of a brain injury are generally irreversible, and the injury continues to worsen as a result of ongoing exposure to trauma. Children in care often suffer from untreated or undertreated chronic illnesses, including, but not restricted to, asthma, eczema, constipation, encoporesis, enuresis, swallow dysfunction, gastro-esophageal reflux disease, recurrent infections, and infestations including scabies and lice (Leslie et al., 2003). At E-PKIC, most of the children we see have multiple cavities that are severe enough to warrant extractions or capping. This fact was the motivation behind the incorporation of dental services into our program, which has proven to be a beneficial expansion of our health-care offerings.

Furthermore, in-care children often have growth and eating issues. Between the two extremes of malnourishment and overeating, obesity is much more common than failure to thrive. Overeating and dysfunctional behaviours related to food (i.e., obsessing about, stealing, hiding, and eating discarded food) are present in approximately 75% of the children we see post-apprehension. Current literature also indicates that the effects of early childhood trauma on the health of an individual are lifelong. Traumatized children have a higher incidence of medical conditions like diabetes, cardiac disease, mental health conditions, and addictions (Perry, 1994; Perry et al., 1995). Children who have lacked basic necessities and have experienced neglect and/or abuse by a trusted caregiver see the world as an unpredictable and unsafe place. They subsequently have difficulty with trust and attachment to others. Without adequate support and treatment, these children are at a high risk of having lifelong dysfunction in their relationships. As previously mentioned, the prevalence of RAD in at-risk child and adolescent populations is a telling example of the long-term adverse effects of neglect or trauma experienced by a young child (Zeanah & Gleason, 2010, pp. 1, 15).

Shifting Practice through the E-PKIC Initiative

Prior to E-PKIC, I was unable to complete a medical follow-up with almost 100% of the children I assessed. Since I have been working in partnership with Region 6, CFSA in the E-PKIC clinic, approximately 80% of the children we serve complete the medical assessments as described above after apprehension. One of the main goals of the E-PKIC program is to provide long-term, consistent, and specialized medical care to children in care. We work within a "medical home" model, meaning that the child's doctor should remain the same regardless of changes in children services workers (CSW), caregivers, and/or placement (Committee on Early Childhood, Adoption and Dependent Care, 2000). From the first assessment, all team members are invited to be involved. This means that the family of origin, children services caregivers, caseworkers, and support workers are invited to participate in the child's initial assessment.

The family of origin is also strongly encouraged to be involved in the medical care of their children while they are followed by our clinic. The advantage of such an approach is that the medical providers are given a more complete medical history and understanding of the challenges faced by the family of origin. Their presence at the initial appointment also expedites the process of obtaining consent for services and arriving at an agreement on the medical plan. Most importantly, I find that a child's sense of security increases when the foster parent/CFSA caregiver meets the family of origin while he/she is present, thus strengthening the relationship between the child and their new caregiver. Also, the relationship between caregivers often improves because they are able to demonstrate to one another the mutual care and concern they have for the child. In my opinion, the current dominant culture of minimal interaction between CFSA caregivers and biological parents is not beneficial to the child. In order for this concept to work, caregivers must be respectful of each other and demonstrate that the child's well-being is the focus of the relationship. In successful situations, the CFSA caregivers become a source of support for the entire family of origin, not just the child in care.

Conclusion

Common sense tells us that a child receives superior health care in a medical home model of care because the health-care providers have sufficient history and knowledge of the child's health to make sound medical decisions. If the child is consistently cared for by one designated physician, repetition of traumatizing and expensive physician visits and medical tests and emergency visits can be avoided. It is also intuitive that if socially vulnerable children and parents are emotionally supported by a team of caring professionals the health of all family members will improve. To my knowledge, there is no current research that proves these assumptions. Literature on this subject is thus clearly warranted. Enhanced community support of the E-PKIC program from the health, justice, and CFSA governmental sectors should be based on the evidence of the need for programs of its type. Documenting more concretely that such a need exists and demonstrating that the health of at-risk families is improved by the program are essential for the expansion of this beneficial and effective approach to better addressing the health care of at-risk populations. Furthermore, generating concrete data indicating the substantial decrease in illness rates, suffering, and health-care costs as a result of E-PKIC is equally important.

Other research questions that warrant further examination in the future include, but are not limited to, these:

- What is the current medical morbidity of children in care in Edmonton, Alberta? This information would inform health-care practices for all at-risk children in the region.
- Are the professionals (health-care providers, lawyers, judges, educators, and child services workers) who deliver services to vulnerable children and families aware of the adverse effects of childhood trauma on the developing brain?
- Are these same professionals aware that the parents of at-risk children likely also suffer from the effects of childhood and lifelong trauma?

Fortunately, I have always worked in a teaching clinic as a salaried physician and therefore I was able to take the time necessary to work with socially vulnerable families. The type of medical financial remuneration I receive has allowed E-PKIC to maintain an open door policy with respect to patients who miss appointments, as well as other unforeseen circumstances. We ask our families to be accountable for the health and well-being of their family. As such, if the child's caregiver is attempting to meet the health needs of the child, we will provide on-going medical care regardless of previous difficulties in health-care delivery. We believe that the acceptance and consistent and clear expectations given to families cared for through the E-PKIC program afford them the confidence to build relationships with the professionals in their lives. I have made it a priority not only to advocate for the health needs of each individual patient, but also to advocate for the health needs of socially vulnerable families at the local and provincial levels of government. Continued advocacy by my colleagues and myself will be needed to support and build upon the positive changes to health-care delivery we are experiencing at the E-PKIC program.

E-PKIC is fortunate to rely on a strong partnership with Region 6 and the CFSA, and our program has benefitted from the support of the Covenant Health Organization. There are thousands of children in care within Region 6, and there are many more socially vulnerable children within this region who are not currently involved with the CFSA. I believe it is possible to take better care of these children by ensuring that their health-care needs are met. Programs like the E-PKIC could be recreated with the investment of appropriate resources. In fact, Calgary has a similar program involving multiple pediatricians who provide comprehensive medical assessment and limited follow-up to children in care. Both Edmonton's and Calgary's PKIC programs are partnerships between local pediatricians and the regional CFSA. In my opinion, partnership between health-care practitioners and the CFSA, collaboration, and the desire to improve the health of vulnerable children should be the foundation of programs such as PKIC. The improved health of at-risk children decreases their suffering and would help to prevent the professional compassion fatigue and burnout of the medical practitioners that care for them. Healthy families use fewer resources and save the government money, and the health of socially vulnerable families will not improve without innovative, thoughtful, and compassionate changes to the systems that serve them.

References

Churchill, W. (1997). *A little matter of genocide: Holocaust and denial in the Americas, 1492 to the present*. San Francisco: City Light Books.

Committee on Early Childhood, Adoption and Dependent Care: American Academy of Pediatrics. (2000). Developmental issues for young children in foster care. *Pediatrics, 106*(5), 1145–1150.

Garner, A., et al. (2012). Early childhood adversity, toxic stress, and the role of the pediatrician: Translating developmental science into lifelong health. *Pediatrics, 129*, e224–e231.

Leslie, L., Hurlburt, M., Landsverk, J., Rolls, J., Wood, P., & Kelleher, K. (2003). Comprehensive assessments for children entering foster care: A national perspective. *Pediatrics, 112*(1.1), 134–142.

Menzies, P. (2010). Intergenerational trauma from a mental health perspective. *Native Social Work Journal, 7*, 63–85.

Mikkonen, J., & Raphael, D. (2010). *Social determinants of health: The Canadian facts*. Toronto: York University School of Health Policy and Management.

Mitchell, T. L., & Maracle, D. T. (2005). Healing the generations: Post-traumatic stress and the health status of Aboriginal populations in Canada. *Journal of Aboriginal Health*, (March), 14–24.

Morrissette, P. J. (1994). The holocaust of First Nations people: Residual effects on parenting and treatment implications. *Contemporary Family Therapy*, 16(5), 381–392.

National Collaborating Centre for Mental Health (NCCMH). (2005). Children and young people with PTSD. In *Post-traumatic stress disorder. The management of PTSD in adults and children in primary and secondary care* (pp. 104–116). London, UK: Gaskell and British Psychological Society.

National Scientific Council on the Developing Child (NSCDC). (2006). Working paper no. 4. Early exposure to toxic substances damages brain architecture. Waltham, MA: NSCDC.

O'Hagan, K. P. (1995). Emotional and psychological abuse — problems of definition. *Child Abuse & Neglect, 19*, 449–461.

Perry, B. D. (1994). Neurobiological sequelae of childhood trauma: Post traumatic stress disorders in children. In M. Murburg (Ed.), *Catecholamine function in post traumatic stress disorder: Emerging concepts* (pp. 253–276). Washington, DC: American Psychiatric Press.

Perry, B. D., Pollard, R. A., Blaicley, T. L., Baker, W. L., & Vigilante, D. (1995). Childhood trauma, the neurobiology of adaptation, and "use-dependent" development of the brain: How "states" become "traits." *Infant Mental Health Journal, 16*(4), 271–291.

Perry, B. D. (2000). Traumatized children: How childhood trauma influences brain development. *The Journal of the California Alliance for the Mentally Ill, 11*(1), 48–51.

Sallnäs, M., Vinnerljung, B., & Kyhle Westermark, P. (2004). Breakdown of teenage placements in Swedish foster and residential care. *Child & Family Social Work, 9*(2), 141–152.

Schore, A. (2001). The effects of early relational trauma on right brain development, affect regulation, and infant mental health. *Infant Mental Health Journal, 22*(1–2), 201–269.

Stannard, D. (1992). *American holocaust: Columbus and the conquest of the New World*. New York: Oxford University Press.

Trickett, P. K., & McBride-Chang, C. (1995). The developmental impact of different forms of child abuse and neglect. *Developmental Reviews, 15*, 311–337.

Zeanah, C., & Gleason, M. (2010). *Reactive attachment disorder: A review for DSM-V*. N.p.: American Psychological Association.

CHAPTER 4

Hearing their Voices: The Experiences of Women with High-risk Substance Misuse Involved with Mentoring Programs to Prevent FASD[1]

Linda Burnside

Fetal alcohol spectrum disorder (FASD) is a condition caused by prenatal exposure to alcohol and is considered to be a condition that can be prevented. The Parent-Child Assistance Program (PCAP) was developed in Seattle in the 1990s to provide women with a mentoring relationship that would reduce the risk of prenatal alcohol exposure for their children. PCAP evaluations demonstrate that mentoring is an effective intervention to assist women with high-risk alcohol misuse issues in altering the life circumstances that create risk to themselves and to their children,

---

Suggested Citation: Burnside, L. (2014). Hearing their voices: The experiences of women with high-risk substance misuse involved with mentoring programs to prevent FASD. In D. Badry, D. Fuchs, H. Montgomery, & S. McKay (Eds.), *Reinvesting in Families: Strengthening Child Welfare Practice for a Brighter Future: Voices from the Prairies* (pp. 63–86). Regina, SK: University of Regina Press.

1   Adapted from Burnside, et al. (2012). *Experiences of Women Involved with Mentoring: Summary of Activities, 2011–2012.* Available at: http://www.canfasd.ca/wp-content/uploads/2013/02/NAT_4_ExperiencesofWomenInvolvedinMentoring_eFinalReport2011-12.pdf

who are vulnerable to being born with FASD (Grant, Ernst, Streissguth, & Stark, 2005; Grant & Huggins, 2013; Grant, Streissguth, & Ernst, 2002; Grant, Pedersen, Whitney, & Ernst, 2007). In particular, the Seattle PCAP interventions were shown to be effective in preventing alcohol/drug exposed births, either by helping women to avoid alcohol and drug use during pregnancy or by helping them to avoid becoming pregnant if they were using alcohol and drugs. Other findings included increased maternal employment, more permanent child custody placements, and increased connections with services. These outcomes help mothers build healthy and productive lives, and improve the quality of the home environment for their children.

Mentoring programs have been established in many communities in northwestern Canada in response to the need to engage women more effectively in recognizing the dangers of alcohol use during pregnancy. Manitoba initiated two programs based on the PCAP model in 1998, and Alberta's first PCAP programs began in 1999. These two provinces have been the leaders in Canada in the provision of PCAP-modelled mentoring programs. There are now more than 20 PCAP or PCAP-like mentoring programs operating in Alberta, and seven in Manitoba, in both urban and rural locations (Government of Alberta Fetal Alcohol Spectrum Disorder Cross-Ministry Committee, 2009; Healthy Child Manitoba, 2009; Henneveld & McFarlane, 2009). Other western provinces, such as British Columbia and Saskatchewan, have also established mentoring programs that draw from the work of the PCAP experience as well as other program influences. Health Canada has also supported First Nations communities in responding to the issue of FASD by funding on-reserve mentoring programs and other interventions since 1999.

This chapter will describe the results of a qualitative study with women who had completed a PCAP mentoring program in Alberta or Manitoba conducted by a research team of the Canada FASD Research Network (CanFASD), a group of formally and informally connected professionals from a range of research sciences in northwestern Canada (information about CanFASD is available at http://www.canfasd.ca). The aim of this study was to learn about the experiences of women through personal interviews, focusing especially on how the mentoring program has made a difference in their lives. The analysis of their experiences led to the identification of common themes and processes of change that provide important insights for mentors, program supervisors, stakeholders, and funders. The women's voices poignantly express the powerful impact that mentoring has had in their lives.

Overview of Study

Methodology
It was anticipated that only a small number of women would be willing to participate in a study of this nature. Many mentoring programs in Manitoba and Alberta have been in existence for less than 10 years, and there are fewer than five graduates per year in some programs, due to the small size of programs and the intensive three-year duration of support that mentors provide to women. Given the challenges in developing trust with women who have often experienced difficulties with formal helping systems, it was also expected that some women would be reticent to talk about their experiences and would decline an invitation to participate in this research. Therefore, in order to attract a sample of 5–12 women, no specific sampling methodology was employed to solicit women from a cross-section of community types (for example, urban- or rural-based), cultural groups, provinces, or programs.

Instead, women were eligible to participate if they had completed a three-year mentoring program in Alberta or Manitoba in the previous 12 months and were willing to be interviewed. Mentoring programs were asked to recruit prospective participants by posting notices in their program waiting rooms, distributing letters of invitation to women who met the research project criteria and were involved in the agency's formal aftercare supports, and making personal contact with women they have mentored who had graduated from the program to provide them with a letter of invitation to participate in the study.

Women who expressed an interest to their contact at their former mentoring program were then contacted by one of the researchers for screening to ensure that they met the study participation criteria and were voluntary participants. Interviews were held at a setting of the woman's choosing: the mentoring program office, a neutral community location, or the woman's home. Each participant signed and was provided with a copy of a detailed letter of consent that was reviewed with the researcher prior to initiating the interview. Each interview lasted from one to two hours in duration and was recorded on a digital audio recorder. Interviews were then transcribed and analyzed.

Limitations
Since voluntary participation was one of the key characteristics that determined participation in the study, the 10 women who agreed to be interviewed for this study cannot be considered a representative sample of the population of women who have completed a mentoring program in Alberta or Manitoba.

Demographics and Characteristics
A total of 10 women agreed to participate in this qualitative study: six from Manitoba and four from Alberta. They ranged in age from 19 to 42 years of age. Three women completed a rural-based mentoring program and seven women completed an urban-based program. At the time of enrollment, seven women were pregnant, and five acknowledged using substances throughout these pregnancies. Seven women were in relationships at admission to the program, although one partner was incarcerated at the time of enrollment. Four of the women described their partners as abusive, and five partners were identified as using substances, with one partner selling drugs in addition to using substances. One woman who was not in a relationship reported having been in an abusive relationship in the past. At the end of the program, five women had partners, with two of these women remaining in the same relationship they had been in at intake into the PCAP program. At enrollment, five women had recently had their children apprehended by child welfare, and one woman was at risk of having her children apprehended. By program completion, all women but one were living with their children.

Discussion of Study Findings

The aim of this qualitative study was to learn about the experiences of women who had completed a PCAP-model mentoring program in Alberta or Manitoba, focusing especially on how the mentoring program had made a difference in their lives. Analysis of the responses of the 10 women who were interviewed for this research resulted in the identification of four distinct phases that were common across their experiences:

1. Engagement with the Program (characterized by one participant's observation, *"I think I hit rock bottom"*);
2. Discoveries through Mentoring (or in one participant's words, *"I wasn't always as broken as I thought I was"*);
3. Changes and Transformations (described by one woman as, *"It literally changed my life"*); and
4. Life after Mentoring (captured by one woman's assertion, *"I take care of myself now"*).

As much as possible, the words of the women themselves are used to articulate their experiences of being mentored. For example, one interview respondent from Manitoba summed up her interpretation of what mentoring was all about as follows:

> *You meet with this lady once a week and she gives you rides that you need or takes you to appointments if you need. She's there whenever you need to talk and gives you information on stuff like parenting and FASD and stuff like that and whatever. It's an awesome program and they don't judge you and it's all confidential and it's awesome. I love it.*

Phase 1: *"I Think I Hit Rock Bottom"*— Engagement with the Program

For all of the women, their lives leading up to enrollment in the mentoring program were characterized as the most desperate of times. They used similar terms to describe the personal challenges they were facing, including having difficulty coping, feeling like giving up, and feeling alone and abandoned. Five women had experienced significant losses just prior to enrollment (the death of a partner by suicide, the death of a parent by homicide, the death of a parent by illness, or the death of a friend by overdose). Additionally, five women had their children apprehended by child welfare just prior to their decision to enroll in the mentoring program, and one had been threatened with apprehension as soon as she delivered her child in hospital. Four women stated that their substance use was at its highest during this time. The profound losses in their lives had taken a toll and left the women with no hope for the future. Comments about this time in their lives included, *"I really, just truly, was a shell and just empty"* and *"I was really afraid that I was about to lose everything"* and *"I knew that if I don't get this help, I'm going to die."*

"This help" was the mentoring program. Many women recognized that they could no longer cope alone and had no other source of support in their lives. Many women identified their children as a primary motivator for enrolling in the mentoring program. They also liked the practical supports that the program offered, such as transportation, information, and support to attend appointments. However, the most important reason they agreed to enroll in the mentoring program was that the offer of support was immediate. One woman stated:

> *I think the hardest time was when I first made that phone call and that time, they came right away. The help started right away. These people are going to be here, they are going to be here to help me, and it just got better.*

Phase 2: *"I Wasn't as Broken as I Always Thought I Was"*—Discoveries through Mentoring

Once women agreed to participate in the mentoring program, they reported that the development of trust was crucial to their ongoing involvement. Their life experiences had left them unable or unwilling to trust others, but despite their dire circumstances, they needed to know that they could trust their mentors. Mentors frequently told women at the start of the program that their involvement was confidential, which meant a lot to the women. They also talked about how important it was not to be judged, as so many had already judged them in their lives. Respondents described the development of trust this way:

> *It was just sudden. It was just...everything is so beneficial. It was just the talking and somebody hearing my side, and the real*

side. It wasn't just someone assuming something and treating me a certain way. They really wanted to know how I was feeling, and I could really open up, whether it was good or bad, and I liked that.

[My mentor] made a commitment to me and she kept it. She said, "I will be here every week and you call me whenever you need," and she kept that commitment and she was always willing to help. She was always willing to help no matter what I needed, and taking me anywhere. She was always there.

The women identified what mentors did as the most significant part of the developing relationship of trust. Specifically, they mentioned the provision of emotional support, encouragement, compliments, and practical assistance (for example, transportation) to access required services (such as medical care and resources like food banks). Most women had never experienced this kind of support before. For example, one woman stated:

Some people, like I said, in the past they try to give me shit. That didn't help me and that didn't change me. It pissed me off. I went and did it even more. But when you have someone like [a mentor] in your life coming to you and saying "Good job, you know you are doing the right thing," it just takes a whole load off every time you meet that person. Every time you are around that person is positive.

Secondly, women identified the characteristics of their mentors that made a difference to them, such as being compassionate, being reliable, and having a big heart. It was these attributes that often led to mentors becoming so close to the women, they were almost like friends. Almost all of the participants described their mentor as being like a friend in many ways, although they were also able to distinguish between personal friends and professionals.

It got more personal and she was more of a sister almost, but on a professional level. She kept her professionalism, but she also took

that one step closer to me. We were friends, almost, and I would
tell her things that I would never tell anybody.

The respondents also appreciated the advice that mentors would give to them. In many cases, these words of advice continued to guide the actions of the women after program completion. One woman explained it was like having her mentor's voice in her head, telling her what to do or how to handle things differently. This was particularly helpful when dealing with child welfare agencies, women reported, as they were reminded to stay calm and advocate for themselves. For example:

Then my meetings with CFS [Child and Family Services]. She
would give me some pointers, like "Maybe you should try it this
way, instead of this" kind of thing, and try to help me do things
differently, in a positive, better way.

Importantly, once trust was established in the relationship between mentor and participant, women were willing to accept challenges from their mentors. On occasion, mentors had to confront the women and push them to do what they needed to do. Women experienced these interactions as difficult, as they were faced with realities they preferred to avoid or had to overcome their fear about something they didn't believe they could manage. Still, these confrontations did not damage the trusting relationship. In fact, the high degree of trust, caring, and respect were the very things that made such confrontations possible.

Usually, [my mentor] was quite direct in her words. Even though
on occasion they could be hurtful, she would tell me before that
"This is going to hurt, but I'm going to say it."

[My mentor] is very opinionated, strong-willed, abrupt, and some-
times ignorant a little bit, but you know, when it comes from a
good place and a good heart, you know that she's only saying it to
make a difference for your life. She just changed everything for me.

Often, the mentor was the only one in the woman's circle who could provide her with the support she needed. One woman described her experience of leaving the province to attend a residential treatment facility, with the support of her mentor:

[My mentor] drove me to the bus, gave me some advice. She hugged me, she was so proud of me and she's like "Oh, I'm so proud of you, do it, do it." She encouraged me so much and she was the only one that was at the bus stop, saying "You can do this. You can do this and I will be there once you come home and I will be waiting for you at the bus stop and I will meet you." And sure enough, when I was done, I finished, and then I came home and she was at the bus stop, and I gave her a big hug and she was all happy.

One of the most important activities of the mentoring program involved the identification and attainment of goals. Many respondents were not accustomed to articulating and working on goals. With encouragement from their mentors, women began to identify goals for themselves and develop plans to work toward them. Examples of goals included improved health care (attending medical appointments, healthy eating, etc.), attending parenting courses, engaging in hobbies, going back to school (for training, literacy, or high school credits), searching for housing, and working toward reunification with their children who were in child welfare care.

We started setting goals. And I never had those before. I didn't even have hobbies. Like, my hobby was drinking and going out every weekend.

Women also expressed their gratitude for the support of their mentors in working with the child welfare system. However, a couple of respondents noted that child welfare workers were not necessarily as pleased to be working with their mentors. Mentors were strong advocates, understood the child welfare system, and were willing to challenge the system on behalf of the women. In some cases, the mentors acted as a second pair of ears to help women remember what was said, and they often helped to interpret technical language and processes for the women.

Child welfare agencies were not generally seen as helpful, the women reported, as their caseworkers just told them to go to addictions treatment, or go to a parenting program, which felt like having to jump through hoops rather than getting real help. Women described their mentors as being more purposeful in helping women to see what they needed to do and why. Mentors were in a key position to facilitate communication between the women and their caseworkers, to ensure that agency expectations were clear and that women's strengths were recognized. As a result, mentors helped the women have faith that they could be successful in regaining custody of their children from child welfare care.

> *People are always paranoid about [child welfare], all the time,*
> *so to see that [my mentor] came in and she was definitely not on*
> *[child welfare's] side was a good thing, and it just opened up all*
> *the trust. Because that's a huge thing, especially when you are*
> *involved in drugs and you don't trust anybody.*

Often, one of child welfare's expectations of the women was completion of a parenting program. The women described needing specific feedback from their mentors about their parenting skills, needing to know that they were good mothers, as they were often unsure they were doing the right thing as parents.

> *I loved hearing that I was a good Mom. I loved hearing that I was*
> *doing it right. And I really needed to hear that, because I didn't*
> *know that.*

Many women reported feeling guilty for having failed their children. Once they were reunited with their children, they often wanted to make amends in some way, even apologizing to their children for their substance misuse. Some participants began to make connections between their own substance use and the unhealthy role modelling it presented to their children. They were concerned with trying to prevent another generation of substance misuse in their own children.

> *If you are teaching them positive and they see you being positive,*
> *then you are going to have a positive outcome for your kids and*
> *your family. But if you are going to sit there and drink in front of*

your kids and they are 7 or 8 years old, your kids are going to drink
in 10 years because they are going to think it's okay, and then they
are going to drink in front of their kids.

However, parenting was not without its significant challenges. Some of their attempts to compensate for their past mistakes were problematic, such as letting their children get away with things and learning that they needed to set consistent limits.

I felt guilty and now it's been over a year and I have had to start
putting my foot down, because I was letting them get away with
way too much.

Other challenges included engaging the necessary supports, whether community services or the assistance of a partner, to ease the burden of parenting. Despite these challenges, many women shared stories of feeling competent and strong as parents, surviving circumstances they might not have coped with well in the past.

There have been times; like just a couple of days ago was the worst
night I have ever had with my kids. Was the worst by far, and I
didn't know how I was going to get through it, but I got through it.
I survived. And then, all of a sudden, the next day was, probably,
the best day, it was just 'wow.'

Women also described their relationships with partners, both before, during, and since completion of the mentoring program. Partner relationships prior to admission to the mentoring program or in existence at the time of program initiation were often characterized by the man's abusive and controlling behaviour, his substance misuse, and his unhelpfulness in parenting or household maintenance. When talking about past relationships with unhealthy partners, the women often referenced how the nature of the relationship affected their self-esteem, their self-care, and their substance use.

Before, it was like, when I was with him, I didn't give a shit. I would
just put my hair up and I don't go shower for two or three days,

because I am always at home, and he kept me at home. And if I did
try to wash up or whatever, "Who are you trying to look good for?"
Now I can do whatever I want.

I told my ex, I said, "You know, someday, somebody is going to
appreciate me," and I said "Somebody is going to love me, some-
body is going to take me, and somebody is going to accept me and
make me feel better and going to appreciate me and take care of
me and love me, and not put me down and make me feel like shit
and treat me like dirt, and leave me and the kids alone all the time
and think about themselves."

Mentors were instrumental in helping women to recognize the abusive
and denigrating characteristics of their relationships, and although they
didn't tell women what to do, for many women, this insight helped them
to end destructive relationships.

I realized telling [my mentor] what was happening to me and
my partner, and she didn't make me change my mind or what-
ever, just made me open my eyes and realize it's not good for
me and my kids to go through that. Like, she gave me resources,
like "Okay, go to this and call this and that." But that's when I
realized, towards the end, like I said I got to snap out of it for
my kids.

Women recognized that they approached new relationships differently, although with hesitation for fear of making the same mistakes
again. They were often encouraged by their mentors to use their insights
to assess their new relationships. Women were often surprised by how
positive relationships with partners could be.

I was already into a year [of the mentoring program] and then
I met somebody. So I talked to [my mentor] about that too,
because I didn't want to start falling into a relationship again
with those signs of abuse, or whatever, and I started talking to
her and I would share those things with her, because she would
know of those signs. And I would tell her how I felt about the whole

situation, and then she's like "Yes, okay, it sounds good. Right on. See, things change, and things will get better." So, I am still with the guy today.

An important area of growth was learning how to deal with and recover from relapses. All 10 women involved in this study acknowledged that relapses were part of their recovery process while in the mentoring program. While one woman stated that she only had one or two relapses, most reported having several through the duration of the program. Some women talked about being able to identify their triggers for relapse as a result of being in the program:

- For one woman, it was nighttime, when she was alone and all the evening parenting and household chores had been done and she was watching television;
- For another, it was whenever she felt alone;
- For another woman, anger was a relapse trigger; and
- For another, it was harder to avoid drinking after her children were apprehended.

Women had enough trust in their mentors to tell them when they had relapsed. They recognized that disclosure about relapses was part of their recovery, that their mentors were not going to judge them but would challenge them to examine the reasons behind their relapses. Sometimes, the relapse was the incident that helped the woman decide that she needed to go into treatment.

I was really feeling guilty that [my mentor] was probably worried. So I remember calling her and she didn't freak out or nothing. She just said, "Do you want me to come and get you? Are you done, are you really done? You don't have to do this alone. We can do this together," so that made it a lot easier. And I just remember my relapses were getting fewer and farther apart because I was happy and I didn't feel like I needed to be sneaky, and I liked the trust that I was getting back in my relationship and stuff. I just liked the person that I was becoming. I just liked it.

[Your mentor] is there for you, like no matter what. Like no matter if you mess up, no matter if you slip, she's still going to help you, and she's not going to abandon you like other people did in your life.

Although relapses did occur, all 10 women talked about ways that they learned to cope with and prevent relapses. In most cases, women used their mentors as initial prevention strategies, by contacting them to overcome feelings of isolation, to seek out support, to cope with a bad day, and sometimes just to get over that moment of craving substances. Many talked about how their mentors were immediate in their responses to calls about needing support to prevent relapse.

When I had a bad day and had nobody to talk to, [my mentor] was there, she was like a phone call away. And she was just there when I felt angry, when I felt alone, when I felt, you know? And when I was starting, when I was home with the kids alone, I was starting to get bored again, and that's when usually an addict starts up again, because they have nothing to do. She came, and I told her. She came right away and got my mind off of it.

I would phone [my mentor] and she would phone me and come and pick me up and take me for coffee, because it takes 15 minutes to get off of craving whatever you had. She's the one who told me that.

One of the major changes women had to make in their lives to prevent relapses pertained to limiting their contact with family members and friends who were risky influences for substance misuse. It took considerable courage and strength to place boundaries around these relationships, and there were significant losses experienced as women disengaged from those who had otherwise been included in their support networks, often leaving them feeling isolated.

I kind of kept my distance and I knew that's what I had to do, is to stay away, because [my sister] could have a slip at any time, and it would be such an easy excuse for us to start doing our thing. And I just knew that was another thing too that you have to stay away from....Like [my mentor] said, you got to stay away and you have to change your friends, and you have to change people in your life, and you have to stay away from things like that. And you will know who your true friends are when they are there going through your healing process.

I am scared to have friends because they might not be suitable to my family. So I am just scared to have people around because if they drink, they are not good, or if they might do drugs. So I keep myself very isolated, and still do. And by having the program, it allowed me not to be isolated, because they were acceptable and they were people I could have in my home, and people we could go to and go to functions with without being judged.

Throughout their interviews, women talked about changes in their substance use, although some women did not attain (nor were they aiming for) full abstinence. However, there was considerable evidence of harm reduction as a result of changes to women's use of substances. In fact, some talked about harm reduction as being the best strategy toward making changes in their use of substances. Many women acknowledged mentors and the mentoring program for helping them to make the decision to enter treatment or change their substance use patterns, one of the key aims of the mentoring program.

With the amount of drugs that I was doing, it was hard for me to just go cold turkey, so we were just going to work on that really slowly.

After leaving the mentorship program, throughout the whole program, I did continue smoking marijuana, but at a lot less rate than what I had for the previous 30 years. But now I have quit that.... Well, I guess it would be about 7 months now, completely.

Women also commented on the effectiveness of their efforts to address their substance misuse (and many did achieve abstinence) and the profound changes in their lives related to substance use:

Drug use has changed definitely, yes. Did I do [addictions] programs when I was [in the mentoring program]?....No, [my mentor] was always trying to get me to go to AA meetings and stuff and I didn't want to. I felt uncomfortable at the time. I was probably still in denial. I guess I didn't want people to know. But since then, I have completed many programs and I have been clean and sober and off drugs.

Made me think a lot differently about drugs and alcohol and more aware of the consequences on parenting. Just the effects of drugs and alcohol have made me more aware, plus growing up with drugs and alcohol — not so much drugs, but a lot of alcohol in my surroundings. And maybe I've learned more about how come I turned out the way I did, or the way I talk to my mom, or the way I treated others and stuff. It made me more aware of that, maybe.

And perhaps most profoundly, the reflections of one woman:

I can't believe though, that today, when you see other addicts doing their drugs, I can't believe that I was there one time, and how much it's a waste, it's just a big waste of money and a big waste of life and time.

Phase 3: *"It Literally Changed my Whole Life"* — Changes and Transformations

The women who participated in this study identified many significant changes that had occurred in their lives, which they attributed to their experience of being mentored. These changes included specific, practical changes, such as:

- participating in programs they might not have accessed previously, such as literacy programs or addictions programs;
- developing insight into themselves, their families, and their substance use;
- learning how to deal with triggers for substance misuse;
- accessing practical supports, such as emergency food and milk, bus tickets, assistance to get to appointments, and

guidance with preparing resumés and conducting a job
search; and

- developing important life skills, such as budgeting, parenting
skills, and consistently using birth control.

Many women spoke about the things they had learned about themselves through the experience of being mentored, especially positive
changes in their attitudes or perspectives on life. Most significantly, they
identified increased self-confidence and self-esteem, feelings of competence and capability, self-acceptance, and a growing sense of self-worth
and maturity.

> *[My mentor] just helped me realize that little flicker of light inside.
> As long as you can feel that, then you will glow and people aren't
> going to see what you think they see, right. They are just going to
> see that kindness, and that lovingness, and smart and stuff like
> that. And that was something I always knew, but coming from
> someone else that also felt like that, it's like, okay then, that must
> be real, so that was huge.*

> *I was capable, and that I was beautiful, and I was worth it, and
> that I was worth it and I was smart. I think that feeling that I was
> smart....Nobody ever really saw that I was smart, but [my mentor]
> saw I was smart.*

> *I know that I am capable of doing things that I didn't know I did.
> And I am my own person.*

These changes were often directly and indirectly attributed to the wom-
en's mentors, leaving many women inspired to want to help other women.

> *The ability to trust, the ability to move on, the ability to have the
> strength even when times are really tough, that there's always a
> way out. There is always somebody there to help you and you just
> need to find it. Teaching me how to access communities, teaching
> me how to ask for help, and I take it with me probably every day,
> what [my mentor] has taught me.*

It kind of inspires me because they help me, and that makes me want to help other women.

Several women characterized the changes they experienced as total transformations, pointing out contrasts from who they had been, to who they are today. These changes occurred at a significant internal level, stimulating faith in themselves, empowerment, and, most importantly, recognition that it is their right to have a good life. Multiple quotes are appropriate to share the voices of women in transformation:

It literally changed my whole life. They gave me hope again. They gave me a faith in myself that had kind of left and, if up to the rest of the people in the world, I still wouldn't have any of that.

I got presented with an Eagle feather, actually, and there was the whole [ceremony] for two hours. It was just for me. Just to say that "You have been coming here for two years and we've watched you grow as a mom, and we've watched you as a person." And to be presented with an Eagle feather is just the biggest honour. And just everything, they made me a medicine bag where there is sage and there is sweetgrass, and it's for me. It was for me, and I have never felt so special, ever, in my life.

I didn't have a lot of faith five years ago, and I watched everybody walk all over me. And within meeting [my mentor], within four months, everything completely turned around and changed, to the point of having my boys back....They helped me get my wings together and helped me set off into flight into a good life. That's basically the way I could describe it.

Knowing that there is a wonderful life out there for me and I'm entitled to it. Life is what you make it. From where I came from before to how I am now, it's just, I don't know, it's so different. I am a totally changed person, not the person I used to be. You know, I have changed every single part of my life.

Interestingly, at the start of the interviews, women often downplayed that they had achieved anything remarkable in their lives, and were skeptical that anyone would be interested in their experiences, which they perceived to be quite ordinary. However, as each interview progressed, each woman expressed a new appreciation for her own journey and accomplishments, recognizing the magnitude of change she had gone through and the courage it took.

Phase 4: *"I Take Care of Myself Now"* — Life after Mentoring

The 10 women who participated in interviews expressed sadness that the mentoring program had ended for them and that they had "graduated." They wished that the program was longer, or that there were other programs or "aftercare" services that were available to them. Despite the transformational changes in their lives, they didn't feel ready for the program to end; they felt that their growth was incomplete and their work was unfinished. And, despite the end of their involvement in the program, they still call their mentors on occasion for advice and support.

> I was kind of disappointed too, because I didn't...like, I know I can still count on them, but I mean, I kind of felt like I was on my own now. And I felt kind of like there was things that I haven't done yet that were my goals, that I didn't get done really.

> It was more than losing a best friend. It was like, I don't even know, like more than a mother. It was kind of like I felt like I was losing everything.

As they elaborated on what the mentoring program meant to them, the women turned to describing the relational dynamics between themselves and their mentors that had been most meaningful. The enduring nature of these relationships, even though the formal aspect of contact had concluded, was poignantly expressed by many women.

> I still know that she's always going to be there if I ever needed to talk, no matter what. But I think she's at ease too, because she sees me doing the right things and she sees me doing good. So I

think she's a little at ease too, and she's like, "Right on, I did some-
thing. I helped somebody."

Despite their sadness at leaving the program, the women acknowledged that they had developed some skills to manage their lives more
independently. For example, they talked about how they had learned
to identify and work toward goals. While some goals had already been
attained during the mentoring program, women were also thinking
about their long-range goals that now seemed possible. For some, these
goals included employment, returning to school, and even becoming
mentors to other women. For others, their goals were more about self-
care: being able to support themselves and their children or getting their
health issues under control. Some women spoke about practical goals,
like getting a driver's license, buying a car, or obtaining their own home.
The women also talked about goals they had for their children, such as
getting an education and playing sports. Some also thought they would
want their children to know about their struggles with alcohol use and
abusive partners, feeling that telling their stories would help their kids
avoid these issues in their own lives.

> *I want them to have [the good] childhood that I had, where they*
> *don't know their mom as an addict. I want to be there for all the*
> *bake sales, I want to be there for all the field trips, I want that spe-*
> *cial feeling that I had, and I want them to know that they always*
> *know where mom is, that security, right? That's what I want, and*
> *that's what I'm going to give them.*

The women also described their current sources of support after completing the mentoring program, and it was evident that mentors continued to play an informal support role for women. Despite the changes they
had made, the skills they had developed, and the dysfunctional relationships they had left, there were still gaps in their support networks that
had not been filled once their mentors left that formal role. Some women
could only identify professionals as the current supports in their lives.

Finally, at the conclusion of the interviews, women were asked if they
had any advice for women who might be in similar life circumstances
who were considering enrolling in a mentoring program, as well as advice

they would give to mentoring programs themselves. For their advice to other women, the respondents were universal in their encouragement for women to join a mentoring program, citing its benefits to women who were in dire circumstances. Many spoke again about the qualities of mentors that made the experience so meaningful, especially the feeling of not being judged, and the opportunity to make real change in one's life. Their advice to women included:

> If you really want to make it and you really want to succeed, anything is pretty much possible when you become part of the program. That they don't leave much room for failure, and when you do, you just start again.

> The mentor program worker won't judge you. She will not judge you, she will be there for you, even if you have slipped, even if you think you don't matter, and just to trust them.

When it came to advice for mentoring programs, many women focused on strategies to make the program more known to women in the community, and the need for aftercare services. In particular, several women noted the critical role that health-care providers play in identifying women who may be using substances during pregnancy and making referrals to mentoring programs. They acknowledged the fear that many women might have about child welfare involvement, which might prevent them from acknowledging their substance misuse, but respondents felt that if health-care practitioners had a better understanding of addictions and presented with a non-judgmental attitude, they would be in a key position to help women get connected to mentoring programs and reduce, if not prevent, alcohol exposure during pregnancy.

Other strategies that were recommended included television and radio ads promoting the program, increased availability of pamphlets, presentations in the community, and a video or audiotape featuring women who have completed a mentoring program that could be shown to other women in addictions treatment programs or other social services environments. They also encouraged reaching out to teenagers who might be pregnant. A couple of the women also talked about how associating the mentoring program with FASD in its advertising was intimidating.

Finally, the women were interested in group mentoring or group support sessions, assuming that the participants were consenting to a group process, since their confidentiality would not be as protected as it is in a one-on-one relationship.

Recommendations

The voices of the women who participated in this study are strong testament to the power of mentoring. Relationships are key and, from what these women described, their mentors were successful in developing trusting relationships that allowed for deep and profound change to occur over time, affecting all aspects of their lives. Significant changes were noted in substance use (using a harm reduction lens), parenting skills, having children returned to their mothers, maintaining better boundaries with others, and finding relationships with partners who are not abusive. These outcomes provide clear advocacy and support for the continuation and expansion of mentoring programs for women with high-risk substance misuse.

However, these women did not feel completely ready for termination at the program's conclusion. They identified gaps in their informal support networks, they worry about relapse, and they are still in the process of achieving their goals. Aftercare supports are critically needed, and while they don't necessarily have to involve the same degree of intensity that mentoring provides, a relational model of service delivery is recommended.

Women reported enrolling in a mentoring program when their lives were most in crisis, when they had reached such a low point that they were at risk of losing (or had already lost) everything. While it is promising that mentoring programs can effectively engage women when they are experiencing such desperate circumstances, it does raise the question of how women might be engaged earlier, before they and their children have endured such deleterious experiences. Some strategies were identified by the women themselves, such as raising the profile of mentoring programs in the community and assisting health-care practitioners to become more cognizant of addictions and mentoring interventions when providing prenatal services, so that referrals can be made more easily.

However, the readiness of women to engage in mentoring is a theme that merits further research, to better understand what helps women engage in services and supports before their lives are in such a state of crisis. These insights would also further our efforts to reduce and prevent prenatal alcohol exposure.

It must also be noted that the women who participated in this study volunteered at the encouragement of their former mentors. Hearing from women who had a successful experience with mentoring may have resulted in a one-sided (albeit positive) view of the strengths and benefits of mentoring. Hearing the voices of women who left the program prematurely, or resisted engagement with the mentoring program, or who were dissatisfied with aspects of the program, would add to our knowledge of how mentoring can best meet the needs of vulnerable women who struggle with substance misuse.

Despite these limitations and gaps in the study, it is fitting to end this discussion of women's experience with mentoring with the words of one "graduate":

You can trust what I am saying for sure, because I have been there.

References

Government of Alberta Fetal Alcohol Spectrum Disorder Cross-Ministry Committee. (2009). *The mentor experience: An Alberta sampler* [Audio Podcast]. Retrieved from http://www.youtube.com/watch?v=13Dw1xCMZFs

Grant, T., Ernst, C. C., Streissguth, A., & Stark, K. (2005). Preventing alcohol and drug exposed births in Washington State: Intervention findings from three Parent-Child Assistance Program sites. *The American Journal of Drug and Alcohol Abuse, 31*, 471–490.

Grant, T., & Huggins, J. E. (2013). Intervention with mothers who abuse alcohol and drugs: How relationship and motivation affect the process of change in an evidence-based model. In N. E. Suchman, M. Pajulo, & L. C. Mayes (Eds.), *Parenting and substance addiction: Developmental approaches to intervention* (pp. 365–385). Oxford: Oxford University Press.

Grant, T., Pedersen, J. Y., Whitney, N., & Ernst, E. (2007). The role of therapeutic intervention with substance abusing mothers: Preventing FASD in the next generation. In K. O'Malley (Ed.), *Attention deficit hyperactivity disorder and fetal alcohol spectrum disorders: The diagnostic, natural history and therapeutic issues throughout the lifespan* (pp. 69–94). Hauppauge, NY: Nova Science Publishers.

Grant, T., Streissguth, A., & Ernst, C. (2002). Benefits and challenges of paraprofessional advocacy with mothers who abuse alcohol and drugs and their children. *Zero to three, 23*(2), 14–20.

Healthy Child Manitoba. (2009). *InSight Training Presentation*, April 2009 [PowerPoint slides]. Winnipeg, MB: Author.

Henneveld, D., & McFarlane, A. (2009). The mentor experience: An Alberta sampler. Retrieved from http://fasd.alberta.ca/documents/May_21_2009.pdf

Determinants of Mental Health Difficulties among Young Aboriginal Children Living Off-reserve

Christine Werk, Xinjie Cui, and Suzanne Tough

Introduction

The purpose of this chapter is to provide insight into the determinants of mental health in young Aboriginal children living off-reserve in Canada. The Aboriginal perspective of health emphasizes the importance of physical, spiritual, emotional, and mental health for child well-being (Trumper, 2004). Mental well-being in childhood is predictive of productivity in society, health, and happiness in adulthood (MHCC, 2012). Thus, encouraging mental health among young children is important for promoting their future mental well-being and for prevention of future societal problems (Babinski, Hartsough, & Lambert, 1999; Heimens Visser, Van Der Ende, Koot, & Verhulst, 2000; WHO, 2003).

Suggested Citation: Werk, C., Cui, X., & Tough, S. (2014). Determinants of mental health difficulties among young Aboriginal children living off-reserve. In D. Badry, D. Fuchs, H. Montgomery, & S. McKay (Eds.), *Reinvesting in Families: Strengthening Child Welfare Practice for a Brighter Future: Voices from the Prairies* (pp. 87–110). Regina, SK: University of Regina Press.

The Alberta Centre for Child, Family & Community Research (ACCFCR) is a not-for-profit charitable organization that is a leader in the development and dissemination of policy-relevant information. Researchers at the ACCFCR had the opportunity in 2009/2010 to perform secondary data analysis on the 2006 Aboriginal Children's Survey (ACS) completed by Statistics Canada. The lead scientist for this analysis was Dr. Werk. Drs. Tough and Cui contributed to development of the research plan, data analysis and interpretation, and manuscript preparation. Data was accessed at the University of Alberta Statistics Canada Research Data Centre. A number of analyses were conducted using the ACS; the mental health analysis is presented in this chapter.

Information about the mental health of young Aboriginal children is sparse, and diagnosed mental health conditions are relatively rare among young children (Cardinal, Schopflocher, Svenson, Morrison, & Laing, 2004). However, school-aged Aboriginal children are slightly more likely to have a mental health condition than their non-Aboriginal peers (Cardinal et al., 2004), and in adolescence and adulthood Aboriginal people are substantially more likely to attempt suicide than their non-Aboriginal peers (Cardinal et al., 2004). Researchers at the ACCFCR wanted to investigate factors associated with early signs of mental health challenges in early childhood, where there are few differences between Aboriginal and non-Aboriginal children (Cardinal et al.). Understanding the risk factors associated with future mental health conditions in young off-reserve Aboriginal children may help identify opportunities for intervention to promote mental health and general well-being throughout childhood.

To better address and potentially reduce mental health challenges, the most important factors associated with poor mental health need to be described. The following analysis was conducted to investigate the key factors associated with mental health difficulties early in the development of some Aboriginal children living off-reserve.

Method

The Aboriginal Children's Survey (ACS), conducted by Statistics Canada, is a survey (based on the 2006 census) of Aboriginal children (aged o to 5) living off-reserve in Canada in 2006. The ACS was developed with the consultation of National Aboriginal Organizations for the purpose of better understanding this young population. Informed consent of the possibility of secondary data use by qualified researchers was obtained following the Tri-Council guidelines (CIHR, 2010). The caregivers of 10,500 off-reserve Aboriginal Canadian children (aged 0 to 5) were surveyed across Canada and represented 135,020 children (O'Donnell, 2008). Non-Aboriginal or on-reserve Aboriginal comparisons were not available for this survey. For more details on the ACS, consult the concepts and methods guide (Statistics Canada, 2008).

The Strengths and Difficulties Questionnaire (SDQ) is an established measure of mental health and was included in the ACS. The SDQ is used to assess prosocial skills, hyperactivity, emotional symptoms, conduct problems, and peer problems in children and youth (Goodman & Goodman, 2009) such as "constantly fidgeting or squirming," "often unhappy, depressed, or tearful," or "considerate of other people's feelings." The SDQ was originally designed for children aged three to four but was used for children aged two to five in the ACS. Thus the SDQ was validated specifically for the ACS population, which led to slightly different item groupings than in past studies (Oliver, Findlay, McIntosh, & Kohen, 2009). These recommended new item groupings were used in the ACCFCR analysis of the 2006 ACS mental health data (see Oliver et al. for all questions and grouping).

A total difficulties score from the SDQ, which was taken by the researchers to represent overall mental health difficulties, was computed from a combination of hyperactivity, emotional, and conduct scores. Because the prosocial scores indicated in the SDQ were consistently high among young Aboriginal children living off-reserve, it was determined that these indicators could not be used to measure mental health. Instead, total difficulty scores rather than prosocial scores were used in conducting the mental health difficulties analysis. Children with high difficulty scores had the top approximately 20% of scores (9 out of 24 or higher). This higher difficulty score subset was compared to the bottom 80% subset of children who had lower difficulty scores, a factor that indicated lower emotional/behavioural difficulties. The highest difficulty scores are referred to in this report as *mental health difficulties* for ease of reporting. Having mental health difficulties by this definition simply means that the children with the highest total difficulty scores were at a higher risk of developing a mental health condition than were children with lower emotional/behavioural difficulty scores.

Difficulty scores were generally low among the survey sample; however, the relationship between mental health difficulty scores and mental health diagnoses has been shown to occur at a constant rate across the range (Goodman & Goodman, 2009), indicating that significant differences in SDQ scores across indicators (e.g., off-reserve Aboriginal children who lived in rental versus owned homes) are meaningful in terms of predicting future mental health disorders.

The statistical software used for all analyses was SAS version 9.2 in combination with SAS-callable SUDAAN, version 10.0. Estimations and regression analyses were conducted using weighted estimates, and variance was computed using ACS survey bootstrapping (1000 weights). Statistical significance was defined as $p < 0.05$.

To assess which determinants of mental health are of primary importance when other factors are taken into account, an adjusted mental health difficulties model was developed. The adjusted mental health difficulties model estimated the likelihood that a child with a given characteristic would experience mental health difficulties, while isolating the effects of other indicators. The constituent elements of the adjusted mental health difficulties model are discussed in the following sections. Percentages and adjusted odds ratios (represented as: adj. OR = #) associated with the adjusted mental health difficulties model are presented in the text.

All factors investigated, with the exception of age and gender, were significantly correlated with mental health difficulties when considered individually. A forward-selection logistic regression was used to determine the factors involved in predicting mental health difficulties (scores 9 or above). Child age and gender were added in Step 1 of the adjusted mental health difficulties model. Responses of "don't know," "refusal," or "not stated" were recoded as "missing" for all indicators before being entered into the model. Age and gender were forced into the model; other indicators significantly correlated with child mental health scores were also included and kept in the model if significant. The following standard Statistics Canada symbols were used to indicate caution with estimates:

- E: The estimate must be used carefully as it is associated with a high level of error; and
- F: The estimate does not meet Statistics Canada's quality standards.

Table 1. Adjusted odds ratios for high mental health difficulty scores, Canadian Aboriginal children aged 2 to 5

Indicator	Reference	Adjusted odds ratio	95% Wald confidence limit
Age 2 to 3	Age 4 to 5	1.1	0.99 - 1.32
Female	Male	0.9	0.82 - 1.07
Visited a psychologist/ psychiatrist	No visits in past 12 months	2.0*	1.27 - 3.21
Good/fair/poor health	Excellent/very good health	1.5*	1.27 - 1.83
Speech/language disorder	No speech/language disorder	1.3*	1.07 - 1.67
Anxiety/depression	Neither anxiety nor depression	8.8*	3.81 - 20.33
Attention deficit disorder	No attention deficit disorder	5.7*	3.23 - 10.07
Rent home	Own home	1.3*	1.06 - 1.47
Three or four people in home	Two people in home	1.1	0.83 - 1.54
Five or more people in home		1.3	0.98 - 1.84
0.1 to 0.5 moves per year	No moves	1.0	0.84 - 1.20
0.51 to 1.0 moves per year		1.1	0.89 - 1.31
1.1 or more moves per year		1.6*	1.22 - 2.03
Regular smoke in home	No regular smoke	1.2*	1.06 - 1.47
Food insecurity	No food insecurity	1.6*	1.25 - 2.06
Respondent 15 to 24 years	Respondent 45 or more years	2.0*	1.27 - 3.01
Respondent 25 to 34 years		1.7*	1.17 - 2.60
Respondent 35 to 44 years		1.5*	1.01 - 2.22

Significantly different from the reference group

Two foster or adoptive parents	Two parents (biological)	1.9*	1.25 - 2.85
Single biological parent		1.3*	1.05 - 1.48
Female less than high school	Female university	1.8*	1.41 - 2.25
Female high school complete		1.4*	1.16 - 1.82
Female non university post-secondary		1.4*	1.09 - 1.73
Daily need to explain	Less than daily need to explain	1.6*	1.25 - 2.09
Less than daily opportunity to watch/learn	Daily opportunity to watch/learn	1.6*	1.12 - 2.22
Less than daily story-telling	Daily story-telling	1.3*	1.06 - 1.53
More than two hours daily screen time	Two hours daily screen time or less	1.5*	1.27 - 1.68

*Significantly different from the reference group

Table 2. Percentage with high mental health difficulty scores by indicators (in logistic odds ratio), Canadian Aboriginal children aged 2 to 5

Indicator	Percentage	Reference Group	Percentage
Age 2 to 3	21.2%	Age 4 to 5	20.3%
Female	19.1%	Male	22.4%
Visited a psychologist/psychiatrist	45.5%	No visits in past 12 months	20.2%
Good/fair/poor health	34.1%	Excellent/very good health	18.7%
Speech/language disorder	33.2%	No speech/language disorder	19.6%
Anxiety/depression	78.0%	Neither anxiety nor depression	20.3%
Attention deficit disorder	72.5%	No Attention deficit disorder	19.9%
Rent home	26.7%	Own home	15.4%
Three or four people in home	19.0%	Two people in home	24.6%
Five or more people in home	22.7%		

0.1 to 0.5 moves per year	19.0%	No moves	17.2%
0.51 to 1.0 moves per year	24.9%		
1.1 or more moves per year	34.2%		
Regular smoke in home	28.8%	No regular smoke	18.9%
Food insecurity	39.4%	No food insecurity	19.7%
Respondent 15 to 24 years	28.4%	Respondent 45 or more years	19.4%
Respondent 25 to 34 years	21.1%		
Respondent 35 to 44 years	16.9%		
Two foster or adoptive parents	33.1%	Two parents (biological)	17.8%
Single biological parent	26.0%		
Female less than high school	29.9%	Female university	12.2%
Female high school complete	21.6%		
Female non university post-secondary	19.4%		
Daily need to explain	21.1%	Less than daily need to explain	17.0%
Less than daily opportunity to watch/learn	27.7%	Daily opportunity to watch/learn	20.5%
Less than daily story-telling	23.9%	Daily story-telling	20.2%
More than two hours daily screen time	24.9%	Two hours daily screen time or less	16.6%

Demographic

Demographic information about the child data utilized for this study indicated their age, gender, and Aboriginal identity. Aboriginal identity was defined by a parent/guardian as identification of the child as First Nations, Métis, or Inuit (Statistics Canada, 2008). Children whose parent or guardian reported that they had an Aboriginal ancestry but were not identified as First Nations, Métis, or Inuit were grouped into an "Aboriginal ancestry" group. A small proportion (3%) of off-reserve Aboriginal children were reported as having more than one Aboriginal identity; these children were counted in each identity group consistent with reports from Statistics Canada (O'Donnell, 2008).

The proportion of mental health difficulties did not vary by either age or gender in the adjusted mental health difficulties model. Even though more children who were identified as First Nations or Inuit had mental health difficulties than all off-reserve Aboriginal children in the study, once other mental health determinants were accounted for, Aboriginal identity was not predictive of mental health difficulties. The lack of predictability of demographic factors indicates that other potentially modifiable factors such as health, family, and living situations are more likely to be associated with mental health difficulties in young Aboriginal children living off-reserve.

Mental Health

Strengths and Difficulty Questionnaire scores have been shown to be predictive of diagnosed clinical mental health disorders (Goodman, Ford, Simmons, Gatward, & Meltzer, 2000), so it was expected that mental health difficulties would be related to a mental health diagnosis. We included a number of mental health factors in the adjusted mental health difficulties model in order to identify predictors above and beyond a mental health diagnosis. A psychologist/psychiatrist visit (yes/no) or a diagnosis of speech/language disorder, autism, fetal alcohol spectrum disorder, anxiety/depression, attention deficit disorder, or cerebral palsy/Down syndrome were included in the adjusted mental health difficulties model.

Within the ACS data, the majority of mental health diagnoses were for speech and language disorders (8.4% of the sample). This is similar to rates for non-Aboriginal children of this age (Law, Boyle, Harris, Harkness, & Nye, 2000). Fetal alcohol spectrum disorders (FASD) were diagnosed in 1.3% of the children in the study and 1% of children had a diagnosis of attention deficit disorder. Less than 1% of off-reserve Aboriginal children in the study had received a diagnosis of anxiety or depression. Diagnoses of cerebral palsy or Down syndrome were also less than 1%.

Off-reserve Aboriginal children who were reported to have visited a psychologist or psychiatrist in the 12 months immediately preceding the ACS were more likely to have mental health difficulties (46%; adj. OR =

2.0) than children with no psychiatric visits (20% of children), which is consistent with the nature of these services. Young off-reserve Aboriginal children with cognitive or mental health conditions were substantially more likely to have mental health difficulties than young off-reserve Aboriginal children with no diagnosed mental health conditions. Speech or language difficulties were associated with mental health difficulties, with 33% of children with a speech or language disorder having mental health difficulties, compared to 20% of children diagnosed with no speech or language disorder (adj. OR = 1.3). The highest rates of mental health difficulties were found among children with a diagnosis of attention deficit disorder or anxiety/depression, though this finding represents only a small proportion of off-reserve Aboriginal children in the study. Seventy-three percent of children with attention deficit disorder (adj. OR = 5.7) and 78% of children with anxiety or depression (adj. OR = 8.8) had mental health difficulties, compared to 20% of children without a diagnosis of attention deficit disorder or anxiety/depression (Tables 1, 2). Neither autism nor FASD was significant in the adjusted mental health difficulties model, once other factors were isolated in the model.

It was not surprising that having a diagnosis of a mental health condition and visits to psychologists or psychiatrists were the strongest predictors of mental health difficulty scores. The mental health difficulties measure was designed to indicate emotional and behavioural difficulties in children, which are characteristic of these disorders. It is interesting, though, that those children diagnosed with FASD or autism had higher mental health difficulty scores but neither condition was significant in the adjusted mental health difficulties model. This either means that other health, living situation, and parent and child indicators were more strongly associated with mental difficulties in young off-reserve Aboriginal children than being diagnosed with FASD or autism or that the sample size was too low to measure an effect for these conditions.

Physical Health

Health conditions have been found to co-occur with mental health disorders (Gonzalez et al., 2012; Spady, Schopflocher, Svenson, & Thompson, 2005); thus, health status (excellent/very good or good/fair/poor health), breastfeeding (ever or not), and birth weight (healthy birth weight 2500 to 4000g, low birth weight less than 2500g, and high birth weight greater than 4000g) were included in the adjusted mental health difficulties model.

Using the adjusted mental health difficulties model, it was evident that better physical health was related to lower mental health difficulties. Off-reserve Aboriginal children who were in excellent or very good health were less likely to experience mental health difficulties (19%) in comparison to children in good, fair, or poor health (34%; adj. OR =1.5; Tables 1, 2). This is consistent with previous findings that children with chronic health conditions were more likely to have psychiatric conditions as well (Hysing, Elgen, Gillberg, & Lundervold, 2007; Hysing, Elgen, Gillberg, & Lundervold, 2009; McDougall et al., 2004). Therefore, evidence-based, accessible, and culturally valued physical health and mental health services for Aboriginal children may improve mental well-being of those experiencing emotional or behavioural challenges. Neither breastfeeding nor birth weight remained significant in the adjusted mental health difficulties model.

Home Environment

A child's home environment, including characteristics of their housing and living situation, may be related to positive child mental health. A number of housing and living situation characteristics have been linked to child mental health challenges, including living in a low-income household (Elberling, Linneberg, Olsen, Goodman, & Skovgaard, 2010; Saab & Klinger, 2010), a large number of children in the household (Najman et al., 2005), poor quality of neighbourhood (Saab & Klinger, 2010), and maternal smoking (Najman et al.). Living in a low-income household has been associated with increased conduct problems or hyperactivity/inattention (Elberling, et al., 2010). In addition, parental smoking has been found to be related to irritability (Johansson, Ludvigsson, & Hermansson, 2008), inattentiveness, and hyperactivity (Polanska et al., 2006; Cho et al., 2010), as well as cognitive, perceptual, and linguistic challenges in children (Polanska et al., 2006; Yolton, Dietrich, Auinger, Lanphear, & Hornung, 2005). Housing and living situation measures are often related to each other; for example, parental smoking has been associated with housing, income, parental age, and low maternal education (Sobotova, Liu, Burakoff, Sevcikova, & Weitzman, 2011).

In using the adjusted mental health difficulties model, home environment factors were assessed together to determine which were most important for off-reserve Aboriginal child mental health. Those assessed were: home in need of repair (major, minor, or none); income status (LICO; families who spend 70% or greater of their before-tax income on basic household necessities); own/rent home; household size (two, three or four, or five or more); number of moves (average per year); regular smoke in home (yes/no); urban/rural region (an urban area is defined as a centre with a population of at least 1,000 persons, with no fewer than 400 individuals per square kilometer); and Canadian region of residence (British Columbia, Alberta, Saskatchewan, Manitoba, Ontario, Quebec, Yukon, Northwest Territories, Nunavut, or the combined Atlantic provinces).

After adjusting for demographic, mental health, and health indicators, certain household characteristics and living situations were found to be associated with mental health difficulties in young Aboriginal children living off-reserve. Off-reserve Aboriginal children whose caregivers owned their homes were less likely to have mental health difficulties (15% of children) than children who lived in rented homes (27%; adj. OR = 1.3). The number of people in the household was significant overall in the adjusted mental health difficulties model, with children living in three to four person homes having the lowest rates of mental health difficulties, but with no two groups significantly different from each other (Tables 1, 2). Aboriginal children living off-reserve who had not moved at all were less likely to have mental health difficulties (17%) compared to children who moved often (34%; high moves; adj. OR = 1.6). Children who lived in homes without regular smoke were less likely to have mental health difficulties (19%) compared to children who lived in homes with regular smoke (29%; adj. OR = 1.2). Income status, home in need of repair, and region of residence (urban/rural and Canadian region) were not significant in the adjusted mental health difficulties model.

Therefore, many household indicators were important for the mental health of Aboriginal children living off-reserve. Smoke in the home was associated with mental health difficulties even when predictors of parental smoke in the home (e.g., housing, parental age, and maternal education (Sobotova et al., 2011)) were controlled for in the adjusted mental health difficulties model. Low income, a well-known determinant of poor mental health (Boyle & Lipman, 2002; Costello et al., 1996), was not related to the mental health of off-reserve Aboriginal children in the current study. This means that other health and housing variables associated with low income (crowding, rent, food insecurity, etc.) were stronger indicators of mental health difficulties of young Aboriginal children living off-reserve. High mobility and household size were also associated with mental health difficulties in this analysis. Therefore, housing and stability appear to be more important for the mental well-being of young off-reserve Aboriginal children than income alone.

Nutrition

Early childhood nutrition, including breastfeeding and choice of food, may also impact the mental health of Aboriginal children. Breastfeeding has been shown to be related to good mental health outcomes in children, including lower rates of child depression (Najman et al., 2005), better motor and communication scores (Oddy et al., 2011), and higher intelligence scores (Kramer et al., 2008). Healthy nutrition throughout childhood is important for controlling weight (Birch, 2006; Epstein, Paluch, Beecher, & Roemmich, 2008), not only to maintain physical health, but also because children who are overweight are at higher risk for low self-esteem and behavioural problems than normal weight children (Reilly et al., 2003). In addition, children who experience hunger and food insecurity are more likely to have mental health challenges (Chen, Wahlqvist, Teng, & Lu, 2009; Willows, Veugelers, Raine, & Kuhle, 2011). Collectively, nutrition and food security may be an important determinant of mental health in young Aboriginal children living off-reserve.

Child nutrition was assessed in part as daily intake of a number of food groups: fruit, vegetables, bread/pasta, milk/milk products, fish/eggs/meat, water, pop/juice, sweets/snacks, and fast food. Parents or guardians also reported whether the child had ever gone hungry because the family ran out of money for food (yes/no), and this was used as a food insecurity indicator.

Off-reserve Aboriginal children who were reported to have experienced food insecurity were more likely to have mental health difficulties (39% of children) than children not reported to have gone hungry (20%; adj. OR = 1.6; Tables 1, 2). No other specific daily nutrition measures were important in the adjusted mental health difficulties model. Food insecurity is associated with high stress (Willows et al., 2011) and therefore mental and behavioural difficulties were expected to be related to food insecurity.

Parents and Family

Parental and family characteristics have been found to influence the mental health of young children. For instance, living in a single parent or no parent (foster/alternative) home increases the risk of mental health challenges (Brand & Brinich, 1999; Elberling et al., 2010; Fagan, Lee, Palkovitz, & Cabrera, 2011). This may be partially due to enhanced challenges, such as higher levels of stress and mental illness and lower levels of social support experienced by single parents (Avison & Davies, 2005; Cairney, Boyle, Offord, & Racine, 2003; DeKlyen, Brooks-Gunn, McLanahan, & Knab, 2006; Tobias, Gerritsen, Kokaua, & Templeton, 2009). In addition, the maltreatment of children that leads to them being placed in foster care may place them at greater risk for mental illness (Kaplow & Widom, 2007; Norman et al., 2012). Higher levels of parental education and older age at parenting have also been associated with lower rates of mental health concerns in children and adolescents (Bowen, Stewart, Baetz, & Muhajarine, 2009; Lung, Shu, Chiang, & Lin, 2009; Rodriquez, da Silva, Bettiol, Barbieri, & Rona, 2011). Therefore, a number of parental characteristics that could also be associated with mental health among young Aboriginal children living off-reserve were included in this analysis.

Parental indicators included in the adjusted mental health difficulties model were age, gender, living arrangement (two parents including at least one biological, a single parent, or two foster parents/alternative living arrangements with relatives or other guardians), and parental education. Highest level of education was computed for female and male parents/guardians separately. Only the responding caregiver gender was provided on the ACS; however, education of the spouse was asked in the survey. Thus, gender of the spouse was assumed to be the opposite of the respondent (e.g., male respondent, female spouse) when computing highest level of education for the spouse.

Maternal, but not paternal, education was associated with mental health difficulties in the adjusted model. Children whose female caregivers had some or completed university education were less likely to have mental health difficulties (12% of children) than children whose female caregivers had less than high school education (30%; adj. OR = 1.8), had completed high school (22%; adj. OR = 1.4), or had some or complete non-university post-secondary education (19%; adj. OR = 1.4; Tables 1, 2). Male caregiver education was also related to mental health difficulties in that male caregivers who had higher levels of education were less likely to have children with mental health difficulties; however, once other indicators were adjusted for, male caregiver education was not predictive of mental health difficulties in young Aboriginal children living off-reserve. This is similar to other research where maternal, but not paternal, education was associated with mental health difficulties (Côté et al., 2007; Lung et al., 2009).

Twenty-eight percent of children with younger caregivers (15 to 24 years) had mental health difficulties compared to 19% of children living with older caregivers (45 or more years; adj. OR = 2.0). When other determinants were included in the adjusted mental health difficulties model, children with caregivers aged 25 to 34 years or 35 to 44 years were more likely to have mental health difficulties (21%, 17% of children, respectively) than children living with an older caregiver (aged 45 or more; 19%; adj. OR = 1.7; adj. OR = 1.5, respectively) though it is not reflected in the percentage for caregivers aged 35 to 44 because the percentages do not isolate the other factors in the model (Tables 1, 2). This may reflect emotional or financial security associated with older age at parenting (MacDougall, Beyene, & Nachtigall, 2012).

Aboriginal children living off-reserve with two parents including at least one biological parent were less likely to experience mental health difficulties (18%) in comparison to children living with a single parent (26%; adj. OR = 1.3) or children living with foster parents, relatives, or in other living situations (33%; adj. OR = 1.9; Tables 1, 2). This is consistent with previous findings of higher rates of emotional and behavioural mental health difficulties among children living with single parents (Elberling et al., 2010; Ford, Collishaw, Meltzer, & Goodman, 2007).

Nurturing

Nurturing is another parental characteristic that is important for child mental health. Positive nurturing such as regular language-based bedtime routines with preschool children including storytelling or singing have been shown to be predictive of better sleep duration and cognitive performance in school-aged children and also with a slightly lower incidence of behavioural problems (Hale, Berger, LeBourgeois, & Brooks-Gunn, 2011). Storytelling is a key feature of Aboriginal culture (NAHO, 2008) and this particular nurturing behaviour may be important for the mental health of young Aboriginal children. In contrast, parental stress and harsh discipline have been linked to both behavioural and emotional problems for children (Bayer, Hiscock, Ukoumunne, Price, & Wake, 2008).

Parents/guardians reported the frequency of a number of nurturing questions, which were grouped into daily or less than daily and included in the adjusted mental health difficulties model. The nurturing questions asked of the caregivers were "how often do you..." explain things to the child, give the child the opportunity to watch you or others do things, encourage the child to try things on his or her own, help the child learn to think and solve problems by telling stories, praise the child with words, and show the child physical affection.

Using the ACS data, the ACCFCR researchers found that certain nurturing indicators were associated with mental health difficulties. For example, slightly more children with parents/guardians who reported explaining things to the child daily had mental health difficulties (21%) than children with parents who explained things less than daily (17%; adj. OR = 1.6). Off-reserve Aboriginal children who had a daily opportunity to watch and learn from parents were less likely to have mental health difficulties (21% of children) than children who did not have a daily opportunities to watch parents (28%; adj. OR = 1.6). Finally, children who were told stories daily were less likely to have mental health difficulties (20%), compared to children who were told stories less than daily (24%; adj. OR = 1.3; Tables 1, 2). Praising and physical affection were related to lower mental health difficulties when considered individually but neither was significant in the adjusted mental health difficulties model. Thus, daily storytelling and providing children with a daily opportunity to watch and learn were positively related to good mental health in young Aboriginal children living off-reserve. Promoting storytelling may also be an easy intervention to implement and evaluate.

Television and Sleep

"Screen time" is defined as time spent watching television, playing video games, or using computers, and the American Pediatric Society recommends no more than two hours per day of screen time for children aged two and older (AAP, 2001; Lipnowski & LeBlanc, 2012). Children who exceed the recommended amount of screen time have less physical activity and higher rates of obesity (Dennison, Erb, & Jenkins, 2002; DuRant, Baranowski, Johnson, & Thompson, 1994; Pagani, Fitzpatrick, Barnett, & Dubow, 2010). Screen time has also been found to be associated with later attention problems, victimization, poor sleep schedules, and cognitive deficits such as attentional problems in children, with a positive gradient of more hours being associated with increased problems (Pagani et al., 2010; Christakis, Zimmerman, DiGiuseppe, & McCarty, 2004; Thompson & Christakis, 2005). In addition, time spent watching television, playing video games, or using a computer is time not participating in other developmentally beneficial activities such as reading, playing with toys, or participating in social interactions with other people (Pagani et al., 2010; Christakis et al., 2004). Therefore, screen time may be one of the factors associated with mental health. Daily hours were grouped into less than or equal to two hours, and three or more hours per day.

Using the adjusted mental health difficulties model, ACCFCR researchers found that screen time was associated with mental health difficulties. Off-reserve Aboriginal children within the daily screen time recommendations were less likely to have mental health difficulties (17%), compared to children who had higher daily screen time (25%; adj. OR = 1.5; Tables 1, 2). High screen time may be detrimental to mental health because time in front of a screen is time not spent engaging in other activities that are important for child development (Christakis et al., 2004; Pagani et al., 2010).

Age-appropriate sleep was a binary measure (yes/no) in our analysis, where *appropriate* was defined by daily sleep for each age range. Children less than two months having 10 or more hours sleep, children aged two to 11 months with 14 to 15 hours sleep, children aged 12 to 35 months with 12 to 14 hours sleep, and children aged 36 to 71 months with 10 to 12 hours daily sleep were deemed to have an *appropriate* amount of sleep (Health Link Alberta, 2004). Age-appropriate sleep was not related to mental health difficulties once other factors were controlled for in the adjusted mental health difficulties model.

General Discussion

Even though the mental health of young off-reserve Aboriginal children was quite good overall, the ACCFCR research team used secondary analysis of the 2006 ACS data to find that many of these children still experienced mental health challenges. Mental health during the early years is vital for child development, so improvements in these early years could have a large impact for this growing population (WHO, 2003).

A number of modifiable factors associated with mental health difficulties in young Aboriginal children living off-reserve were identified. Examples of modifiable factors that were found in this study are maternal education, storytelling, learning opportunities, screen time, and food insecurity. These or other factors could be addressed to provide more focused support for the promotion of good mental health in young Aboriginal children living off-reserve. Changes in policy or programs may be an opportunity to address some of these factors to reduce the proportion of young Aboriginal children living off-reserve in Canada experiencing mental health difficulties.

Limitations

No non-Aboriginal comparison group was available for statistical comparisons. It cannot be assumed that Aboriginal identity would or would not be associated with mental health difficulties among those living off-reserve. In addition, mental health difficulty indicators were only available for age two to five in the Aboriginal Children's Survey; thus, the mental health of younger Aboriginal children could not be determined. Further research should include a non-Aboriginal comparison group and include a longitudinal focus to be able to determine predictors of mental health in these young children.

The ACS was a post-censal survey, and the census was relatively complete, but some individuals may not have been considered for the survey because they chose not to report Aboriginal status on the census. The sampling methods utilized by Statistics Canada for the 2006 Census are well-established, but there is still a possibility that the sample was biased and may not accurately represent all off-reserve Aboriginal children living in Canada. The SDQ was statistically validated for the sample of Aboriginal children living off-reserve, but an investigation of the cultural relevance of the instrument would be valuable for future research and understanding of early mental well-being in this population.

Acknowledgements

A special thanks to Dr. Navjot Lamba, lead of the ACS research team, and to Dr. Leslie Twilley and Tara Hanson for providing comments, which improved the report. Additional thanks go to Irene Wong at Statistics Canada's Research Data Centre, who assisted with data analyses, and to Dr. Jeffrey Bakal, who provided advice on statistical techniques.

Data for this report comes from the 2006 Statistics Canada Aboriginal Children's Survey, which was accessed at the University of Alberta Research Data Centre. While the research and analysis are based on data from Statistics Canada, the opinions expressed do not represent the views of Statistics Canada.

References

AAP (American Academy of Pediatrics; Committee on Public Education). (2001). Children, adolescents, and television. *Pediatrics, 107*(2), 423–426.

Avison, W. R., & Davies, L. (2005). Family structure, gender, and health in the context of the life course. *Journals of Gerontology, 60B*(Special Issue II), 113–116.

Babinski, L. M., Hartsough, C. S., & Lambert, N. M. (1999). Childhood conduct problems, hyperactivity-impulsivity, and inattention as predictors of adult criminal activity. *Journal of Child Psychology and Psychiatry, 40*(3), 347–355.

Bayer, J. K., Hiscock, H., Ukoumunne, O. C., Price, A., & Wake, M. (2008). Early childhood aetiology of mental health problems: A longitudinal population-based study. *Journal of Child Psychology & Psychiatry, 49*(11), 1166–1174. doi:10.1111/j.1469-7610.2008.01943.x

Birch, L. L. (2006). Child feeding practices and the etiology of obesity. *Obesity, 14*(3), 343–344. doi:10.1038/oby.2006.45

Bowen, A., Stewart, N., Baetz, M., & Muhajarine, N. (2009). Antenatal depression in socially high-risk women in Canada. *Journal of Epidemiology and Community Health, 63*, 414–-416. doi:10.1136/jech.2008.078832

Boyle, M. H., & Lipman, E. L. (2002). Do places matter? Socioeconomic disadvantage and behavioral problems of children in Canada. *Journal of Consulting and Clinical Psychology, 70*, 378–389. doi:10.1037//0022-006X.70.2.378

Brand, A. E., & Brinich, P. M. (1999). Behavior problems and mental health contacts in adopted, foster, and nonadopted children. *Journal of Clinical Psychiatry, 40*(8), 1221–1229.

Cairney, J., Boyle, M., Offord, D. R., & Racine, Y. (2003). Stress, social support and depression in single and married mothers. *Social Psychiatry and Psychiatric Epidemiology, 38*, 442–449. doi:10.1007/s00127-003-0661-0

CIHR (Canadian Institutes of Health Research, Natural Sciences and Engineering Research Council of Canada, and Social Sciences and Humanities Research Council of Canada). (2010). *Tri-Council Policy Statement: Ethical Conduct for Research Involving Humans*, December 2010.

Cardinal, J. C., Schopflocher, D. P., Svenson, L. W., Morrison, K. B., & Laing, L. (2004). *First Nations in Alberta: A focus on health service use*. Edmonton: Alberta Health and Wellness.

Chen, L., Wahlqvist, M. L., Teng, N.-C., & Lu, H.-M. (2009). Imputed food insecurity as a predictor of disease and mental health in Taiwanese elementary school children. *Asia Pacific Journal of Clinical Nutrition, 18*(4), 605–619.

Cho, S.-C., Kim, B.-N., Hong, Y.-C., Shin, M.-S., Yoo, H. J., Kim, J.-W., ...Kim, H.-W. (2010). Effect of environmental exposure to lead and tobacco smoke on inattentive and hyperactive symptoms and neurocognitive performance in children. *Journal of Child Psychology and Psychiatry, 51*(9), 1050–1057. doi:10.1111/j.1469-7610.2010.02250.x

Christakis, D. A., Zimmerman, F. J., DiGiuseppe, D. L., & McCarty, C. A. (2004). Early television exposure and subsequent attentional problems in children. *Pediatrics, 113*(4), 708–713.

Costello, E. J., Angold, A., Burns, B. J., Stangl, D. K., Tweed, D. L., Erkanli, A., & Worthman, C. M. (1996). The Great Smoky Mountains study of youth: Goals, design, methods, and the prevalence of DSM-III-R disorders. *Archives of General Psychiatry, 53*(12), 1129–1136.

Côté, S. M., Boivin, M., Nagin, D. S., Japel, C., Xu, Q., Zoccolillo, M., ...Tremblay, R. E. (2007). The role of maternal education and nonmaternal care services in the prevention of children's physical aggression problems. *Archives of General Psychiatry, 64*(11), 1305–1312.

Dennison, B. A., Erb, T. A., & Jenkins, P. L. (2002). Television viewing and television in bedroom associated with overweight risk among low-income preschool children. *Pediatrics, 109*(6), 1028–1035.

DeKlyen, M., Brooks-Gunn, J., McLanahan, S., & Knab, J. (2006). The mental health of married, cohabiting, and non-coresident parents with infants. *American Journal of Public Health, 96*, 1836–1841. doi:10.2105/AJPH.2004.049296

DuRant, R. H., Baranowski, T., Johnson, M., & Thompson, W. O. (1994). The relationship among television watching, physical activity, and body composition of young children. *Pediatrics, 94*(4), 449–455.

Elberling, H., Linneberg, A., Olsen, E. M., Goodman, R., & Skovgaard, A. M. (2010). The prevalence of SDQ-measured mental health problems at age 5–7 years and identification of predictors from birth to preschool age in a Danish birth cohort: The Copenhagen Child Cohort 2000. *European Child & Adolescent Psychiatry, 19*(9), 725–735. doi:10.1007/s00787-010-0110-z

Epstein, L. H., Paluch, R. A., Beecher, M. D., & Roemmich, J. N. (2008). Increasing healthy eating vs. reducing high energy-dense foods to treat pediatric obesity. *Obesity, 16*(2), 318–326.

Fagan, J., Lee, Y., Palkovitz, R., & Cabrera, N. (2011). Mediators of the relationship between stable nonresident households and toddler outcomes. *Journal of Family Issues, 32*(11), 1543–1568. doi:10.1177/0192513X11400172

Ford, T., Collishaw, S., Meltzer, H., & Goodman, R. (2007). A prospective study of childhood psychopathology: Independent predictors of change over three years. *Social Psychiatry and Psychiatric Epidemiology, 42*, 953–961.

Gonzalez, A., Boyle, M. H., Kyu, H. H., Georgiades, K., Duncan, L., & MacMillan, H. L. (2012). Childhood and family influences on depression, chronic physical conditions, and their comorbidity: Findings from the Ontario child health study. *Journal of Psychiatric Research, 46*, 1475–1482.

Goodman, A., & Goodman, R. (2009). Strengths and difficulties questionnaire as a dimensional measure of child mental health. *Journal of the American Academy of Child and Adolescent Psychiatry, 48*(4), 400–403. doi:10.1097/CHI.0b013e3181985068

Goodman, R., Ford, T., Simmons, H., Gatward, R., & Meltzer, H. (2000). Using the strengths and difficulties questionnaire (SDQ) to screen for child psychiatric disorders in a community sample. *British Journal of Psychiatry, 177,* 534–539.

Hale, L., Berger, L. M., LeBourgeois, M. K., & Brooks-Gunn, J. (2011). A longitudinal study of preschoolers' language-based bedtime routines, sleep duration and well-being. *Journal of Family Psychology, 25*(3), 423–433. doi:10.1037/a0023564

Health Link Alberta. (2004). *Frequently asked questions about children and sleep.* Retrieved from http://www.healthlinkalberta.ca/Topic. asp?GUID=%7B9040F2A8-46D5-446C-B0CD-AA2BDA1088FC%7D

Heimens Visser, J., Van Der Ende, J., Koot, H. M., & Verhulst, F. C. (2000). Predictors of psychopathology in young adults referred to mental health services in childhood or adolescence. *British Journal of Psychiatry, 177,* 59–65. doi:10.1192/bjp.177.1.59

Hysing, M., Elgen, I., Gillberg, C., & Lundervold, A. J. (2007). Chronic physical illness and mental health in children. Results from a large-scale population study. *Journal of Child Psychology and Psychiatry, 48*(8), 785–792. doi:10.1111/j.1469-7610.2007.01755.x

Hysing, M., Elgen, I., Gillberg, C., & Lundervold, A. J. (2009). Emotional and behavioural problems in subgroups of children with chronic illness: Results from a larger-scale population. *Child: Care, Health, and Development, 35*(4), 527–533. doi:10.1111/j.1365-2214.2009.00967.x

Johansson, A., Ludvigsson, J., & Hermansson, G. (2008). Adverse health effects related to tobacco smoke exposure in a cohort of three-year olds. *Acta Paediatrica, 97,* 354–357. doi:10.1111/j.1651-2227.2007.00619.x

Kaplow, J. B., & Widom, C. S. (2007). Age of onset of child maltreatment predicts long-term mental health outcomes. *Journal of Abnormal Psychology, 116*(1), 176–187. doi:10.1037/0021-843X.116.1.176

Kramer, M. S., Aboud, F., Mironova, E., Vanilovich, I., Platt, R. W., Matush, L., … Shapiro, S. (2008). Breastfeeding and child cognitive development. *Archives of General Psychiatry, 65*(5), 578–584.

Law, J., Boyle, J., Harris, F., Harkness, A., & Nye, C. (2000). Prevalence and natural history of primary speech and language delay: Findings from a systematic review of the literature. *International Journal of Language and Communication Disorders, 35*(2), 165–188.

Lipnowski, S., & LeBlanc, C. (2012). Healthy active living: Physical activity guidelines for children and adolescents. *Paediatric and Child Health, 17*(4), 209–210.

Lung, F.-W., Shu, B.-C., Chiang, T.-L., & Lin, S.-J. (2009). Parental mental health, education, age at childbirth and child development from six to 18 months. *Acta Paediatrica, 98*, 834–841. doi: 10.1111/j.1651-2227.2008.01166.x

MacDougall, K., Beyene, Y., & Nachtigall, R. D. (2012). 'Inconvenient biology:' Advantages and disadvantages of first-time parenting after age 40 using in vitro fertilization. *Human Reproduction, 27*(4), 1058–1065.

McDougall, J., King, G., De Wit, D., Miller, L., Hong, S., Offord, D., ...Meyer, K. (2004). Chronic physical health conditions and disability among Canadian school-aged children: A national profile. *Disability and Rehabilitation, 26*(1), 35–45. doi:10.1080/09638280410001645076

MHCC (Mental Health Commission of Canada). (2012). *Why investing in mental health will contribute to Canada's economic prosperity and to the sustainability of our health care system.* Retrieved from the Mental Health Commission of Canada website strategy.mentalhealthcommission.ca/pdf/case-for-investment-en.pdf

NAHO (Métis Centre, National Aboriginal Health Organization). (2008). In the words of our ancestors: Métis health and healing. Ottawa: National Aboriginal Health Organization.

Najman, J., Hallam, D., Bor, W., O'Callaghan, M., Williams, G., & Shuttlewood, G. (2005). Predictors of depression in very young children. *Social Psychiatry & Psychiatric Epidemiology, 40*(5), 367–374. doi:10.1007/s00127-005-0895-0

Norman, R. E., Byambaa, M., De, R., Butchart, A., Scott, J., & Vos, T. (2012). The long-term health consequences of child physical abuse, emotional abuse, and neglect: A systematic review and meta-analysis. *PLOS Medicine, 9*(11), 1–31. doi:10.1371/journal.pmed.1001349

O'Donnell, V. (2008). Selected findings of the Aboriginal Children's Survey 2006: Family and community. *Canadian Social Trends, Catalogue no. 11-008*, 64–72. Retrieved from the Statistics Canada website http://www5.statcan.gc.ca/bsolc/olc-cel/olc-cel?catno=89-634-x&lang=eng

Oddy, W. H., Robinson, M., Kendall, G. E., Li, J., Zubrick, S. R., & Stanley, F. J. (2011). Breastfeeding and early child development: A prospective cohort study. *Acta Paediatrica, 100*, 992–999. doi:10.1111/j.1651-2227.2011.02199.x

Oliver, L., Findlay, L., McIntosh, C., & Kohen, D. (2009). *Evaluation of the Strengths and Difficulties Questionnaire: Aboriginal Children's Survey 2006.* (Catalogue 89-634-x2009008). Retrieved from the Statistics Canada website http://www5.statcan.gc.ca/bsolc/olc-cel/olc-cel?catno=89-634-x2009008&lang=eng

Pagani, L. S., Fitzpatrick, C., Barnett, T. A., & Dubow, E. (2010). Prospective associations between early childhood television exposure and academic, psychosocial, and physical well-being by middle childhood. *Archives in Pediatric and Adolescent Medicine, 164*(5), 425–431.

Polanska, K., Hanke, W., Ronchetti, R., Van, D. H., Zuurbier, M., Koppe, J. G., & Bartonova, A. (2006). Environmental tobacco smoke exposure and children's health. *Acta Paediatrica.Supplement, 95,* 86–92. doi:10.1080/08035320600886562

Reilly, J. J., Methven, E., McDowell, Z. C., Hacking, B., Alexander, D., Stewart, L., & Kelnar, C. J. H. (2003). Health consequences of obesity. *Archives of Disorders in Childhood, 88,* 748–752.

Rodriguez, J., da Silva, A., Bettiol, H., Barbieri, M., & Rona, R. (2011). The impact of perinatal and socioeconomic factors on mental health problems of children from a poor Brazilian city: A longitudinal study. *Social Psychiatry & Psychiatric Epidemiology, 46*(5), 381–391. doi:10.1007/s00127-010-0202-6

Saab, H., & Klinger, D. (2010). School differences in adolescent health and well-being: Findings from the Canadian health behaviour in school-aged children study. *Social Science & Medicine, 70,* 850–858. doi:10.1016/j.socscimed.2009.11.012

Sobotova, L., Liu, Y.-H., Burakoff, A., Sevcikova, L., & Weitzman, M. (2011). Household exposure to secondhand smoke is associated with decreased physical and mental health of mothers in the USA. *Maternal Child Health Journal, 15,* 128–137. doi:10.1007/s10995-009-0549-z

Spady, D. W., Schopflocher, D. P., Svenson, L. W., & Thompson, A. H. (2005). Medical and psychiatric comorbidity and health care use among children 6 to 17 years old. *Archives of Pediatrics and Adolescent Medicine, 159,* 231–237.

Statistics Canada. (2008). *Aboriginal Children's Survey, 2006.* (Catalogue number 8-5300-506). Retrieved from the Statistics Canada website http://www5.statcan.gc.ca/bsolc/olc-cel/olc-cel?catno=89-634-x&lang=eng

Thompson, D. A., & Christakis, D. A. (2005). The association between television viewing and irregular sleep schedules among children less than 3 years of age. *Pediatrics, 116,* 851–856. doi:10.1542/peds.2004-2788

Tobias, M., Gerritsen, S., Kokaua, J., & Templeton, R. (2009). Psychiatric illness among a nationally representative sample of sole and partnered parents in New Zealand. *Australian and New Zealand Journal of Psychiatry, 43,* 136–144.

Trumper, R. (2004). Health status and health needs of Aboriginal children and youth: Literature review. Retrieved from the First Nations First Portal website http://www.fsin.com/healthandsocial/childportal/detail.php?firstLevel=&secondLevel=&currentItemId=277

Willows, N., Veugelers, P., Raine, K., & Kuhle, S. (2011). Associations between household food insecurity and health outcomes in the Aboriginal population (excluding reserves). *Health Reports, 22*(2), 82-003-XPE.

WHO (World Health Organization). (2003). *Investing in mental health.* Retrieved
from the World Health Organization Department of Mental Health and
Substance Abuse website www.who.int/mental_health/media/investing_
mnh.pdf

Yolton, K., Dietrich, K., Auinger, P., Lanphear, B. P., & Hornung, R. (2005).
Exposure to environmental tobacco smoke and cognitive abilities among U.S.
children and adolescents. *Environmental Health Perspectives, 113*(1), 98–103.
doi:10.1289/ehp.7210

Research *with*, not *on*: Community-based Aboriginal Health Research through the "Voices and PHACES" Study

Amrita Roy, Wilfreda Thurston, Lynden (Lindsay) Crowshoe, David Turner, and Bonnie Healy

Introduction

Prenatal depression is a significant issue in Canada, where approximately 10% of pregnant women will experience depression (PHAC, 2005). Prevalence may be much higher in disadvantaged and marginalized groups, such as Aboriginal populations (Bowen & Muhajarine, 2006a); however, there is a paucity of research on prenatal depression in Aboriginal women. To support the development of evidence-based population health interventions, the project team proposed a program of research to examine prenatal depression among Aboriginal women from a population-health perspective. As the first step, we launched a qualitative study named "Voices and PHACES," with PHACES standing for "Prenatal Health in Aboriginal Communities and EnvironmentS."

Suggested Citation: Roy, A., Thurston, W., Crowshoe, L., Turner, D., & Healy, B. (2014). Research *with*, not *on*: Community-based Aboriginal health research through the "Voices and PHACES" study. In D. Badry, D. Fuchs, H. Montgomery, & S. McKay (Eds.), *Reinvesting in Families: Strengthening Child Welfare Practice for a Brighter Future: Voices from the Prairies* (pp. 111–132). Regina, SK: University of Regina Press.

In response to the sad history of exploitation of, and harm to, Aboriginal communities through academic research, there is growing recognition of the importance of community-based approaches and academic-community partnerships. While the benefits of community-based research are generally unquestionable, its execution can often be challenging. This chapter describes the process followed in the "Voices and PHACES" study to engage, and work in partnership with, communities and policy-makers. The chapter also discusses challenges we faced and how we addressed them, and offers recommendations for researchers and community members considering this type of research.

Research *with* (not *on*) Aboriginal Communities

Savan and Sider define community-based research (CBR) as "a range of research approaches that link community members and external researchers in investigations that promote progressive social change as well as deeper understanding of specific issues important to communities" (2003, p. 33). CBR recognizes the value of different sources of knowledge and different methods of knowledge acquisition, and also mandates multiple means of dissemination to facilitate the application of research results for meaningful social change (Scott & MacKean, 2007).

Israel and colleagues situate CBR in public health by highlighting the focus "on social, structural, and physical environmental inequities through active involvement of community members, organizational representatives, and researchers in all aspects of the research process" (1998, p. 173). In public health, CBR goes hand-in-hand with health promotion, which is "the process of enabling people to increase control over, and to improve, their health" (p. 1) through the strategies of building healthy public policy, creating supportive environments, strengthening community action, developing personal skills, and reorienting health services (WHO, 1986). In this regard, Israel and colleagues (1998) point out that CBR is particularly significant for marginalized communities whose members have limited access to power and resources. The impact of the history of colonization on Aboriginal peoples in Canada can be seen in the disproportionate number of health and social problems they face. While the health inequities facing Aboriginal populations are daunting, Aboriginal individuals and communities also have considerable strength and resilience (Dion Stout & Kipling, 2003; Wesley-Esquimaux & Smolewski, 2004). This community capacity facilitates health promotion as a means to address the health inequities at hand. There is ample evidence that community participation can result in better policies, programs, and other interventions (Lombe & Sherraden, 2008; Thurston, Dutton, & Emery, 2012). Indeed, one of the reasons why certain programs have had limited success in alleviating the health inequities faced by Aboriginal peoples is the failure to take local context, culture, and means of knowledge exchange into consideration in design and evaluation (Smylie et al., 2009). Health research endeavours that have the goal of health promotion in Aboriginal communities must engage with the fact that "contemporary health knowledge and health behavior among Indigenous individuals and communities are influenced by an interplay of pre-colonial systems of health, historic and ongoing processes of colonization, and exposure to non-Indigenous systems of health" (p. 437); this interplay varies across communities, based on local context (Smylie et al., 2009). By facilitating engagement with local context, CBR yields "the potential to design more effective public policies [and] to successfully advocate for policy change" (Ritas, 2003, p. 4).

According to the Royal Commission on Aboriginal Peoples (RCAP) (1996), Aboriginal people have had little chance to challenge misinformation and ethnocentric or racist interpretations of research results. The First Nations Centre (2007) reported that historical research practices were "disrespectful, damaging and stigmatizing" (p. 3). The result is that research had "acquired a bad name," with outcomes that were "as often as not, misguided and harmful" (Castellano, 2004, p. 98). In addition to coping with problematic research practices and outcomes, Aboriginal communities have had little control over the research process (First Nations Centre, 2007). RCAP found that research concerning Aboriginal peoples has usually originated from outside the Aboriginal community and has usually been conducted by non-Aboriginal individuals. The lack of control within the research process and exclusion from determining research in general have been likened to historical colonial policies directed towards Aboriginal populations within Canada (Castellano & Reading, 2010). Furthermore, Durst argued that research, in regards to Aboriginal populations, has historically been used as "an instrument of oppression, imperialism and colonialism" (as cited in First Nations Centre, 2007, p. 3).

In response to the adverse processes and outcomes from historical research practices, Aboriginal communities have begun to demand an ethical basis for research rooted in self-determination. In general, Aboriginal populations require that health research benefits Aboriginal peoples, that Aboriginal peoples be full partners in health research at all stages, and that Aboriginal peoples *own, control, access, and possess* (OCAP) health research data. OCAP outlines key principles of a critical framework for research (First Nations Centre, 2007; Schnarch, 2004). The First Nations principles of OCAP, as trademarked by the First Nations Information Governance Centre (2010), stem specifically from First Nations groups' historical ways of knowing; other Aboriginal groups may have different approaches. However, research practices that are respectful, participatory, and beneficial to the communities they involve can be applied broadly to all Aboriginal populations. The *Tri-Council Policy Statement: Ethical Conduct for Research Involving Humans* (TCPS) also includes a chapter focused on applying the TCPS policy provisions within Aboriginal contexts. The TCPS is intended to provide guidance to researchers to ensure that research "involving Aboriginal peoples is premised on respectful relationships" (CIHR, NSERC, and SSHRC, 2010).

In summary, Aboriginal health research endeavours must ensure that the research process does not replicate the very processes and outcomes of colonization that the research is seeking to address (Martin, 2008; Tuhiwai Smith, 2006; Varcoe et al., 2011). To this end, a decolonizing approach to research is warranted that involves "critical examination and dismantling of individual and systemic assumptions and power relationships, including the suppression of Indigenous systems of knowledge" (Smylie et al., 2009, p. 437). CBR plays a critical role in this regard. We accordingly used CBR in the research project described in this paper to facilitate an ethical approach that was respectful of the OCAP principles.

The "Voices and PHACES" Study

Depression carries consequences for health and well-being. The health consequences of prenatal and postpartum maternal depression can also be found in the baby and other family members, making it a significant maternal-child health concern. The associated continuous elevation of stress-related hormones has serious implications; for example, it can contribute to adverse pregnancy outcomes such as preterm birth and low birth weight (Swaab, Bao, & Lucassen, 2005; Bowen & Muhajarine, 2006b), and can preprogram a fetus to be at increased risk for depression and anxiety later in life (Swaab, Bao, & Lucassen, 2005). Pregnant women who are depressed are also more likely to engage in unhealthy coping behaviours such as smoking, alcohol consumption, and illicit drug use, and less likely to use prenatal health services (Bowen & Muhajarine, 2006b). Women with prenatal depression are more likely to experience postpartum depression (Bowen & Muhajarine, 2006b; Beck, 2006). Maternal depression can impact the mother's interactions with her infant, her partner, and her other children, yielding negative effects on the children's long-term cognitive and behavioural development (Bowen & Muhajarine, 2006b; Beck, 2006). Thus, good maternal mental health is critical for the physical, mental, and psychosocial health of the entire family. In this regard, programs, policies, and services that enhance maternal mental health during pregnancy can serve as a preventive tool for many of the issues identified by the Government of Alberta's Ministry of Children and Youth Services (now part of Alberta Human Services) in its 2010 Business Plan.

The Ministry of Children and Youth Services of Alberta and the Alberta Centre for Child, Family and Community Research (ACCFCR) have both identified Aboriginal maternal-child health issues as being of particular concern (Government of Alberta, 2010; Tough, 2009). Not only do Aboriginal populations in Canada experience greater health and social inequities relative to other Canadians, but many of the risk factors and health consequences associated with prenatal depression are more prevalent among Aboriginal populations (Bennett, 2005), suggesting that prenatal depression should be assessed. However, empirical research on the determinants of depression among pregnant Aboriginal women is limited. Population-level studies to date on all types of depression have found that socio-economic disadvantage and chronic psychosocial stress are major risk factors (Bowen & Muhajarine, 2006b). It is also clear, however, that the causal pathways of depression, both at the clinical and the population levels, are complex. Given the unique historical and present-day social context of Aboriginal peoples, it would be erroneous to assume that the results of studies in non-Aboriginal populations can be directly applied to Aboriginal populations. Notably, Aboriginal women experience intersecting stressors from race, gender, social exclusion, and intergenerational trauma from the legacy of residential schools and other occurrences of colonization (Bennett, 2005; Sotero, 2006). Research that takes these factors into consideration is therefore crucial for the development of effective and evidence-based policies, programs, and services for this population.

To address the above, we launched the "Voices and PHACES" study as a first step in a proposed program of research on prenatal depression and Aboriginal women. "Voices and PHACES" is a constructivist-grounded theory study involving semi-structured interviews with pregnant Aboriginal women and health-service and social service professionals who work with them in the Calgary area. Through these interviews, the objectives are to gain insight on: (a) the factors that impact maternal mental well-being during pregnancy; (b) the social context in which Aboriginal women live their lives; (c) the appropriateness and adequacy of existing programs and services; and (d) how these programs and services can be improved or expanded to better meet the women's needs.

At the time of submission of this chapter (June 2013), data gathering for "Voices and PHACES" is still in progress. Interviews with twelve pregnant Aboriginal women and twelve professionals have been completed. Preliminary results point to a number of risk factors that are consistent with prenatal depression studies in other populations, including stressful life events, social and economic factors, negative previous pregnancy experiences, and experiences of violence and abuse. However, risk factors related to this population's unique social and historical context are also apparent, including experiences with the child welfare system, family members' residential school experiences, historical (intergenerational) trauma, stigma, racism, and sexism. Negative coping mechanisms for stress identified in the interviews include substance abuse. Positive coping mechanisms include social support and access to Aboriginal traditional practices, which appear protective. While services in Calgary are working well in certain ways, the preliminary results suggest there is a need for more culturally appropriate and safe services, better networking among agencies, and interventions with service providers to reduce stigma. Once all interviews are completed and the data fully analyzed, a theoretical framework will be proposed on the determinants of depression in this population. This framework will be translated into key recommendations for dissemination to stakeholders, and will form the basis for future stages of our proposed program of research.

In the early stages of conceiving this study, University of Calgary researchers decided to engage with community organizations and stakeholders, and pursue academic-community partnerships for a community-based approach to the research. One reason for this decision was ethical concerns about how research should be done *with* Aboriginal peoples, rather than *on* them. A community-based approach was pursued to ensure research that was respectful of the principles of OCAP and of the guidelines laid out in the TCPS. Another reason was sensitivity to the complexity of gender issues for Aboriginal communities (Huhndorf & Suzack, 2010; Varcoe et al., 2011) and the historic role of community in advancing change, especially for women. Thirdly, ethical and practical considerations for reaching and recruiting the target samples played a role. Recruitment of both pregnant women and service professionals for the study is being done through clinics and agencies in and around the city of Calgary. Recruitment strategies vary between sites: display of posters and pamphlets in high-traffic areas; distribution of pamphlets by clinic or agency staff to individual patients or clients who may be eligible to participate (the prospective participants then contact research study staff for more information if interested); and, presence of research study staff on-site to speak with prospective participants directly. Fourth, the organizations play an integral role in addressing potential participant distress. In the event of participant distress during the interview process, the interviewers are to contact the "point person" identified in each organization who agreed to facilitate access to counselling and other services for distressed participants. These precautions were considered necessary given the varying levels of vulnerability among our target population, and the sensitivity of some of the questions being asked in the interviews. Finally, apart from success in recruitment, it was also important to the academic researchers that the products of the study be meaningful for eventual knowledge translation into beneficial programs and policies. Thus, the engagement of relevant stakeholders as partners was recognized as important.

Community-based Approach and Academic-community Partnerships in "Voices and PHACES"

For the sake of simplicity, we have dichotomized "academic" and "community" parties in our discussions below, with "academic" signalling those who entered the research via their role at the university. This dichotomy should not be interpreted to suggest a hierarchy between parties; indeed, at the heart of CBR is recognition of the equal value of the contributions of all parties. Furthermore, the distinction between "academic" and "community" is not always clear in CBR; in the case of "Voices and PHACES," one of the academic research team members (L. Crowshoe) is also a local First Nations person. He is thus a member of both the university and the community, and brings both perspectives to the research.

Community-based approaches to research vary with the contexts and settings involved. In the case of "Voices and PHACES," the formation of the study's academic-community partnerships was initiated by the academic researchers, rather than by the community parties involved. However, once they were approached, there was immediate interest by the community members in the topic and the proposed preliminary outline for the study. Some proponents of community-based research would insist that it must be initiated strictly by a community to be truly community-based; we, however, do not hold that position, and instead posit that academic researchers can serve as allies to communities who may not always have the resources (including time and training) in place to readily initiate rigorous research. Savan and Sider (2003) also embrace a more inclusive definition of CBR; in their discussion of the range of possible approaches to CBR, they highlight that partnerships between university researchers and community entities are quite common in CBR initiatives. Thus, the defining dynamic of CBR is in the nature of the partnership between academic and community entities, and the values honoured, rather than strictly around the question of which entity initiated the research. Flexibility of methods is one important value (Anderson, Khan, & Reimer-Kirkham, 2011).

Community engagement in "Voices and PHACES" is present in the five community organizations (health clinics and social service agencies) in the city of Calgary that are the core community partner agencies for the study. Secondly, there is the involvement of Aboriginal community members and Elders, and the government of Alberta, in advisory capacities. Thirdly, there is an explicit commitment to the dissemination of study results to relevant stakeholders, in forms that are useful for knowledge translation. We have worked to ensure involvement of community members, organizations, and stakeholders from government in the decision-making surrounding the design, implementation, dissemination, and governance of the study.

Community Organizations

Early in the study's conception, the academic researchers approached various community organizations in the city of Calgary that work with Aboriginal women. Five organizations joined as partners and supplied letters of partnership: Inn from the Cold, Awo Taan Healing Lodge, Calgary Urban Projects Society / CUPS, Elbow River Healing Lodge (of Alberta Health Services), and the Adult Aboriginal Mental Health Program (of Alberta Health Services). One or more of the academic researchers had previous relationships with leaders in these organizations. The letters laid out the terms of reference agreed upon for the partnership, and copies are kept on file by each partner. Formalizing the partnerships was viewed as important (Scott & Thurston, 1997) because the relationship involved much more than a "letter of support." The letters were included in applications for research ethics board approval and for funding. At this time, 13 other organizations have also joined the study as additional recruitment sites. Although not as deeply involved in the study as the five partner organizations, they have expressed enthusiasm for the research and an interest in receiving the report of the final results.

Research Team and Oversight Committee

The research team includes both academic and non-academic members: academic members are researchers at the University of Calgary (one doctoral student and five faculty members in the Faculty of Medicine); non-academic members are representatives from the five partner community organizations. The research team brings complementary expertise to the table, enabling both rigorous and feasible research, and research that is responsive to community needs and different models of service delivery, relevant for eventual knowledge translation, and therefore useful for practical application by front-line service providers.

The project's oversight committee consists of five individuals, four of whom are Aboriginal community members from the Calgary area. The fifth member is a representative from the Ministry of Human Services of the Government of Alberta. The role of the oversight committee is to provide guidance to ensure that the research is ethical, appropriate, and meaningful for Aboriginal communities, that all interactions with individuals and communities are culturally appropriate and culturally safe (congruent with Aboriginal cultural practices, and conducted in a manner in which individuals and communities feel empowered and respected), that the principles of OCAP are observed, and that the research is meaningful from a policy perspective.

Two of the four Aboriginal community members on the oversight committee are Elders, meaning they are respected advisors, helpers, and ceremonial leaders in their communities (Stiegelbauer, 1996). In addition to offering guidance and oversight along with other committee members, the Elders support the research team in conducting the research in a manner that resonates with traditional perspectives of the Elders' communities. They also help support traditional Aboriginal team processes and protocols at study meetings and other study-related events. Because Elders may not belong to an institution or program that pays their salary, it may be appropriate for researchers to give an honorarium for their involvement. We included this honorarium cost as an item in the budget in our application for grant funding, to enable us to do so.

Because the study is focused on urban Aboriginal women who come from many locations in Alberta and possibly other provinces, how best to institute a formal community-based ethical review process was a dilemma. The oversight committee has been advising us in regards to ethical considerations specific to Aboriginal communities, as well as in the interpretation, validation, and dissemination of results. At the time of this study's initiation in 2011, there was no mechanism in place at the University of Calgary for community-based ethical review of studies focused on urban Aboriginal populations. More recently, the Institute of Public Health's Group for Research with Aboriginal Peoples for Health (GRAPH) has established a community advisory board that can offer review of research projects. Additionally, the University of Calgary's Conjoint Health Research Ethics Board (CHREB) now has representatives from the Alberta First Nations Information Governance

Centre. One of these is co-chair of the oversight committee of our study, and it was initially through involvement with our project that she met with and came to serve on CHREB. The latter demonstrates the power of relationships in creating an institutional environment where CBR can be strengthened.

Governance and Communications

The study's governance process includes three general meetings, where the research team and oversight committee attend together, allowing for interactive discussions and exchanges of ideas and viewpoints. To date, the first of the three planned general meetings has occurred. At this first meeting, discussions were focused on the processes for recruitment and data gathering, as well as the wording and content of the interview guides and the consent forms. The second general meeting, which will be held when the interviews are close to completion, will be devoted to group analysis. During this meeting, the lead researchers will present preliminary codes and themes from the interviews, and seek reflection from attendees on relationships among codes, themes, and overall interpretation. The third general meeting will be held towards the end of the study, and the dissemination plan for the research findings to both academic and community audiences will be discussed. In this regard, the non-academic team members and the oversight committee, in particular, will play a valuable role in the translation of research findings into key recommendations for policy and programs, which will be disseminated to community and governmental agencies in the final report. Additional meetings, teleconference calls, and email conversations are conducted as needed outside of these general meetings. In this way, all parties involved have an opportunity to contribute meaningfully to decisions.

Dissemination to Stakeholders

In order for research findings to make a true difference, they must be disseminated widely, and to the appropriate audiences. Research results will be disseminated in academic venues such as peer-reviewed journals, academic conferences, and presentations. Additionally, the research findings will be disseminated to stakeholders. To this end, a gathering (of managers and service providers from clinical and social service agencies in and around Calgary, representatives from Aboriginal organizations, Aboriginal community members, and pregnant Aboriginal women) is planned for the end of the study to share findings and recommendations. The gathering will include an opportunity for attendees to share their thoughts and reflections about the statements and recommendations in the report; the final report will be modified as appropriate, based on feedback received. That report will be submitted to community partners, funders, and the Government of Alberta. Additionally, the report will be made more widely available to those interested, notably gathering attendees and the participants in the study. The contents of the report will also be shared through oral presentations to staff members and patients/clients alike at the partner organizations. Finally, the report will be presented to the educational offices of the Faculty of Medicine at the University of Calgary, and the Faculties of Nursing at each of University of Calgary and Mount Royal University, so that they may consider the findings in their curricula.

We also want to make the study results accessible for Aboriginal women themselves. We expect to deliver oral presentations tailored specifically for Aboriginal patients and clients at clinics and agencies. If it proves feasible to do so, we are also considering the possibility of creating a short video to be uploaded to YouTube, which would convey the results in simple terms and in an engaging manner.

Challenges Encountered in "Voices and PHACES"

Structures in academia around project funding and ethical approval, and the various policies and procedures of financial and human resources departments at universities, can make CBR more difficult. The structures and policies are intended to protect both academic researchers and community members; however, they can create obstacles vis-à-vis relationships with community partners, who may not always understand the reasons for the complex processes at hand. Most notably, the various procedures that need to be followed have lengthy turnaround times; this can lead to long gaps of time when it may feel to the community partners like "nothing is happening." It is generally expected that partnerships with community agencies be fully and concretely established in advance of submitting both funding applications and applications for research ethics board approval. This can put the community partners "on hold" for lengthy periods of time when success is not guaranteed.

In our case, community members did not have the time to work on writing up the application for project funding, though academic members did keep them informed of its content and its progress. We were very fortunate to secure funding, as funding competitions are highly competitive in Canada, with low success rates. Academic researchers have had to develop "thick skins" to deal with this high rate of rejection; community members, on the other hand, may get discouraged by the often blunt style of criticism of academic peer reviewers, which can risk the burgeoning relationship among partners. Although this did not occur with "Voices and PHACES," it has proven to be a difficulty in other CBR projects in which the authors have been involved.

Research ethics board approval at our institution can take anywhere from six weeks to six months, depending on the specific issues in the research, and also on the workload of the ethics review board at the time of submission. The original ethics application for "Voices and PHACES" took less time than usual (about four weeks from time of formal submission), due to efforts on the part of the board's then-chair to expedite review of graduate students' dissertation projects. However, ethics modification applications submitted more recently (to add new recruitment sites) have taken up to six weeks for approval, despite the new sites being fairly similar to original sites. As turnaround time is due to workload volume of the research ethics board, it is difficult to predict how long the process will take, which can lead to frustration, especially for community partners.

In a process involving so many steps—securing funding through a successful grant application, obtaining ethics approval (funds cannot be accessed before then), having funds released following the appropriate university financial services process, and recruiting and hiring study staff following the appropriate university human resources process—many months pass during this lengthy, rigorous process from application to implementation. Changes in staff, capacity, and enthusiasm may occur at the partner agencies during this long period. These changes can complicate the dynamics of project management. In "Voices and PHACES," there were staff changes at one of our community partner agencies during the interim period of time, and an individual who had enthusiastically endorsed the partnership was no longer in that managerial position. The new person was not familiar with the research partnership agreement that had been struck many months before, so some confusion and some tension resulted. Changes in space-use needs at one of the partner agencies meant that a concern developed around doing interviews on-site, whereas that was the original plan. In the intervening months, one of the agencies had a negative experience with another (unrelated) research project, and became hesitant to maintain involvement in the "Voices and PHACES" project. We addressed all of these issues with open dialogue and discussion, listening carefully to concerns, and offering clarification and assurances as possible. For example, some of the concerns that surfaced in the above scenarios included concerns around how much time agency staff would have to invest in recruiting for the study (we were able to reach an understanding on the limits in this regard), and concerns around clients feeling uncomfortable at being approached on-site by study staff (for the agency expressing this concern, we agreed that posters and pamphlets would be the principal recruitment strategy). In some cases, we reworked the initial partnership agreement to address new circumstances (e.g., the altered availability of rooms on-site for interviews). As Varcoe and colleagues (2011) report, these "experiences illustrate how trust is never a given, but rather, is created though attention to relationships and reflexivity" (p. 225). The importance of relationship development cannot be overstressed; this is particularly true for CBR involving Aboriginal peoples, for whom relatedness is a major component of traditional ways of knowing (Tuhiwai Smith, 2006).

The need for developing and maintaining a diverse set of human relationships is one reason that CBR is considerably more time-consuming than many other research designs, and involves extra steps for academic researchers above and beyond those otherwise required in the research-intensive environment. Because people in community agencies are busy with other priorities, it can often take multiple contacts across several weeks just to arrange an initial meeting or conversation. In addition, community organizations also have their own formal governance structures, and it can take several weeks as various levels of agency leadership review and approve a proposed partnership. In "Voices and

PHACES," this phenomenon of multiple follow-ups being required (and long wait times for responses) has continued throughout the partnership, even though the enthusiastic support is still there among agencies. We strive to demonstrate "respect, relevance, reciprocity, and responsibility" (Varcoe et al., 2011, p. 226) by accommodating the agencies' and community members' needs whenever possible, so as to facilitate their involvement (e.g., issuing friendly follow-ups and reminders, going to agencies for meetings rather than making them come to us, and working around their schedules and availabilities).

CBR is a particularly challenging form of research for doctoral students, who face fairly stringent requirements for degree completion, as well as institutional requirements directed at the educational process. At the helm of "Voices and PHACES" is a doctoral student who has had to revise graduation timelines, and revise plans surrounding the other components of her dissertation, around the progress of "Voices and PHACES." Her supervisory committee members have been flexible, understanding, and supportive. They have permitted her, for example, to amend the other projects in her original dissertation proposal, so as to allow her to still graduate in a reasonable period of time. Some supervisory committee members also have existing relationships with some of the community partner agencies, due to involvement in other (separate) research studies or due to other professional connections; this connectedness has helped in the relationship-building and trust-development processes required in CBR.

Scientific and community perspectives can often conflict. For instance, ethical considerations around research participant confidentiality and autonomy can conflict with the desire of helping professionals at agencies or clinics to access information revealed in interviews, for the sake of incorporating it into treatment or rehabilitation plans. For example, "Voices and PHACES" participants are administered the Edinburgh Postnatal Depression Scale as part of the interview, and multiple partner organizations requested that we share each woman's score with her physician or counsellor. While we understood the good intentions of the clinics and agencies in this regard, we had to decline this request. We engaged in open dialogue to explain the ethical reasons that constrained us and to work with the organizations to find alternatives that respected all perspectives. The alternative we were able to implement instead was to tell research participants their scores on the scale in question, and to suggest to the participants that they could choose whether or not to share the score with their helping professionals.

One of the challenges of CBR is being clear on who makes up the community. Aboriginal communities are diverse, especially in urban settings. Academic communities (departments, disciplines, universities) are also diverse. When large, multidisciplinary groups try to come to consensus, it helps to have a spirit of respect and compromise at the table. One example we experienced was the recommendation from some of our community members that we use the medicine wheel to frame a particular question in the interview guide, to make it culturally appropriate. Other members were concerned that participants who were not immersed in their traditional culture would be confused, and even offended, by this approach. Our compromise was to have the interviewer ask the participant about their familiarity and comfort with the medicine wheel framework, and then proceed to ask the question accordingly. Group dynamics in large, multidisciplinary teams also can be a challenge at meetings. As some team members were more talkative and dominated discussions at the first general meeting, we provided the opportunity to contribute outside of the meeting by following up with individual members afterwards to get additional feedback one-to-one. Multidisciplinary discussions can become challenging due to differing areas of expertise. To assist community members, we prepare lay-language versions of documents initially written in scientific language (e.g., research proposals), so that they are not inhibited by the technical jargon. At the same time, community partners educate the academic partners about Aboriginal culture, jurisdictional issues, and practical concerns around connecting with patients and clients, as well as other matters. When approached with mutual respect, the challenges of multidisciplinary discussions can be overcome, and the benefits reaped for all involved.

Reflections and Recommendations

Our experiences with the "Voices and PHACES" study resonate with experiences reported by others who have engaged in CBR (Israel et al., 1998; Savan & Sider, 2003). CBR involves many extra steps above and beyond those entailed in more "traditional" research methods; these can lead academic researchers to shy away from pursuing CBR. As noted earlier, the demands of CBR can raise particular concerns when considering such an approach as part of a graduate student dissertation. Given the complexity, uncertainty, and extra completion time that CBR adds to a dissertation, there may seem to be little incentive for a graduate student to opt for such a project. The doctoral student leading "Voices and PHACES" (A. Roy) has indeed faced unique challenges in her dissertation relative to her classmates who have pursued more traditional dissertation projects. She has, however, also relished the unparalleled opportunity that the experience has provided her, with respect to building skills in project development and management, and in collaborative research. These skills will be critical for success in her future career in academic research and medicine, in which she hopes to continue working in partnership with Aboriginal communities both as a population health researcher and as a physician. We have found that, while difficult, the challenges associated with CBR are surmountable. Based on our experiences, we can offer some recommendations to readers who are contemplating CBR.

- *Draft and agree upon formal terms of reference for partnerships, in writing.* Having a written account can help ensure clarity, and it can serve as a written record for future reference by all parties involved. The latter is particularly relevant in light of the length of time that can pass between the forging of partnerships and the start of data gathering.
- *Approach conflicting ideas or opinions with a spirit of compromise, whenever possible.* When it is not possible to compromise, communicate the reason (e.g., university policies, agency policies, budget constraints, etc.) to defuse the potential for misunderstandings and hurt feelings. Furthermore, never be afraid to ask for flexibility at the institutional level; such requests may have positive results, and may also provide education on CBR that may facilitate its acceptance.
- *Maintain clear and open communication, and encourage back-and-forth dialogue.* Ensure that everyone has the opportunity to both hear and be heard, and to contribute meaningfully and equitably to decisions. Keeping everyone "on the same page," so to speak, requires active effort. For academic researchers, use of lay

language to communicate scientific ideas to community partners is integral. Attaching deadlines to tasks and issuing friendly reminders in regards to the progress of tasks can also be helpful for keeping everyone on track. "Checking in" in order to offer support to facilitate task completion is appreciated by community members; for many of them, research activities are often volunteer endeavours, above and beyond their normal job duties.

- *Patience and flexibility are important.* CBR can be time-consuming, complex, and unpredictable. It is advisable to factor possible delays into projected timelines, and to be prepared to "return to the drawing board" should circumstances around the partnerships change. In this regard, fostering a culture of forgiveness and mutual accountability can help.
- *Mutual respect is integral.* CBR unites academic researchers and community members around a common goal: conducting meaningful inquiry to lead ultimately to beneficial outcomes. Every partner has a role to play in the research, and every partner's contribution is of value for the realization of the research objectives.
- A further recommendation we can offer to academic researchers on CBR in Aboriginal contexts is to *learn about cultural protocols specific to the community* (or communities) involved, notably around how to respectfully approach Elders to participate. Firstly, it is advisable to ask multiple sources about how to identify Elders, as there is variation both between and within communities as to recognition of Elder status. Norms and traditions also vary by community regarding how to approach Elders. In many First Nations communities, it is traditional to approach Elders with tobacco or other sacred items (e.g., cloth items specific to the Elder's tribal culture) when making a request for their involvement (Stiegelbauer, 1996). If unsure, ask: in our experience, Aboriginal community members are more than happy to explain their cultural protocols (and to forgive inadvertent transgressions), when approached respectfully by researchers who have a sincere interest and a genuine desire to work in a true partnership.

Conclusion

As with any relationship, challenges can occur in academic-community partnerships. These can be addressed through an approach characterized by mutual respect, cooperation, and clear communication. Academic-community partnerships facilitate research that is valid, respectful, and meaningful for "real world" usage. Community partners bring to the table critical perspectives on community needs and contexts, and valuable insight on knowledge translation. Academic partners bring to the table the formal skills and tools required for rigorous, valid research. In combining these strengths, CBR can yield tangible benefits for individuals and populations. The question of benefit is particularly pertinent in the context of Aboriginal health research, in light of the troubling historical record that exists around research about these populations. Along with benefits stemming from the knowledge gained from the research results, there are also broader benefits to the community associated with the participation and capacity-building involved in the research process. For non-Aboriginal external researchers, CBR is also an opportunity to learn about reconciliation. In these ways, CBR that follows the principles of OCAP can be a powerful counter to the legacy of colonization.

Acknowledgements

We are indebted to the women and the professionals who are sharing their stories as participants in the "Voices and PHACES" study. We also wish to recognize the contributions of the staff at the community partner agencies and recruitment sites; the academic and non-academic research team members; the oversight committee members; and the study's research coordinator and research assistants. Finally, we gratefully acknowledge the support of our funding sources: Investigator-Driven Small Grant, from the Alberta Centre for Child, Family and Community Research; Frederick Banting and Charles Best Canada Graduate Scholarship Doctoral Award, from the Canadian Institutes of Health Research (CIHR); Izaak Walton Killam Memorial Scholarship, from the Killam Trusts; MD-PhD Studentship, from Alberta Innovates-Health Solutions (AIHS); Scobey Hartley Doctoral Award, from the Alberta Centre for Child, Family and

Community Research; Alberta Award for the Study of Canadian Human
Rights and Multiculturalism (doctoral scholarship), from the Government
of Alberta; and Achievers in Medical Science doctoral scholarships, from
the University of Calgary.

References

Anderson, J. M., Khan, K. B., & Reimer-Kirkham, S. (2011). Community research
    from a post-colonial feminist perspective: Exemplars from health research
    in Canada and India. In G. Creese & W. Frisby (Eds.), *Feminist community
    research: Case studies and methodologies* (pp. 16–36). Vancouver, BC:
    University of British Columbia Press.
Beck, C. T. (2006). Postpartum depression: It isn't just the blues. *American
    Journal of Nursing, 106,* 40–50.
Bennett, M. (2005). Annotated bibliography of Aboriginal women's health
    and healing research. Vancouver: Aboriginal Women's Health and Healing
    Research Group.
Bowen, A., & Muhajarine, N. (2006a). Prevalence of antenatal depression in
    women enrolled in an outreach program in Canada. *Journal of Obstetric,
    Gynecologic, and Neonatal Nursing, 35,* 491–498.
Bowen, A., & Muhajarine, N. (2006b). Antenatal depression. *Canadian Nurse,
    102,* 26–30.
Castellano, M. B. (2004). Ethics of Aboriginal research. *Journal of Aboriginal
    Health, 1*(1), 98–114.
Castellano, M. B., & Reading, J. (2010). Policy writing as dialogue: Drafting
    an Aboriginal chapter for Canada's Tri-Council Policy Statement: Ethical
    conduct for research involving humans. *The International Indigenous Policy
    Journal, 1*(2), 1.
CIHR, NSERCC, & SSHRC (Canadian Institutes of Health Research, Natural
    Sciences and Engineering Research Council of Canada, and Social Sciences
    and Humanities Research Council of Canada). (2010). *Tri-Council Policy
    Statement: Ethical Conduct for Research Involving Humans,* December 2010.
    Retrieved January 25, 2013, from http://www.pre.ethics.gc.ca/pdf/eng/tcps2/
    TCPS_2_FINAL_Web.pdf
Dion Stout, M., & Kipling, G. (2003). Aboriginal people, resilience and the
    residential school legacy. Ottawa, ON: Aboriginal Healing Foundation.
First Nations Centre. (2007). *OCAP: Ownership, control, access and possession.*
    Sanctioned by the First Nations Information Governance Committee,
    Assembly of First Nations. Ottawa: National Aboriginal Health Organization.

First Nations Information Governance Centre. (2010). *The First Nations Principles of OCAP^{TM}*. Retrieved February 1, 2013, from http://www.fnigc.ca/node/2

Government of Alberta. (2010). *Children and Youth Services Business Plan 2010–2013*. Retrieved April 1, 2011, from http://www.finance.alberta.ca/publications/budget/budget2010/children-youth-services.pdf

Huhndorf, S. M., & Suzack, C. (2010). Indigenous feminism: Theorizing the issues. In C. Suzack, S. M. Huhndorf, J. Perreault, & J. Barman (Eds.), *Indigenous women and feminism: Politics, activism, culture* (pp. 1–15). Vancouver, BC: University of British Columbia Press.

Israel, B. A., Schultz, A. J., Parker, E. A., & Becker, A. B. (1998). Review of community-based research: Assessing partnership approaches to improve public health. *Annual Review of Public Health, 19,* 173–202.

Lombe, M., & Sherraden, M. (2008). Inclusion in the policy process: An agenda for participation of the marginalized. *Journal of Policy Practice, 7*(2), 299–213.

Martin, K. L. (2008). Please knock before you enter: Aboriginal regulation of outsiders and the implications for researchers. Teneriffe, Qld: Post Press.

PHAC (Public Health Agency of Canada). (2005). *Depression in pregnancy*. Retrieved January 5, 2007, from http://www.phac-aspc.gc.ca/mh-sm/preg_dep_e.html

Royal Commission on Aboriginal Peoples (RCAP). (1996). Appendix E: Ethical guidelines for research. In *Report of the Royal Commission on Aboriginal Peoples. Vol 5. Renewal: A twenty-year commitment*. Ottawa: The Commission; 1996, updated February 8, 2006. Retrieved January 25, 2013, from http://www.collectionscanada.gc.ca/webarchives/20071124125036/http://www.ainc-inac.gc.ca/ch//sg/ska5e_e.html

Ritas, C. (2003). *Speaking truth, creating power: A guide to policy work for community-based participatory research practitioners*. Community-Campus Partnerships for Health. Retrieved from http://depts.washington.edu/ccph/pdf files/Ritas.pdf

Savan, B., & Sider, D. (2003). Contrasting approaches to community-based research and a case study of community sustainability in Toronto, Canada. *Local Environment, 8*(3), 303–316.

Schnarch, B. (2004). Ownership, control, access, and possession (OCAP) or self-determination applied to research. *Journal of Aboriginal Health,* (January), 81.

Scott, C., & MacKean, G. (2007). Strengthening community action: Public participation and partnerships for health. In A. R. Vollman, E. T. Anderson, & J. McFarlane (Eds.), *Canadian community as partner: Theory and multidisciplinary practice* (2nd Ed.) (pp. 113–136). Philadelphia: Lippincott, Williams & Wilkins.

Scott, C. M., & Thurston, W. E. (1997). A framework for the development of community health agency partnerships. *Canadian Journal of Public Health, 88*(6), 416–420.

Smylie, J., Kaplan-Myrth, N., & McShane, K. (2009). Indigenous knowledge translation: Baseline findings in a qualitative study of the pathways of health knowledge in three Indigenous communities in Canada. *Health Promotion Practice, 10*, 436–446.

Sotero, M. (2006). A conceptual model of historical trauma: Implications for public health practice and research. *Journal of Health Disparities Research and Practice, 1*, 93–108.

Stiegelbauer, S. M. (1996). What is an Elder? What do Elders do? First Nation Elders as teachers in culture-based urban organizations. *The Canadian Journal of Native Studies, 16*(1), 37–66.

Swaab, D. F., Bao, A. M., & Lucassen, P. J. (2005). The stress system in the human brain in depression and neurodegeneration. *Ageing Research Reviews, 4*, 141–194.

Thurston, W. E., Dutton, D. J., & Emery, H. E. (2012). Building healthy public policy and introduction to economic thinking. In A. R. Vollman, E. T. Anderson, & J. McFarlane (Eds.), *Canadian community as partner: Theory and multidisciplinary practice* (3rd Ed.) (pp.125–139). Philadelphia: Wolters Kluwer Health/Lippincott Williams & Wilkins.

Tough, S. (2009). Call to action: Improving First Nations, Inuit and Métis maternal and child health in Canada. Calgary, AB: The Alberta Centre for Child, Family and Community Research.

Tuhiwai Smith, L. (2006). Decolonizing methodologies: Research and Indigenous peoples. New York: Zed Books.

Varcoe, C., Brown, H., Calam, B., Buchanan, M. J., & Newman, V. (2011). Capacity building is a two-way street: Learning from doing research within Aboriginal communities. In G. Creese & W. Frisby (Eds.), *Feminist community research: Case studies and methodologies* (pp. 210–230). Vancouver, BC: University of British Columbia Press.

Wesley-Esquimaux, C. C., & Smolewski, M. (2004). *Historic trauma and Aboriginal healing*. Ottawa, ON: Aboriginal Healing Foundation.

WHO (World Health Organization). (1986). *The Ottawa Charter for Health Promotion*. Retrieved January 22, 2013, from http://www.who.int/healthpromotion/conferences/previous/ottawa/en/

The Youth Restorative Action Project: Evaluating Effectiveness as a Youth-run Program

Elly Park, Katie Gutteridge, Auralia Brooke, and Erik Bisanz

Introduction

The Youth Restorative Action Project (YRAP) is a youth justice committee in Edmonton, Alberta, sanctioned under section 18 of the Youth Criminal Justice Act to provide programs and services to youth involved in the criminal justice system. Traditionally, youth justice committees are asked to provide sentencing advisory to the courts as well as the administration of extrajudicial sanctions programs. However, in many cases, YRAP has gone beyond these roles to support young people—both victims and offenders—in other ways. Specific examples include its development of a one-to-one mentorship program, its ongoing close partnerships with youth servicing agencies, and its advocacy work with youth in child welfare, education, and other social systems. In addition, for the past 10

Suggested Citation: Park, E., Gutteridge, K., Brooke, A., & Bisanz, E. (2014). The Youth Restorative Action Project: Evaluating effectiveness as a youth-run program. In D. Badry, D. Fuchs, H. Montgomery, & S. McKay (Eds.), *Reinvesting in Families: Strengthening Child Welfare Practice for a Brighter Future: Voices from the Prairies* (pp. 133–154). Regina, SK: University of Regina Press.

years YRAP has been Canada's only youth-run youth justice committee. YRAP, as an organization, has a unique membership composition, and the creativity of its structure is one-of-a-kind within our current justice system. In this chapter, we, as volunteers of YRAP, draw on findings from a recent internal program evaluation[1] (Hyun & Gutteridge, 2012) as a means to understand the successes and challenges of YRAP in terms of its innovative approach to youth mentorship, the unique organizational culture YRAP offers, and the questions surrounding its identity as a restorative justice committee. Throughout the chapter we refer to some of the specific questions and concerns raised by evaluation respondents and how they relate to our current operations.

Objectives and Activities[2]

The Youth Restorative Action Project (YRAP) is a youth justice committee founded and run by Edmonton youth. YRAP is mandated to work with young people who have caused harm while being affected by a variety of significant social issues such as intolerance, racism, substance abuse, homelessness, family violence, and prostitution. YRAP offers an opportunity for youth to take responsibility for their actions and to move forward in positive ways. YRAP was officially sanctioned as a justice committee in 2003 and has dealt with over 300 cases of all levels of severity.

Objectives

YRAP strives to bring about constructive outcomes for those affected by criminal activity. In accordance with the Youth Criminal Justice Act and principles of restorative justice, YRAP aims to create meaningful consequences that are educational and rehabilitative rather than punitive. Clients are referred to YRAP when they have ongoing underlying factors that make their lives unstable. Often for the young person to be able to take responsibility and for consequences to be meaningful, he or she must first have a level of support and stability, and to this end YRAP

---

1   This program evaluation can be accessed through YRAP's website at www.yrap.org.
2   The information in this section on objectives and activities is from YRAP's website (www.yrap.org).

provides some support and advocacy for the young person while they are a part of the program. In all instances YRAP considers long-term consequences and outcomes.

YRAP also encourages and supports victims of crime to have a greater level of involvement in the judicial process than through traditional courts. Some of those who are harmed by a young person's crime would rather not be involved any further, while others find a great deal of closure in coming to understand why they were harmed and perhaps to prevent it from happening again. Should the victim choose, their input could be passed on to the court and even included in YRAP's sentencing recommendations. Notably, victims are able to choose to be involved, based on their comfort level and on what would be helpful and meaningful to them. This can take a variety of forms such as a simple phone conversation, writing a letter, or participating in mediation with the accused. YRAP members are aware that every person has particular needs and are prepared to be extremely flexible.

Activities

YRAP carries out many legal responsibilities, including sentencing and extrajudicial sanctions, judicial interim releases, the supervision of community service and probation orders, treatment plans, and mediation. It also has an active role in the community, supporting other youth initiatives, promoting education and engagement of youth, and creating awareness and public discussion surrounding youth-related issues. YRAP collaborates with a variety of governmental and non-governmental organizations to support youth.

YRAP takes referrals for a variety of reasons. The most common referrals are for:

- *Sentence advisory.* Once a young person has been found to be guilty of an offense, YRAP gathers information and makes recommendations for constructive and appropriate consequences. YRAP typically offers to follow up with the recommendations (via mentorship, support, connecting youth with other agencies, etc.).
- *Developing and supervising the completion of extrajudicial sanctions.* The extrajudicial sanctions program is an alternative

to the traditional court process for young people who qualify, usually for those charged with more minor offenses, who have no prior criminal record or a minor one, and who have admitted their role in their offenses.

- *Making detailed plans for a young person's interim release (bail).* YRAP will gather information about the young person's life and make recommendations on what conditions could be put on the release in order to give the young person the best chance of success.

Those who take part in the YRAP process will meet with a youth panel and possibly the victim of their offenses; they will discuss their personal circumstances and possible consequences. In all cases, YRAP offers one-to-one mentorship for the duration of the young person's involvement in YRAP. Continued involvement allows for the young person to have a stable individual in their lives who is able to assist them in the court system as well as with any other issues that undermine their stability.

YRAP works closely with the young person in order to come up with recommendations. In most cases, YRAP also consults the important people in the young person's life, such as family members, social workers, key workers at group homes or correctional centres, prosecution and defense lawyers involved with the criminal case, and any victims of the crime. During the meeting with the youth panel, participants will discuss past and present situations, the incident itself, and possible ways to repair the harm that has been done. Based on this information, the panel generates appropriate conditions or consequences that are presented as recommendations to the court.

Although YRAP is known for its role in the court system as a sanctioned youth justice committee, the members of YRAP have long believed that the above goals are also served well both by increasing public understanding of important issues as well as by engaging youth so that they become invested in positive activities in the community. It is for this reason that YRAP has often been involved in hosting and supporting art shows, educational workshops, musical events, artistic films, and other public events. YRAP also has an annual fundraising charity gala that showcases the achievements of young people in the community.

Youth-led Approach

YRAP is a justice committee that is also a registered non-profit organization. Its board of directors, voting members, and youth mentors are
all under the age of 25. This by-youth-for-youth model is built into the
organization's mandate, and has garnered the organization international
acclaim. As previously mentioned, it is the only entirely youth-run youth
justice committee in Canada, and YRAP has been used to advise other
committees interested in developing similar youth-led models. Recently,
YRAP volunteers carried out an internal program evaluation (Hyun
& Gutteridge, 2012) to get a clearer sense of the organization from the
perspectives of referred youth who are considered 'at risk' and participate in YRAP, volunteers who work with vulnerable youth, and partners
in the community. In this program evaluation, a member of a partner
agency stated: "You can go to any conference across Canada that focuses
on restorative justice and YRAP will be brought up. And the reason it
is brought up is primarily because of its acceptance of youth and youth
having a role in the decision-making process" (p. 17).

YRAP's youth-run approach was initially envisioned as a means to
bridge the gap between the adult-run justice and child welfare systems,
and the youth they serve. It was also intended to help youth volunteers
relate with their clients, and vice versa—there was even the hope that
clients would open up to and trust the youth volunteers more, by the
very fact that they were of similar age. One of the volunteers interviewed for the program evaluation optimistically stated, "I would like
to think [we are] more flexible—willing to meet the youth where they
are at and understand the barriers they may have in dealing with their
charges" (p. 12).

Yet, according to the evaluation, it appears that YRAP's youth-led
model has impacted its practice in other, perhaps more significant,
ways—for example, in its optimistic and common-sense approach to
meeting the needs of youth in Edmonton. In fact, many of the supports
that YRAP offers are not built directly into the organization's mandate,
but rather came about as YRAP's youth volunteers responded to what
they saw as unmet needs of their clients. When communication broke
down between a youth and his social worker, volunteers picked up the
phone. When a youth was accepted into treatment, but had no family

to drive her to southern Alberta, volunteers jumped in their cars. When a youth spent his birthday in jail, volunteers popped in for a visit. For some volunteers, when they encountered a youth struggling to meet even more basic needs—for example, food or clothing—they felt it was their responsibility to help out.

Strengths and Weaknesses of the Youth Approach

Being a small, youth-led organization that is operational based on independent fundraising and donations allows YRAP to approach social problems with a distinct set of strengths. The organization is able to be highly flexible, to adapt to different circumstances, and to personalize services for individuals. Its young members are often very eager and idealistic, and do not suffer from the same stress and burnout that some workers in human services face (Maslach, 2003). Youth members have fewer barriers in relating to other youth, and may be a refreshing alternative for those who are involved with many workers and professionals and no longer respond to more mainstream interventions.

In particular, YRAP's very nature creates a potential for positive youth engagement and empowerment. This is true of the youth that YRAP serves, as well as the organization's youth volunteers. Many of the current youth volunteers are passionate about working with vulnerable youth and other marginalized individuals and hope to continue this work in the criminal justice system or social services field in the future. Chances are many of the volunteers will soon be lawyers, social workers, teachers, and health-care providers working within our city. In this way, YRAP offers an opportunity to educate and empower the next generation of community leaders in diverse ways.

The recent evaluation indicates that many volunteers felt their involvement with YRAP has changed the way they understand youth in Edmonton. As one volunteer said: "Before working for YRAP, I was naive in my understanding of at-risk youth. After working with many at-risk youth one on one, I have been exposed to many of their stories and life experiences that really opened my eyes to how life really is" (p. 11). Another volunteer stated, "[Volunteering with YRAP] has helped me understand youth issues, and this understanding affects how I conduct my job as a peace officer. I feel I have a unique perspective that others in my field do not have" (p. 11).

Interviews from the program evaluation elucidated the double-edged sword of an entirely youth-based organization with regard to sustainability: "The greatest strength of YRAP is the youth, without a doubt....The greatest weakness of YRAP is the youth" (p. 17). These comments highlight the need for YRAP to better understand and engage with itself as a youth-run organization that is unique in its field on a national level. As such, it might be beneficial for staff to compare struggles of more typical community non-profits with its own to see where its youth is a benefit and where it requires support and planning in order to remain an asset. There is frequent turnover due to YRAP's age cap of 25, which could threaten the stability that a healthy organization needs, as well as the consistency that its clients deserve. However, while it has the high turnover rate expected of an average non-profit organization, it has steadily increased its capacity and membership over the past several years. Likewise, volunteers are able to participate as "adult advisors" even after the age of 25. Although older volunteers are not able to sit on the board or be voting members, there are a number of supporters who remain actively involved and uphold the youth-led structure of YRAP. The enthusiasm of its youth is contagious and motivating, and the organization has managed to recruit adequate replacements for turnover through support from community partners as well as YRAP members themselves.

On the other hand, YRAP's youth-led nature seems to carry with it some inherent risks. Its members lack the training and experience possessed by most workers who have to deal with similar social problems on a regular basis. While YRAP volunteers do receive training on issues concerning personal boundaries and safety, one partner in the community suggested that volunteers might unknowingly be putting themselves in danger (Hyun & Gutteridge, 2012). The major concern expressed was that the continuous and seemingly limitless helping model may lend itself to the overextension of volunteers' time and energy. A community partner asked, "What are your boundaries? What if something goes wrong?" (Hyun & Gutteridge, 2012, p. 18). Overall, his suggestion was that youth volunteers and mentors were not equipped to do the work they set out to do.

Finally, YRAP is not solely a mentorship program, and it must balance supporting high-needs youth with the obligations to stakeholders and the community that come with being a youth justice committee that uses a restorative process. The evaluation revealed a sense of uncertainty about YRAP's purpose among certain members and partners. Some community partners were unclear on what the current objectives of YRAP are (Hyun & Gutteridge, 2012). As one partner stated, "There seems to be some confusion with what YRAP is trying to do lately. Their goals are unclear and it seems that volunteers are trying to be social workers, but do not have training to do this" (p. 18). Although YRAP has a very unique position in the court system, there is an expressed need to clarify and explicate what its mandate is today. Developing a mission statement and clearly outlining a collective set of goals has been a recent undertaking, a direct outcome of the program evaluation findings.

Peer Mentoring in YRAP

The evaluation findings highlighted the importance of mentoring in the program, as well as the potential pitfalls that arise when using peer mentoring in the context of working with young offenders in a judicial process. The evaluation also highlighted YRAP's unique role as a youth-led group that works on the front lines with serious social problems. YRAP's mentoring process in particular provides an interesting insight into how the non-professional youth organization has adapted to the demands of its front-line work.

At YRAP, "mentoring" refers to a supported peer relationship between a youth client who has been charged with a criminal offense under the Youth Criminal Justice Act (therefore aged 12 to17 at the time of the charge), and a youth member of the YRAP program who has volunteered for a mentorship role (aged 15 to 25). In YRAP, the mentor is considered to be a peer and an equal to the client, but he or she is in a more stable place in life and also has training and support from the organization and its partners, such as other youth justice committees, other non-profit organizations who work with youth, and the legal representatives who work with youth. All clients are offered a youth mentor, but they are under no obligation to develop any sort of relationship with that mentor.

YRAP accepts a wide variety of youth as referrals from the courts, schools, or community agencies. These youth are from different ethnic and socioeconomic backgrounds, and participation, as recommended by the referral source, is contingent mostly on the youth's situation rather than the severity of the offense. Often the referral is made because a referrer feels that the youth needs greater support, or that the legal and/or social situation of the youth requires a higher degree of flexibility on behalf of the service provider than is common in other human services organizations. As a result of the lack of other suitable programs, many youth in very difficult life circumstances are referred to YRAP. Often referrals are made specifically because a youth has had limited success with other agencies, or the youth seems to be in a particularly poor situation and needs additional support.

The result is that YRAP is a non-professional youth organization that is routinely asked to be involved with some of the most difficult situations that adult professionals have to deal with. As such, it contends with many of the same pressures as other groups who work in criminal justice and child welfare systems. These include managing risk to members who work and volunteer in the community, managing emotional stress and burnout, being able to carry out the objectives of the work in the community, and coping with crises as they arrive. YRAP's position as a youth-driven project with an age cap also means that it must be especially diligent in providing consistency for youth members and clients, maintaining acceptable boundaries, and working effectively with other agencies whose members may be more experienced and may be less flexible. In addition, if YRAP intends to remain independent and youth-led, it must resist pressures to become yet another arm of the existing adult system (Hogeveen, 2005).

A few key elements of YRAP's organizational structure and culture allow this group of non-professional youth volunteers to handle some of the most difficult cases that the justice system has to offer. These are its flexibility, strong internal culture, and support network of members and non-members.

Structure and Supports

YRAP consists of a body of youth volunteers, a small number of paid coordinators who help to direct activities, and an elected board of youth members that oversees the activities of the program. YRAP's coordinators handle intakes and build relationships with all parties involved in a situation before matching a mentor to work more closely with the youth. Coordinators are almost always very seasoned volunteer mentors who are hired based on relevant experience, often from YRAP's own mentoring pool. Following the matching, the coordinator continues to be involved with the mentor and client, making sure that the mentor and client both feel supported and continue to work on court objectives, allowing the mentor to focus almost exclusively on building a supportive relationship. Mentors are told that YRAP is much like a hammock or a net; members take on whatever they are able to, and if they begin to feel overwhelmed, other members and coordinators can step in to take some of the pressure away from the overwhelmed mentor. By the time mentorship has begun, the youth client will have met a coordinator (or two, in a more difficult situation), as well as other members during the panel process. This means that several YRAP members in addition to the coordinators will know about the youth's circumstances and will be familiar to the youth, and may step in to support if need be.

Culture, Values, and Training

In addition to the structure of the mentoring program, there are less concrete elements of YRAP's organizational structure that help to address some of the factors that it faces given its unique position in society. Both inside and outside of the organization, YRAP's strength is based on the quality of relationships, interaction with community partners, and engagement of its members. Past mentors and coordinators have also made themselves available to support in times of need. One of YRAP's values involves building capacities in its youth members that will be of use throughout their participation and when they leave the program, and so many former YRAP volunteers have moved on to related fields and offer support and insight to members still in the program. As well, YRAP's "adult advisors" are often able to offer a variety of supports including advice on legal or emotional matters that a client or mentor may face. The organization has accumulated goodwill in several organizations and is able to get advice and support on short notice from many experienced people in related fields (Hyun & Gutteridge, 2012).

YRAP members may have different emotional engagement with their clients than workers with different organizations, perhaps due to their youthful naiveté. As pointed out by one partner in the evaluation, YRAP members are young and often have not taken on more cynical attitudes of some workers in human services (Hyun & Gutteridge, 2012). Mentors are also given a wide range of ways to support clients, which may alleviate some of the stress from a perceived lack of efficacy that affects those with inflexible roles in human services work (Spencer, 2007). Unlike workers who work full days and are unreachable after office hours, mentors are able to set up their interactions around their life's schedule and that of the client. As well, unlike workers who are associated with large institutions like Family and Children's Services, YRAP members are usually seen as neutral parties who are not paid to spend time with youth, which leads to less conflict and strain on relationships.

YRAP provides training sessions that focus on practical advice and real scenarios that have happened to mentors. Although they are often involved with youth in difficult circumstances, members are repeatedly reminded that their job is to be a friend, role model, and support rather than an intervention worker. They are asked to work within their own personal limits, and to request support and guidance if they do not feel able to handle any situation. They are encouraged to engage with youth clients using their own interests and strengths, making each mentor an expert in what they need to be able to interact with youth.

Moving Forward and Embracing Both Potential and Criticism

The kinds of questions and criticisms that have been raised in the program evaluation speak to the pressures that YRAP is adapting to. Much of the structure and training described has been implemented in response to past challenges and input from volunteers, partners, and clients. These changes were very recent at the time of the evaluation, and it remains to be seen how they impact YRAP's ability to effectively deliver service.

The YRAP mentor orientation booklet starts off with a list of the most important things for a mentor to know. One of the points begins with the line, "You're not superman. In fact, that's kind of your super power." This sums up both the spirit and modus operandi of the program. This is peer mentoring based on the premise that an equal, unconditionally supportive relationship can have huge payoffs that are different than what professional interventions can offer.

YRAP has the potential to be a lively program that can connect with youth in ways that other agencies cannot. Its strength lies not in experts or vast resources, but in engaging the passion, interest, and commitment of the youth members and clients alike. Members are encouraged to acknowledge and embrace their own limitations, making it easy both to ask for support and to model good behaviour in difficult circumstances for clients. They are not expected to be able to provide the same level of expertise as professionals, but rather to do their best, be honest in their failures, and to grow alongside their clients. To some extent, this informal structure of YRAP within the traditional justice system has come from its foundation in restorative justice principles.

Organizational Spirit

This section of the chapter takes a closer look at possible applications for YRAP's evaluation findings in the areas of youth leadership, succession and retention for non-profit organizations, and innovation and flexibility within organizational culture and structure. YRAP, as a distinctive kind of organization, presents a unique opportunity to study the benefits and tensions of youth-run initiatives, both for the members themselves as described above and for their community. A non-hierarchical organization within which the majority of work is planned and executed by motivated youth volunteers, YRAP represents a different approach to community justice programming and, indeed, not-for-profit programming in general. As iterated throughout the program evaluation interview responses, the organization has a unique capacity for individualized solutions to problems that meet collective goals (Hyun & Gutteridge, 2012). This capacity can be attributed to its structure, to the youthfulness of its members, and to their approach to the problems of justice programming.

Leadership

The field of positive youth development has become a pillar of community development and of educational programming. Its value to succession strategies, healthy civic life, and learning institutions is well-demonstrated (Mohamed & Wheeler, 2001). The literature shows that good leadership programming allows youth to synthesize experience into knowledge through successful, self-directed initiatives (Hamilton, 1990; Zeldin, McDaniel, Topitzes, & Calvert, 2000). For youth, their feelings of agency and self-worth, their confidence and motivation to see a project through, are dependent on investment, a sense of direct impact, and their self-perception as an important agent of change within the scope of their endeavours (American Youth Policy Forum, 1997). Because of its age cap of 25 years, a side benefit of YRAP is that youth have the opportunity to take on serious responsibilities without necessarily going through the formal and intense screening, training, and grooming process that is required of youth in other volunteering positions. This is significant both because it affirms that leadership opportunities can be directly integrated with active programming, and that all youth, regardless of their grades, stability, or other qualifications for participation in programs like Junior Achievement, have the potential to contribute to their community as mentors and leaders. Kozol (2005) suggests it is more than just a side benefit; it is a key component of producing thoughtful citizens:

> *Much of the rhetoric of "rigor" and "high standards" that we hear so frequently, no matter how egalitarian in spirit it may sound to some, is fatally belied by practices that vulgarize the intellects of children and take from their education far too many of the opportunities for cultural and critical reflectiveness without which citizens become receptacles for other people's ideologies and ways of looking at the world but lack the independent spirits to create their own. (p. 98)*

Innovation and Flexibility

YRAP members have expressed that one of the most valuable aspects of YRAP is its flexible organizational structure. While it seems that many non-profit organizations struggle with the question of how to nurture autonomy and allow employees and members to find their niche within the work, YRAP's natural environment is an innovative, collective process built on the notion that each individual within the organization comes to the table as themselves, with a unique contribution to and path into the work.

This organizational culture may seem to be simply a pleasant, non-essential benefit of the way YRAP functions, but in actuality it has a traceable effect on both the success of the cases the organization processes and the satisfaction of those involved with YRAP, both its members and its youth referrals. By finding a way to allow individuals to define and expand their own capacities, the organization maximizes its efficiency and is able to innovate and evolve in ways that escape larger bureaucratic institutions. However as partner organizations have suggested, this flexibility and youthfulness can also become a risk if not planned for and incorporated into a larger vision of the organization's capacity and mandate.

An examination of one particular core value and one key assumption that lie at the heart of this innovative structure might be useful here. The value in question is that of individualized representation. Each person within the structure represents, to the best and most respectful extent possible, their own experiences and unique capacities. The sister assumption to this is that each individual will represent their values with the same end goals: respectful support of the youth they serve. For many organizations, building on this assumption is quite a leap of faith—almost a liability. We must ask, then, how YRAP has become a recognized and respected community partner (Agano, 2009) when its very foundation depends on a sort of abstract faith in the goodness of the human beings it hires and works with. What aspects of this process are central to its success? Are those attributes, as the evaluation has suggested, also long-term liabilities? (Hyun & Gutteridge, 2012).

The answer to these questions perhaps can be found in YRAP's communications procedures and organizational structure. Its non-hierarchical group framework, along with the use of collaboration and a combination of resources to solve problems, provides a strong balancing force to the individualized agency that mentors and coordinators have. Combined with a culture of direct group communication during the decision-making process, this structure is a safeguard against poor individual judgement, but one that still permits experimentation and gives members room to expand their own capacities and push their limits. The interplay of trust and individual representation, collectivism, and transparent communication, together has created the unique space referred to above—an organization limited only by its imagination.

The goal now must be to evolve, to sustain those practices that are critical to its uniqueness, and to support internal processes where vulnerability is identified. This combination of recognizing strengths and supporting vulnerabilities or liabilities could allow this organization to grow without restructuring or losing its flexibility and unique leadership qualities. In order for this to happen, the organization must recognize its structure as an asset and analyze it for strengths and weaknesses just the way it would analyze any aspect of its programming.

YRAP in Relation to Restorative Justice Models

Braithwaite (1996) shares an example where an informal meeting with the victim, young offender, and other community members (the offender's family members, a support for the victim, and a facilitator) takes place with an opportunity to openly talk about what happened and how it affected those involved. The participants come up with a way for the youth to pay the victim back, and the relationships between the youth and family members are restored. This alternative to having the offender go to court, receive a sentence, and spend time in a juvenile detention centre presents a specific case where few would disagree with the assertion that the informal, restorative approach is a better option for everyone involved.

In many ways, YRAP exemplifies the alternative, informal approach described above. YRAP encourages healing and the restoration of healthy relationships and communities by involving family, friends, and community members who have been impacted by the crime. Yet, the program evaluation has raised concerns about whether YRAP engages in true restorative justice practice, given the advocacy and support YRAP offers to the youth offenders, as well as the relatively low level of victim participation (Hyun & Gutteridge, 2012). In addition, concerns have been raised concerning YRAP's role within the criminal justice system, including the suggestion that youth justice committees, restorative or not, act not as an alternative to the current system, but rather as a cost-efficient way of dispersing the caseload.

Are We a Restorative Justice Program?

Restorative justice has been described as the antithesis of retributive justice; the goal of the former is to heal, whereas the goal of the latter is to punish (Zehr, 1995). Some clear distinctions between these practices are the use of an informal, conference-style meeting, rather than a formal criminal trial, and encouraging openness rather than having strict rules and regulations to follow. By this definition, YRAP certainly does engage in restorative justice practices.

However, concerns have been raised over the advocacy and support YRAP offers youth offenders. The suggestion has been made that in offering such extensive support to the youth offenders, YRAP fails to represent the concerns of the victims and the community at large. The YRAP mentorship program works specifically with the offenders—many of whom are considered high-risk. YRAP believes that by supporting these youth in making positive connections to their community and changes in their lives it is, in fact, representing the concerns of the victims and the community at large.

Obviously, restorative practice must take into account the needs of all stakeholders. YRAP believes that its process does maintain fairness and equality for all involved. The mentoring of the youth offender begins after the panel process. This allows a coordinator to first meet with those impacted by the offense, build a trusting relationship with those involved, learn more details about the offense, and work towards creating a panel where those involved feel as safe and comfortable as possible and participate to the degree that they feel able. It is only once a resolution is made that is to the satisfaction of all those involved that the matter is sent back to court for a final decision, and the youth is matched with a mentor.

In this configuration, there are at least three checks in the process that are intended to maintain fairness and accountability of those involved. The chairperson of the panel guides the process and ensures that those present feel as though they have been heard and are satisfied by the resolution. The YRAP coordinator serves as the keeper of the larger process; he or she actively engages with all the different stakeholders and endeavours to address the needs of those involved. The court then judges whether the resolution is reasonable and is acceptable from a legal perspective and ensures that the rights and safety of those involved are not compromised and that harmful precedents are not being set by the restorative process.

What Might be Missing: Victim Empowerment

The face-to-face encounter that takes place during a panel with the youth offender, YRAP members, community members, and possibly the victim(s) has been promoted as a key factor in providing healing to victims, and victim satisfaction is used as a measure of effectiveness (Bazemore & Green, 2007; Gromet & Darley, 2006; Strang et al., 2006). A sense of empowerment is reinforced through active participation by members of the community and the participants of the crime (Braithwaite, 1996). Although maximum participation of stakeholders is considered ideal for active involvement in the restorative process (Bazemore & Green, 2007), there are concerns about re-victimizing by sharing the details of the incident and triggering feelings of anxiety and fear by seeing the offender (LaPrairie, 1998). In fact, despite the potential benefits of participating, research suggests that the rates of victim participation remain very low (Stahlkopf, 2009; Strang et al., 2006).

The same is true for YRAP, where actual attendance of victims at the panel meetings is uncommon. The YRAP process offers the opportunity for victims to be involved in whatever way is meaningful to them, provided that it does not pose a risk of causing further harm. If a victim does not want to participate in a face-to-face meeting or if a YRAP coordinator determines that this is not a good idea, the victim can be involved in other ways. Some choose to write letters, or to share their experience with a coordinator to pass on in the panel. YRAP members adapt to the needs of the victims, and victims have participated in creative ways, such as selecting readings or poetry to be shared to express their thoughts. In most cases, the victims express concern about the youth and want the youth to receive rehabilitation and support, rather than punishment.

Relationship as the Key to Community

The emphasis on a collective dimension to restorative justice is essential to understanding the collective responsibility in restorative procedures (Harris, 2004). A community is generally understood to be beneficial for all of its members because it is providing support, gathering people with common interests, and fostering relationships. When the term community is used in restorative justice programs, it must be qualified and explicit. The idea of community in relation to the other stakeholders, where the community includes those who have an authentic and ongoing interest in the healing and restoration process, should be clear and apparent. Always open-ended, it is a more revisionary way to negotiate new communal forms of being with others without being violent, destructive, or harmful (Couzens-Hoy, 2004). Concentrating on communality, being open without boundaries, creates the possibility for restorative justice to become transformative (Woolford & Ratner, 2008).

When youth justice committees form to offer alternative measures that include the youth and other participants, such as the Youth Restorative Action Project (YRAP), the regulations outlined in the Youth Criminal Justice Act limit the power that these committees have (Hogeveen, 2006). Nevertheless, the growing attention to and interest in restorative justice practice (Tomporowski, Buck, Bargen, & Binder, 2011) is a hopeful sign that critical discourse about the transformative potential of restorative justice initiatives in Canada and their role in addressing social inequalities and systemic imbalances will begin to occur in and amongst community organizations.

An Alternative Program or Extension of the System?

Pavlich (2005) has described restorative justice initiatives as more *appendages* of the criminal justice system rather than *alternatives* to it. Coinciding with Pavlich's view, one partner in the community stated in a program evaluation that YRAP could not be considered an alternative, but more of a branching out of the traditional criminal justice system (Hyun & Gutteridge, 2012). Community-based restorative justice committees have become a strategy to take the burden off the retributive justice system and reduce legal costs by using volunteer-based organizations to take on client caseloads (Dhami & Joy, 2007; Pavlich, 2005).

Woolford and Ratner (2008) have argued that "formal" and "informal" justices are indeed intertwined. Formal justice refers to traditional practices, including legal representation, court proceedings, and incarceration, while informal justice is an alternative process and often includes mediation and restorative justice practices (Woolford & Ratner, 2008). The informal-formal justice complex is described as "the cultural, economic, and political relations within the juridical field through which punitive and restorative justice forms coexist and reinforce one another, despite their apparent competition" (Woolford & Ratner, 2008, p. 32). Pavlich (2005) maintains that restorative justice is not truly an alternative justice because it seems only to exist in relation to the justice system it is trying to replace. He discusses the paradoxes of restorative justice and argues that restorative justice defines itself as being outside of the criminal justice system, but resorts to the same concepts and terminology as this very system (Pavlich, 2005).

YRAP is an example of this tension between informal and formal justice practices. Although the committee is given the significant responsibility of coming up with sentencing recommendations and alternatives to spending time in custody for the youth, the ultimate decision is made in court by a judge. The judge has a copy of the report created by a YRAP member at the panel, but the report provides only a limited amount of information, which the judge uses to make the final ruling. Meaningful consequences and healing the harm that has been done to community members are important aspects of YRAP's mandate, but these efforts can be thwarted by the court's verdict.

Is Our Restorative Approach Working?

Restorative justice is extremely difficult to evaluate. Although healing and restoration are fundamental outcomes of restorative justice, outcome measures in studies on the effectiveness of restorative justice practices often rely on rigid guidelines of retributive practices such as recidivism and restitution compliance (Latimer, Dowden, & Muise, 2005). That said, when comparing outcomes, restorative justice programs do tend to produce higher rates of victim and offender satisfaction and decreased rates of recidivism.

Of course, such measures also significantly depend on the severity of the crime, the history of the offender, and the supports in place during transition. With YRAP in particular, it is difficult to compare the effectiveness of YRAP to other youth justice programs, because of the relative seriousness and complexity of many YRAP referrals. The aim of our program evaluation was to get an idea of what people within YRAP, partnering organizations of YRAP, and clients who were involved with YRAP thought about YRAP itself and about its effectiveness (Hyun & Gutteridge, 2012). The findings pointed to a lack of understanding of what restorative justice is and doubt concerning whether YRAP met the criteria found in restorative justice literature.

Conclusion

YRAP is not necessarily doing things for youth that no other agency does, but it is doing things in a way that no other agency does, due to the fact that it is youth-led. Volunteers meet each client with an openness to support that person in any way they can—without concern for definitional roles, policy, or agency directives. As one member said regarding certain mainstream agencies, "There are so many good people wanting good things and being stymied for some pretty poor reasons" (Hyun & Gutteridge, 2012, p.13). By contrast, YRAP's approach is simple: a community of youth takes responsibility for youth and helps out in whatever way possible (Hyun & Gutteridge, 2012).

The struggle of successive generations of youth members at YRAP is how to take advantage of the huge potential that their unique organization offers, while still managing the risk that is inherent in doing such work. The organization's approach involves an organizational structure that focuses on support, community, and building capacities among youth, as well as relying on support from experienced members of the wider community. While it has inherent limitations, YRAP serves as a very interesting example of how one small youth organization has been able to create a robust program that works with some of the most difficult cases in the youth justice system. All this considered, there remains one significant benefit of YRAP's by-youth, for-youth model: the positive engagement of youth in our community and the education and empowerment of the next generation of community leaders.

References

Agano Consulting. (2009). *Youth restorative action project: A study report for the National Anti-racism Council of Canada.* Canada: Department of Justice.

American Youth Policy Forum. (1997). *Some things do make a difference for youth: A compendium of youth programs and practices.* Washington, DC: American Youth Policy Forum.

Bazemore, G., & Green, D. L. (2007). "Yardsticks" for victim sensitive process: Principle-based standards for gauging the integrity of restorative justice process. *Victims & Offenders, 2*(3), 289–301. doi:10.1080/15564880701404031

Braithwaite, J. (1996). *Restorative justice and a better future, Dorothy J. Killam memorial lecture* (Manuscript). Presented at Dalhousie University, Halifax, Nova Scotia, on October, 17, 1996.

Couzens-Hoy, D. (2004). Levinas and Derrida: "Ethical resistance." In *Critical resistance: From poststructuralism to post-critique* (pp. 149–190). Cambridge, MA: MIT Press.

Dhami, M. K., & Joy, P. (2007). Challenges to establishing volunteer-run, community-based restorative justice programs. *Contemporary Justice Review, 10*(1), 9–22. doi: 10.1080/10282580601157455

Gromet, D. M., & Darley, J. M. (2006). Restoration and retribution: How including retributive components affects the acceptability of restorative justice procedures. *Social Justice Research, 19*(4), 395–432.

Hamilton, S. (1990). *Apprenticeship for adulthood.* Cambridge: Harvard University Press.

Harris, M. K. (2004). An expansive, transformative view of restorative justice. *Contemporary Justice Review, 7*(1), 117–141.

Hogeveen, B. (2005). Toward "safer" and "better" communities?: Canada's Youth Criminal Justice Act, aboriginal youth and the processes of exclusion. *Critical Criminology, 13*(3), 287–305. doi: 10.1007/s10612-005-3185-y

Hogeveen, B. (2006). Unsettling youth justice and cultural norms: The youth restorative action project. *Journal of Youth Studies, 9*(1), 47–66.

Hyun, E., & Gutteridge, K. (2012). *YRAP program evaluation report* (Unpublished work). Youth Restorative Action Project, Edmonton, Alberta.

Kozol, J. (2005). *The shame of the nation: The restoration of apartheid schooling in America.* New York: Crown Publishers.

LaPrairie, C. (1998). The "new" justice: Some implications for Aboriginal communities. *Canadian Journal of Criminology, 40*(1), 61–79.

Latimer, J., Dowden, C., & Muise, D. (2005). The effectiveness of restorative justice practices: A meta-analysis. *The Prison Journal, 85*(2), 127–144. doi: 10.1177/0032885505276969

Maslach, C. (2003). Job burnout: New directions in research and intervention. *Current Directions in Psychological Science, 12*(5), 189–192. doi: 10.1111/1467-8721.01258

Mohamed, I., & Wheeler, W. (2001). *Broadening the bounds of youth development: Youth as engaged citizens.* Chevy Chase, MD: The Innovation Center and the Ford Foundation.

Pavlich, G. C. (2005). *Governing paradoxes of restorative justice.* London: Glass House Press.

Spencer, R. (2007). "It's not what I expected": A qualitative study of youth mentoring relationship failures. *Journal of Adolescent Research, 22*(4), 331–354. doi: 10.1177/0743558407301915

Stahlkopf, C. (2009). Restorative justice, rhetoric, or reality? Conferencing with young offenders. *Contemporary Justice Review, 12*(3), 231–251. doi: 10.1080/10282580903105756

Strang, H., Sherman, L., Angel, C. M., Woods, D. J., Bennett, S., Newbury-Birch, D., & Inkpen, N. (2006). Victim evaluations of face-to-face restorative justice conferences: A quasi-experimental analysis. *Journal of Social Issues, 62*(2), 281–306. doi:10.1111/j.1540-4560.2006.00451.x

Tomporowski, B., Buck, M., Bargen, C., & Binder, V. (2011). Reflections on the past, present, and future of restorative justice in Canada. *Alberta Law Review, 48*(4), 815–829.

Woolford, A. J., & Ratner, R. (2008). *Informal reckonings: Conflict resolution in mediation, restorative justice and reparations.* Abingdon, UK: Routledge-Cavendish.

Zehr, H. (1995). Justice paradigm shift? Values and visions in the reform process. *Conflict Resolution Quarterly, 12*(3), 207–216. doi: 10.1002/crq.3900120303

Zeldin, S., McDaniel, A. K., Topitzes, D., Calvert, M. (2000). *Youth in decision-making: A study on the impacts of youth on adults and organizations.* Madison: National 4-H Council.

CHAPTER 8

Outcomes-based Service Delivery (OBSD): The Process and Outcomes of Collaboration

Susan Gardiner, Bruce MacLaurin, and Jon Reeves

Introduction

Over the past 20 years, Canadian child welfare jurisdictions have faced an ongoing challenge to meet the needs of children and families in a timely and effective manner. This period saw a significant increase in the number of children referred for investigation and the number of children in care (Trocmé et al., 2010). In addition, there was a sharp increase in the cost of child welfare intervention in Canadian jurisdictions (McKenzie, 2011). Waldfogel's critique of the child welfare system at the end of the twentieth century identified several key concerns related to capacity, specifically the question of which children and families were truly in need of child welfare investigation and which interventions were best designed to serve their needs. This critique also challenged the continued use of a single-practice orientation requiring all families and children referred

Suggested Citation: Gardiner, S., MacLaurin, B., & Reeves, J. (2014). Outcomes-based Service Delivery (OBSD): The process and outcomes of collaboration. In D. Badry, D. Fuchs, H. Montgomery, & S. McKay (Eds.), *Reinvesting in Families: Strengthening Child Welfare Practice for a Brighter Future: Voices from the Prairies* (pp. 155–182). Regina, SK: University of Regina Press.

to undergo a fairly authoritarian investigation process (Waldfogel, 1998). This trend has raised a number of questions about the utility and effectiveness of existing structures and objectives of provincial and territorial child welfare services in Canada (Provincial and Territorial Directors of Child Welfare & Rogers, 2003), resulting in the development of new policy and practice initiatives designed to better meet the needs of children and families at risk. Outcomes-based Service Delivery (OBSD) is one recent and well-documented example in Alberta (Brodziak, 2010; Gardiner & Hachkowski, 2011), and will be the primary focus of this chapter.

This chapter briefly reviews the historical foundation of child welfare legislation in Canada, followed by a review of some of the key events that resulted in change to the public and professional views of the best interests of children. This work represents a collaborative endeavour between a legislated child protection body, the research sector, and a non-profit agency, with a joint commitment to developing a research-to-practice, outcomes-based initiative. The authors will provide a summary of Alberta's experience with child welfare policy reform leading up to the current development of Outcomes-based Service Delivery (OBSD). A case study will be presented on the development and implementation of the Forest Lawn pilot site, followed by an examination of preliminary data on outcomes and lessons learned from this process.

Evolution of Child Welfare in Canada

Early Legislation and Practice

Child welfare practice in Canada was built upon the child-saving as well as the child-rescue movements, two distinct, yet overlapping, child welfare reform groups initiated in the United States in the nineteenth century to address the needs of children and families at risk of abuse or neglect (Bullen, 1991; Costin, 1985; Rosen, 1998). The doctrine of parens patriae provided the context for government intervention to address issues of harsh discipline or physical injury during the late 1800s (Costin, Karger, & Stoesz, 1996; Jordan, 1998).

The first humane society in Canada was developed in Toronto in 1887 by J. J. Kelso and was a voluntary organization designed to protect women, children, and animals (MacLaurin, 2005). In 1888, the initial Canadian child welfare legislation was enacted—the Act for the Protection and Reformation of Neglected Children—followed by the Act for the Prevention of Cruelty to and Better Protection of Children, introduced and approved in 1893 (Bullen, 1991). The Toronto Children's Aid Society was founded in 1891, followed shortly by the first children's shelter for neglected youth in 1892 (Jones & Rutman, 1981). Alberta's first child welfare legislation was the Children's Protection Act, enacted in 1909, four years after Alberta became a province (Knitel, 2003; Reichwein, 2002). Child welfare systems continued to be developed at the provincial and, later, territorial level and were based upon the jurisdictional needs and legislation specific to the region (Bala, 2004).

Canadian child welfare policy and practice during the first half of the twentieth century was primarily designed to have decisions about the well-being of children rest within the family (Bala, 2004). Following the start of the 1960s, however, great change occurred in child welfare legislation, policy, and practice in most provinces and territories in Canada in response to a growing body of evidence related to child maltreatment and to evolving definitions of best practice. These changes continue to impact current Canadian policy and practice.

Evidence of Different Types of Maltreatment
The battered child syndrome was identified during the mid-twentieth century, as medical technology developed sufficiently to distinguish intentional physical harm from accidental injury (Kempe, Silverman, Steele, Droegemueller, & Silver, 1962). X-rays allowed professionals to view a child's bone fracture within the larger context of historical injury, and investigations for child physical abuse increased following this point. Reports of child sexual abuse also increased dramatically during the early 1980s, as researchers and practitioners learned more about intra-familial and extra-familial sexual abuse, factors that support or challenge timely disclosures, as well as the key elements of a coordinated professional response (Bagley, 1983; Bala, 2004; Committee on Sexual Offences Against Children and Youths, 1984). Since the 1990s, there has been growing acknowledgement that other forms of maltreatment, including neglect, emotional maltreatment, and child witness to intimate partner violence, were quickly becoming the types of maltreatment that were driving child welfare caseloads across Canada (Trocmé, Fallon,

MacLaurin, & Neves, 2005; Trocmé et al., 2010). Child welfare services continue to be challenged by the growing recognition and awareness of each of these forms of maltreatment.

Foster Care Drift and Permanency

During the 1960s and 1970s, children were placed in child welfare care at a rate much higher than in previous or subsequent decades (Trocmé, Fallon, Nutter, MacLaurin, & Thompson, 1999). Children placed in care were at risk of staying in care for long periods despite evidence that indicated children who remained in care for an extended period had reduced chances of permanency through adoption or reunification and were at risk of drifting through multiple foster care placements before aging out of the system (Barth, Courtney, Duerr-Berrick, & Albert, 1994; Maluccio, Fein, & Olmstead, 1986). The Richard Cardinal inquest that occurred in Alberta during the early 1980s highlighted some specific failures of the child welfare system, including the lack of a clear permanency plan, numerous placement changes, and the lack of accountability and documentation in the years leading up to Richard Cardinal's death (Thomlison, 1984). Permanency planning was a response developed in most child welfare jurisdictions, with the expectation that a clear and comprehensive plan of action is required for each child coming into contact with the state; the plan must detail specific actions to achieve a permanent placement while reducing the negative impact of extended periods in care (MacLaurin & Bala, 2004). Maintaining permanency continues to be a critical element of child welfare practice in the twenty-first century.

Overrepresentation of Aboriginal Children in Child Welfare Care

Aboriginal children are overrepresented in the numbers of out-of-home care across most provinces and territories of Canada. This issue is best viewed within the context of the residential school movement that led to generations of children who experienced a range of abuse and neglect as well as the loss of culture and language (Fournier & Crey, 1997; Milloy, 1999; Sinha et al., 2011). The Sixties Scoop described a period beginning in the 1960s and continuing to the early 1970s that saw the responsibility of First Nations child welfare shift from the educational system to the child welfare system (Sinha et al., 2011). Sinha and colleagues summarized that the overrepresentation of Aboriginal children in child welfare care is explained by a range of issues external to the needs of the child at risk. This includes funding and practice models that prioritized out-of-home placement versus early intervention approaches, as well as a lack of professional appreciation and understanding of the contextual and cultural issues for First Nations peoples. Ensuring that children investigated by child welfare maintain contact with their family, culture, and communities is a critical priority and outcome for child welfare success in the twenty-first century (Trocmé et al., 2009).

Balancing Family Preservation with Safety of the Child

Family preservation was identified as a critical policy initiative during the 1980s in response to the increasing rates of children placed in care during previous decades. This policy initiative acknowledged that a child's relationship with his or her parents and caregivers was paramount, and efforts were redirected to ensure a timely return to the family home (MacLaurin & Bala, 2004). This shift led to the development of numerous family support and reunification programs to facilitate effective family connections (Morton & Grigsby, 1993; Wells & Biegel, 1991; Whittaker, Kinney, Tracy, & Booth, 1990). The family preservation approach was based upon the family welfare orientation to child welfare, which identifies that the family is the best place for a child to be raised and that extensive state involvement is most useful when it is directed to supporting the continued involvement of the family or return to the family when placement occurs (Fox-Harding, 1997). One immediate result of this family preservation practice orientation was that the number of children in care decreased in most child welfare jurisdictions in Canada (Trocmé et al., 1999). The role of the family continues to be firmly established in most provincial and territorial legislation in Canada and is a priority for services as well as outcome success.

An ongoing debate has continued regarding the relative benefits of family preservation efforts as a primary alternative to out-of-home care (Altstein & McRoy, 2000). The balance between the benefits of maintaining a child's connection with family versus the risk of further maltreatment or fatality is a critical factor in the decision-making process. The Gove Inquiry challenged existing perspectives on family preservation and the child welfare system in British Columbia in the mid-1990s (Gove, 1995a, 1995b), while fatality reviews in Ontario in the late 1990s led to a child welfare policy swing back to a prioritization for child safety as the paramount concern for decision-making (Trocmé, 1997). Discussions about how to meet the best interests of the child continue during the twenty-first century (Bala, 2004).

Best Interests of the Child

This principle of best interest of the child has gained importance in decision-making and policy formulation for provincial child welfare legislation in Canada and also in the international context for the United Nations Convention on the Rights of the Child (Alberta Government, 1984, 2004; British Columbia Government, 1996; Ontario Government, 1996, 2000; United Nations Committee on the Rights of the Child, 1990). This concept has long been criticized in the literature for lacking specific guidelines to assist decision-makers in the process of determining the best outcome for children at risk. In addition, the concept adopts different meanings during shifts in child welfare policy and services in Canada during the twentieth century. Child welfare perspectives on how best to meet the best interests of the child are seen to drive the shifts in policy and highlight the debate between the level of intervention (interventionist versus non-interventionist models) (Armitage, 1993), the location of intervention (family versus out-of-home placement) (Altstein & McRoy, 2000), and the paramount concerns of legislation (child safety versus family integrity) (Bala, 1999).

Current Alberta Legislation, Policy, and Practice

Child Intervention, the name used for child welfare services in Alberta, is designed to support the health and well-being of children and families (Alberta Human Services, 2012). Child Intervention provides programs and services that support children to grow up in safe, nurturing homes where they are cared for, loved, encouraged, and provided with opportunities to achieve their potential. The current configuration of Child Intervention is the result of ongoing change to legislation, policy, and practice since the initial legislation in the early twentieth century.

Over the past 15 years, there have been numerous changes to legislation, policy, practice, and delivery systems in Alberta, including the development of the Alberta Response Model (ARM), the implementation of the Child and Youth and Family Enhancement Act (CYFEA), the intro-duction of the Casework Practice Model (CWPM), and the development of Outcomes-based Service Delivery (OBSD).

The Alberta Response Model

The Alberta Response Model was first established in 2001 and set a new direction for the delivery of child intervention services in the province. The model provided a foundation for an integrated, community-based approach to address the short-term and long-term needs of children and families (Anselmo, Pickford, & Goodman, 2003). The Alberta Response Model was based on a philosophy of family-centred practice with child-centred outcomes. This model proposed two approaches that would decrease the likelihood that vulnerable children would need further child protection services. These included 1) developing an available and com-prehensive system of community-based supports; and 2) encouraging early permanency by promoting a variety of care options to give children safe, nurturing, and permanent homes. The principles established in the Alberta Response Model provided a strategic direction for the province's child intervention system over the last decade (Government of Alberta, 2004). Select principles include

- *Differential Response:* There is growing awareness that different circumstances require different types of intervention and investigation. As well, families have different needs at different times in their lives. A thorough and detailed assessment at the beginning of the intervention process allows caseworkers to engage with children and families and connect them with the resources and intervention services they need.
- *Early Intervention:* Meaningful engagement with families and community stakeholders is facilitated by an early intervention orientation. Connecting families with services that meet their needs can help with early resolution and continued success.
- *Community Partnerships:* An emphasis on strong community partnerships supports families to connect with services that can help them address critical challenges, including homelessness, family violence, addiction, substance abuse, poverty, and physical and mental health issues.

- *Permanency Planning:* A focus on timely permanency planning supports children to maintain or develop stable, nurturing relationships and permanent homes required to support their sense of belonging and longer-term well-being and development.
- *Family Involvement:* Maintaining and enhancing genuine family involvement assists children to achieve long-term success as healthy, well-adjusted, competent adults. An essential element of this involvement is that parents and families are actively engaged in planning and decision-making throughout the continuum of intervention involvement.
- *Evaluation and Measurement:* An ongoing commitment to evaluation and measurement of services is required in order to establish better outcomes for children and families at risk.

Child, Youth and Family Enhancement Act, 2004

The key principles of the Alberta Response Model were embedded in legislation with the enactment of the Child, Youth and Family Enhancement Act in 2004 (Alberta Government, 2004). Section 2 of the Act, "Matters to Be Considered," outlines principles that call for an evidence-based orientation to practice. The CYFEA affirmed the importance of the family and the role of child intervention in supporting the family, and recognized that children need stable, permanent, nurturing relationships. The Act directs that children should be informed of their rights and that all services should be provided with the least disruption to the child. As well, the legislation acknowledged the importance of engaging with children and their families and ensuring that their opinions are heard.

The CYFEA legislation included several significant improvements to the previous legislation (Alberta Government, 2004). Examples of changes include:

- Legislated reduction in the time that a child could be in care until permanency is achieved;
- Legislated differential response allowing for intervention and child protection services, as well as the ability to provide earlier services;
- Legislated emphasis on Aboriginal involvement in case planning and decision making regarding Aboriginal children;

- Legislated alternative dispute resolution mechanism to support early dispute resolution
- Improved access to adoption records;
- Provision of special rights, called procedural rights, to youth.

With the proclamation of the new legislation, there was a need to ensure that practice was aligned with principles and tenets of the Child, Youth and Family Enhancement Act. This led to the development and implementation of a research-based model of practice called the Casework Practice Model (CWPM).

The Casework Practice Model, 2006

The Casework Practice Model, a collaborative, decision-based orientation to practice was initiated in 2006 (Alberta Children's Services, 2006). The model identified assessment, engagement, and collaboration as the key pillars of effective casework practice and provided clear expectations regarding casework processes. This approach was designed to help caseworkers use consistent, evidence-based practice to achieve optimal outcomes for children. This approach embraced a family-centred orientation to practice with child-centred outcomes.

Shift to an Outcomes Orientation to Services

There is agreement that children and youth in all Canadian provinces and territories deserve timely access to effective resources to promote optimal well-being and development. The question of whether children and families are well served by systems of care, however, has historically been overshadowed by the urgency to help children at risk (Trocmé, MacLaurin, & Fallon, 2000). As a result, over recent years there is growing consensus about the value of measuring outcomes for children and youth experiencing child welfare concerns, since outcome measurement can clearly demonstrate which interventions are most useful for which populations and for what presenting concerns (Trocmé et al., 2000; Trocmé et al., 2009).

The National Child Welfare Outcomes Indicator Matrix or National Outcomes Matrix (NOM) is one framework for tracking outcomes for children, youth, and families involved in child welfare (Trocmé et al., 2000; Trocmé et al., 2009). Developed through a series of consultations initiated by the provincial and territorial directors of Child Welfare and Human Resources Development Canada, the NOM provides a framework for tracking outcomes for children and families receiving child welfare services. The elements of NOM reflect the complexity and challenge experienced by child welfare authorities in ensuring a balance between maintaining a child's immediate need for protection; the child's long-term requirement for a nurturing and stable home; a family with potential for growth; and the community's capacity to meet a child's needs. The NOM includes four nested domains: child safety, child well-being, permanence, and family and community support. A total of 10 outcome indicators were chosen based on select criteria regarding whether the data was generally available on information systems, could be clearly defined, and was most useful to stakeholders. This framework has been adopted by the Alberta government for reporting on the indicators of child welfare success and has been used as a foundation for the development of Outcomes-based Service Delivery (OBSD).

Outcomes-based Service Delivery

Alberta Human Services developed the Outcomes-based Service Delivery (OBSD) initiative in 2009 (Brodziak, 2010), and this initiative was designed to better meet the needs of vulnerable children and families. In May of 2009, Alberta sponsored a provincial forum on "Improving Outcomes for Children, Youth and Families," which brought together academic and practice experts from across North America to present leading research on the topic of outcomes-based service delivery. This forum launched the start-up of OBSD for the province of Alberta and highlighted current Canadian research in child intervention, trends regarding children, youth, and families involved in child intervention, and leading practice and research in providing child intervention services.

Using the learning generated at the 2008 forum, as well as a thorough and critical review of the work accomplished in other jurisdictions on OBSD, Alberta Human Services adopted a number of principles to guide the initial start-up of OBSD in Alberta. Brodziak (2010) provides a summary of the key underlying principles of OBSD, which include

- Lead Agency Model: one agency provides a continuum of services to the family;
- Outcomes Focused: outcomes are clearly articulated and defined;
- New Contracting Model: financial contracting is tied to outcomes, not outputs, and the contracting methods allow greater flexibility for service delivery to achieve outcomes;
- Evaluation: clearer data-tracking and evaluation systems are established to measure achievement of outcomes.

Outcomes-based service delivery moves the focus of serving at-risk children and families away from identifying what specific services are provided and towards identifying what the results of the service should be. OBSD focuses on implementing evidence-based practices and services through collaborative partnership to achieve mutually agreed-upon outcomes. OBSD also builds on the philosophy of the Casework Practice Model (assessment, collaboration, and engagement) and supports system-wide evolution, ranging from thorough assessment to how collaborative case planning and service delivery will achieve desired child and family outcomes. Contracted agencies play an important role in the provision of services. Under outcomes-based service delivery, agencies possess the flexibility to adjust their services to meet those outcomes, as they will have more opportunities to provide input into case planning.

Regional Implementation of Outcomes-based Service Delivery, 2009
In early 2009, Calgary and Area Child and Family Services moved forward on implementing OBSD in the region. The Calgary region provides child intervention services through a network of community-based service sites, and each site has a geographical or community-based service delivery area. Prior to starting the tender process for identifying a lead agency, the Calgary region held an internal tender process in which community-based service delivery sites submitted proposals on how OBSD would be implemented in the specific site. The Forest Lawn service delivery site proposal was successful and was chosen to implement phase one of OBSD with the lead agency that was to be selected.

Following the subsequent tender process for the lead agency, Wood's Homes was selected, and a joint services delivery model was started in the

Forest Lawn office in July 2009. The initial work in phase one dealt with establishing clear roles and responsibilities for service delivery, reviewing financial arrangements, implementing data collection systems, and developing infrastructures to ensure services delivery was ongoing. With the establishment of ongoing process and practice, the focus then shifted to improving practice to meet identified outcomes for children, youth, and families. Over the past three years, OBSD has continued to evolve and adapt, using data to assist in practice, integrating evidence-based practices, and improving fiscal process to lead to improved outcomes. This focus on improving practice and process is showing early promise. The measurement of practice outcomes is showing that fewer children are being provided services, more children are staying at home while being provided services, children and families are involved for a shorter time, and fewer families are returning for service.

Outcomes-based Service Delivery: A Case Study

The Tender Process

In January 2009, Wood's Homes responded to the Calgary-based tender opportunity to develop Outcomes-based Services Delivery, given the appeal of possibilities inherent in working towards transformational change in system delivery processes and in anticipating innovation from a focus on outcomes. This seemed an important moment in time to address the critical issues for vulnerable children and families, to work collaboratively towards real change, and to find new ways to improve results for children and families.

There were exciting factors in the tender process itself, as Calgary and Area Child and Family Services had also run an internal competition and the first site was chosen on the basis of demonstrating a clear understanding of the conceptual framework related to new service delivery, as well as readiness for change. This was a very important step. Traditional contracting processes are typically one-sided; that is, agencies typically apply through various procurement methods to the funder and the funder chooses the vendor. Rarely is the funder also expected either to demonstrate readiness for change or also clearly expected to embrace new ways of working. This feature of the initial selection process was very important as the work developed. The idea that any failure in implementation would be a joint failure was a fundamentally important starting place and guiding principle as the work unfolded.

The tender itself demanded some clarity around a vision for change, including what services would be offered, and how and when. Services have traditionally been offered in silos, with each service operating separately, leaving families to negotiate a labyrinth of different services. This opportunity represented a way to tailor services to address the families' needs in more flexible ways, to connect services, and, more importantly, to increase the families' voice and choice as a main priority in planning supports. Central to the initial planning was the idea of providing services close to the time of child protection involvement, being clear about the risk issues, and engaging families in finding solutions. There is now considerable international support for child welfare reform directed at recognizing the fundamental connection to and importance of family (Lonne, Parton, Thomson, & Harries, 2009).

Wood's Homes

Wood's Homes is a nationally accredited multi-service organization providing a wide variety of services for children, youth, and families with presenting concerns that include mental health concerns, child maltreatment issues, serious behavioural issues, school problems, and family disruption. Wood's Homes began in 1914 in Alberta and will celebrate 100 years of service in 2014. At present, Wood's Homes operates over 30 programs, in Calgary principally, but also at Fort McMurray, Lethbridge, Canmore, and Strathmore in Alberta, and Fort Smith in the Northwest Territories. With over 350 staff and a current operating budget of approximately $29 million per annum, Wood's Homes has developed a continuum of services to lessen gaps in service, to promote ease of access and flexibility, and to adapt to the ever-changing needs of families and the communities. Wood's Homes' philosophy and mandate is based on responding when families need help and providing the most accessible, effective, and high-quality help possible.

At the time of the tender, the shift to an outcomes focus fit with Wood's Homes' organizational priorities. The work within Outcomes-based Service Delivery could increase capacity to focus on improving outcomes; to explore different business models; to develop greater flexibility in service delivery; and to develop as a collaborative partner. An in-house research department had been in place for 10 years. As a result, there was an internal culture that recognized the power of data in defining success, in developing rigour in program delivery, and in facing the facts where programs were not working. Wood's Homes also had an entrepreneurial spirit based on over 20 years of experience running fee-for-service programs. This work allowed for creative new programs and for change over time as the market determined viability.

The risks of pursuing this opportunity were also fodder for great debate. Prominent in the discussion were not only financial and business risks but also practice risks, given the potential hazards of being an early adapter of a new direction. The financial and business risks were mostly related to complicated funding and lack of understanding related to controls over the factors that made up the case rate. The case rate model, discussions of risk and reward, and financial penalties for poor outcomes posed significant financial risks. The early agreement was a no-risk and no-reward process of discovery with clear understanding of the financial limitations both organizations could tolerate.

The Lead Agency Model had been chosen as the business model, and this meant substantial change in how services were procured and provided. From a broad menu of choice, including all available service providers and services within the Calgary Region, services within the Lead Agency Model would be procured and provided by Wood's Homes. Some services would be subcontracted to other organizations on the basis of need and organizational fit. The initial discussions on lead agency models were cause for tension with all service providers. Worry regarding how this model would impact the current business and contractual relationships with the Child Welfare funder dominated many discussions. Issues related to business threats, competition, mergers, acquisitions, and change management all surfaced. Fear about the loss of business as well as of privatization was evident. Over the past three years, these fears have subsided to a great extent. The pace of change has been relatively slow within the Calgary context. The impact of the pilot site has not been significant enough to impact the business of other services. A larger parallel system has run alongside the demonstration sites. And this has presented both opportunity for development and challenges related to change management.

The Beginning of Outcomes-based Service Delivery Systems at the Forest Lawn Site

Articulation of a Shared Vision and the Development of Collaborative Processes

The development of a shared vision has been identified as a critical element in the change processes related to child welfare reform (Child Welfare Information Gateway, 2008), and it is an important starting place in the development of a collaborative service. A shared vision includes agreement on common goals, values, and principles that guide the work.

The tender process set the stage for early discussions and agreement about the vision of the work. There was initially wide agreement between the staff at all levels around basic principles and values. As it quickly became apparent, though, it was harder to define what this meant for staff at the front line. In addition, launch and learn is a relatively weak management imperative. It was not a whole-hearted commitment to a new direction but rather a process of discovery. As such, it created confusion for what this meant in relation to the families and children being seen.

In the early stages of this change process, it was necessary to *begin* the work in order to *determine* the work, as it were. While the benefits for new practice were obvious very early on, the details of how things could work needed to be fleshed out. The setting was an active learning environment with child protection cases and the need for due care even as a change process was under way. There were many cases where the solutions seemed obvious, where creative practice produced early results, and where collaboration produced quick wins. There were other cases, more complicated or higher risk, where the going was much tougher. As the courts and other service providers were also involved and the pressure mounted, so did the conflict between the teams.

The need for policy to support the change process, the need to re-examine existing training, and the need to modify support structures, such as databases, was obvious. Confusion over roles and responsibilities quickly evolved. There was, and is, considerable tension related to confusion about the rules of engagement and indeed about the shared vision. A process of articulating the work began: Who was to do what when?

The development of collaborative processes helped in some regard to clarify roles and responsibilities, but this work is still very much a moving target. And it may well be that in these early days of the development of an outcomes-based service delivery system, our efforts to improve communication and coordination remain an important starting point. Fully collaborative efforts will follow, as the policies, systems, and structures are developed to fully support a collaborative operating environment.

Service Delivery Capacity

The first cycle of the Alberta Incidence Study of Reported Child Abuse and Neglect (AIS-2003) provided a base for program planning with this population (MacLaurin, Trocmé, Fallon, et al., 2006). The AIS-2003 found that referrals to services beyond the parameters of child welfare involvement were made in 73% of substantiated investigations, and these services typically included in-home parent support programs, family or parent counselling, drug or alcohol counselling, psychiatric or psychological counselling, child-focused referrals, and cultural supports. In addition, almost one-fifth of these substantiated investigations resulted in the child being placed outside of their home in either formal (12%) or informal (8%) care (MacLaurin et al., 2006).

For Wood's Homes, there was a need to develop new capacity. More comprehensive networks of services were needed, as service was provided to families from opening to closing. For cases that remained in parental care, the work seemed straightforward. For cases where out-of-home placement was needed, the work was more complex. More service providers were involved, and it required more time to develop shared visions. Instead of providers offering a variety of independent services, the work was developing integrated services as a part of an intervention plan over an episode of care. Largely, the provider network offered services in areas outside of Wood's Homes expertise, such as domestic violence counselling, addictions or mental health services, pediatric or medical support, or additional out-of-home placements, such as foster care or treatment services. Because this is a pilot project within the context of an existing delivery system, a clear idea of how to work collaboratively towards single intervention plans is only beginning to emerge.

Developing new practice also meant focusing on a clinical framework that could engage families, provide safety for children, and address child protection needs, while also demonstrating outcomes. Service delivery in this instance was not simply providing services but rather developing a framework for clinical practice and outcome measurement. There has been considerable work in child protection practice reform, with clear recommendations for improvements in the ways we engage families while addressing child protection concerns. (See for example Lonne et al., 2009; Department of Education, 2011). Thus, a search began for a clinical framework to assist with developing an approach for our work.

The work of Turnell and Edwards (1999) emerged as a clear choice. Foundational ideas from the Signs of Safety approach, related to balancing risk with safety, seemed to be a good starting place in shifting practice. In addition, this work is strengths-based and focuses on family voice as a critical element. Finding the work of Turnell and Edwards was an important starting point, and considerable discussion over the past three years was needed to gain agreement from the region, to provide training for our staff groups, and to begin to utilize this approach as a tool. It is fair to say that these are still early days in adopting this way of working; at the same time, though, the promise in this approach is considerable. Many jurisdictions are beginning to adopt the Signs of Safety approach, and there is considerable support within the literature for the focus on engaging families, being clear with families about what the issues are, and what needs to change (Turnell, 2010).

A basic Family Support model was chosen as a service delivery starting place. This model could be employed whether children were at home or in out-of-home placements. And services could be offered in integrated ways using a single case plan. The name of the service became the Family Support Network. Family Support typically includes the following as core elements:

- Home Visiting and Concrete Services (e.g., food, transportation);
- Child Development and Screening;
- Parent Training and Education; and
- Social, Emotional and Educational Support for Parents (Crampton & Riley-Behringer, 2012, p. 85).

For the region, as with the lead agency, there was the need to examine how the Casework Practice Model (CWPM) would be implemented through OBSD. The need to clarify practice and administrative processes was evident in the establishment of the partnership with Wood's Homes.

Although the CWPM provides a clear foundation for practice, there was a need to articulate and clarify the delegated roles and functions child intervention staff must perform and which roles and functions agency staff can perform. The legislative action under the CYFE Act cannot be delegated to agency staff; therefore, the need to have clearly defined roles and responsibilities has been a key focus at the service delivery site with the agency. This process has challenged the region to articulate and describe how we practice and provide child intervention services. This definition and role clarification of practice has been an ongoing process and challenge, and has led to the region clearly defining child intervention practice and developing processes to improve practice across the region.

Business Processes and Financial Systems
A very complex (at least relative to previous arrangements) financial system was developed as a starting place. All expenditures were tracked according to the client's usage, and one unintended outcome was adding new administrative burdens without improving outcomes. This area also created considerable confusion for both staff groups. Conflict developed around issues related to who gets to decide what services will be provided and who has to pay for what. In the interest of developing competence in direct services, while gaining experience with costs, a block-funded model was adapted and existing contractual agreements with the region were utilized. This process resulted in greater risk management for Wood's Homes, a better sense of what money was being spent, and a reduction in the day-to-day conflict.

Creation of an Outcomes-based Measurement and Management System
Outcomes measurement in this work has been largely influenced by findings from the Canadian Incidence Study of Reported Child Abuse and Neglect (Trocmé et al., 2010), as well as ideas related to defining what success should look like for vulnerable children who come in contact with the child welfare system, as outlined by the National Outcomes Matrix (NOM) (Trocmé et al., 2009). The Canadian Incidence Study has also been useful in examining the methods used to train staff to gather data and to ensure acceptable levels of data collection. The National Outcomes Matrix provided the foundation for a multi-level approach to tracking

client outcomes. This approach focused on two levels of data that would include outcomes-based case planning measures for clinical practice as well as systems-based cohort data. Wood's Homes focused on gathering client-level data related to well-being and engagement at a child and family level. The region has focused on gathering and analysing cohort data as indicators to achieving outcomes as defined in OBSD. The intent is to reach a point where these two levels of data are integrated, resulting in a consolidated outcomes measurement system.

It was important to choose tools that had clinical utility and could inform the work with families as opposed to simply measuring results. A system was designed that could be reasonably easy to learn and administer. After some considerable search, measures were chosen that looked at overall family capacity (Family Assessment Form; Children's Bureau of Southern California, 1997), developmental screening for young children (Ages and Stages Questionnaires; Squires et al., 1997), and problem-based screening for school-aged children and adolescents (Preschool and Early Childhood Functional Assessment Scale and the Child and Adolescent Functional Assessment Scale; Hodges, 1989; 1994). It has taken time to select these instruments, to train staff to use them, to develop report formats, and to reliably collect data in a systematic way. And, it is fair to say, the building phase of this system is still under way.

The greatest success with data collection is related to instruments already in use. This reflects existing organizational capacity related to training, data collecting, and data analysis. The chart below illustrates greater success with the Preschool and Early Childhood Functional Assessment Scale (PECFAS) and the Child and Adolescent Functional Assessment Scale (CAFAS) related to training and data collection that have been in place internally for the past 10 years. New tools required the development of training, reporting formats, data collection methodology, and so forth. And over a three-year period, consistent utilization of tools and data collection is highly dependent on caseload growth, staff turnover, and management focus. While the data can provide important feedback on performance, measures are often seen as secondary in practice, and this is an area for further staff training and development. The following chart illustrates some success with continuous improvement and also some challenges in getting a system to the point of providing reliable feedback that can facilitate improvement.

Table 1. Developing an Outcomes Measurement System

	2009-2010	2010-2011	2011-2012
Total Children Served	100	216	310
Closed Files	31 children (17 families)	82 children (38 families)	117 children (68 families)
Ages and Stages Pretests *	68% (20/34)	80% (18/20)	56% (26/46)
PECFAS/CAFAS Pretests	74% (48/65)	97% (38/39)	86% (61/71)
Family Assessment Form Pretests **	Not Applicable	57% (22/38)	63% (42/67)

* *Implemented January, 2010*
** *Implemented March, 2010*

As the number of children served grew and the pace of the day-to-day work increased, the work to develop a measurement system grew more challenging. Staff turnover was a large factor in continuous improvement and the development of capacity. This work is ongoing. Systems related to staff training, data collection, and data analysis are being built. While there is quantitative growth (i.e., more instruments overall are being completed), the completion rate does not yet meet internal quality standards.

The data that is emerging is important to ongoing program development. The tools inform the work done with children and families and, as such, are important in establishing a clearer sense of risk and safety factors.

Identification and Management of Financial, Operational, and Risk Issues
At the end of three years, approximately 500 children and their families have been seen. Families are being seen early in their child welfare experience, and a broad range and depth of family problems are obvious. For the most part, the risk issues related to a new service delivery system are becoming clearer with experience. Financial considerations/constraints, legal and child protection issues, and realistic expectations of service delivery all present risks to program delivery. It is important to be aware of and monitor possible risks and to engage in risk mitigation as needed. Other efforts at outcomes-based service delivery note steep learning curves related to financial risk, contract terms, and overall funding levels (Lamothe, 2011). And, it is fair to say, this is still an area of

significant concern over the long haul. In the short term, efforts to reduce financial risk on both sides, through financial agreements that support stability while developing experience, have been effective in reducing tension. That being said, there are important differences being made for children and their families. The results related to reductions in the number of children coming into care and in the length of time they are involved in care are important beginnings. Refining the practice, developing greater capacity in work with families and in collaboration, will lead to further improvements.

Forest Lawn Site: Outcomes Measurement
Using the National Outcomes Matrix (Trocmé et al., 2009) as a foundation for the development of an outcomes measurement and tracking system in OBSD, the partnership has been collecting information to determine if the outcomes under the Child, Youth and Family Enhancement Act (The Act) are being met. Systems data related to number of files opening, days in care, and length of stay in care were collected from existing provincial data banks. The CYFE Act (Alberta Government, 2004) has five high-level outcomes that relate well to outcomes highlighted by the National Outcomes Matrix (Trocmé et al., 2009) and include

- Vulnerable children have the support they need to live successfully in their communities;
- Children in temporary care are quickly reunited with their families;
- Children in permanent care are quickly placed in permanent homes;
- Youth make successful transitions to adulthood; and
- Aboriginal children live in culturally appropriate homes in which their unique heritage, spirituality, traditions, and cultural identity are respected and fostered.

Regarding these outcomes the region has been gathering proxy data to measure the outcomes for over two years. The focus for data collection and analysis has been using systems data already collected and aligning them with the outcomes as proxy measures. The data is then compared to the rest of the region in the same time frames as a way to measure improvements.

When controlling for Aboriginal children and youth, the OBSD project at the Forest Lawn site is revealing some interesting preliminary findings. The project has opened fewer files for assessment, works with more children and youth at home, returns the same number of children and youth back home, has less reoccurrence, and is achieving these results in a shorter period of time. Below is an overview of the data results for the period of April 1, 2011, to March 31, 2012.

Table 2. Comparison of OBSD Site to Rest of Calgary Region Sites

	OBSD	Rest of the Region
Closed at Assessment	87%	77%
Children Staying at Home	89%	88%
Children returning home	67%	72%
Recurrence	4.50%	6.10%
Placement Mix	No difference between sites	
Duration in Preservation *	144 days	195 days
Duration in Recurrence **	297 days	326 days

* OBSD 35% less
** OBSD 10% less

Although the preliminary results are promising, the results must be interpreted with caution. The sample size is small, the work sites are not identical, and each site has unique characteristics that impact practices and results. The OBSD partnership will need to continue to work on common and consistent process to collect and analysis results.

Summary and Key Learnings

History

Launching and Learning was an important starting place in beginning to develop new practice. While there have been strengths and weaknesses with this approach, at the end of three years, we have a clearer idea of what is needed for a broader-scale implementation and, more importantly, for continuous improvement within our Forest Lawn site. We see this work as developmental. Our original visions have remained important, and implementation has created many challenges, some anticipated, others unanticipated. The results are, thus far, promising enough to continue developing this new area of work.

Practice

OBSD has led to a focus on articulating and improving the practice of regional and agency staff. This focus has pushed each organization to articulate, examine, and justify how services need to be delivered. This has been significant and should not be underestimated; having a clear and well-defined model of practice provided a solid foundation for improving services to children, youth, and families.

Business Model

Initially the region and Wood's Homes spent considerable time and energy in developing a financial model that would be suitable for OBSD. Given the case rate funding formula, the initial financial model placed emphasis on financial monitoring and risk. This at times moved the focus from collaborative practice to administrative process. The ability to have a financial model that is flexible in managing fiscal risk and encouraging good practice is key to meeting our outcomes. This is work in progress, and negotiation and flexibility are the keys to success.

Outcomes Evaluation

It was necessary, right from the start of the project, to understand and articulate outcomes. There needs to be a balance between having good data collection systems, having data that measures outcomes, and having resources to collect and analyze the data. Using and enhancing systems already in place and aligning these systems with outcomes have proven to be successful in measuring outcomes.

Limitations

Outcomes-based Service Delivery is at a preliminary stage of development, and the utility of this child welfare practice reform needs to be assessed and evaluated in a variety of practice and research settings (Lonne et al., 2009; Lamothe, 2011). The preliminary data presented in this chapter provides important evidence that supports continuing development of this initiative. At the same time, the strength of this evidence is limited by several factors. These are still early days in our work and the results are also based on a short time frame. Data is compiled on the basis of closed files, and more time is needed to capture files of longer duration. As well, larger samples over more time will be needed. The data collection and analysis processes are also under development. Refining these processes and developing understanding will lead to greater clarity with respect to understanding the data.

Conclusions

At the end of the initial three years of the Calgary and Area Child and Family Services initiative to implement outcomes-based service delivery in their region, strong collaborative foundations have been built and the work that lies ahead is clearer. The original vision and thinking are still very relevant. Implementation and capacity-building remain sustaining, captivating, and exciting challenges.

References

Alberta Children's Services. (2006). A new casework practice model. Edmonton: Child Intervention Planning and Implementation Office, Program Quality and Standards Division.

Alberta Government. (1984). Child Welfare Act. Edmonton: Queen's Printer.

Alberta Government. (2004). Child, Youth and Family Enhancement Act, Revised Statutes of Alberta 2000, Chapter C-12 and Alberta Government 1984, Child Welfare Act. Edmonton, AB: Government of Alberta.

Alberta Government (2004). *Overview of changes to the child, youth and family enhancement Act, August, 2004.* Edmonton: Queen's Printer.

Alberta Human Services. (2012). *Child intervention.* Edmonton: Queen's Printer.

Altstein, H., & McRoy, R. (2000). *Does family preservation serve a child's best interests?* Washington, DC: Georgetown University Press.

Anselmo, S., Pickford, R., & Goodman, P. (2003). Alberta response model: Transforming outcomes for children and youth. In N. Trocmé, D. Knoke, & C. Roy (Eds.), *Community collaboration and differential response: Canadian and international research and emerging models of practice* (pp. 98–104). Ottawa, ON: Centre of Excellence for Child Welfare, Child Welfare League of Canada.

Armitage, A. (1993). The policy and legislative context. In B. Wharf (Ed.), *Rethinking child welfare in Canada* (pp. 37-63). Toronto: McClelland and Stewart, Inc.

Bagley, C. (1983). *Child sexual abuse: A child welfare perspective*. Calgary: University of Calgary.

Bala, N. (1999). Reforming Ontario's child and family services act: Is the pendulum swinging back too far? *Canadian Family Law Quarterly, 17*, 121–173.

Bala, N. (2004). Child welfare law in Canada: An introduction. In N. Bala, M. K. Zapf, R. J. Williams, R. Vogl, & J. P. Hornick (Eds.), *Canadian child welfare law* (pp. 1–26). Toronto: Thompson Educational Publishing Inc.

Barth, R. P., Courtney, M., Duerr-Berrick, J., & Albert, V. (1994). *From child abuse to permanency planning*. New York: Aldine de Gruyter, Inc.

British Columbia Government. (1996). Child, Family and Community Services Act. Victoria: Queen's Printer.

Brodziak, J. (2010). Outcomes based service delivery — On the ground. *Alberta Association of Services for Children and Families Journal, 3*, 19–25.

Bullen, J. (1991). J. J. Kelso and the "new" child-savers: The genesis of the children's aid movement in Ontario. In R. Smandych, G. Dodds, & A. Esau (Eds.), *Dimensions of childhood: Essays on the history of children and youth in Canada* (pp. 135–58). Winnipeg: Legal Research Institute of the University of Manitoba.

Child Welfare Information Gateway. (2008). *Systems of care*. February 2008. Retrieved January 23, 2009, from http:www.childwelfare.gov/pubs/soc

Children's Bureau of Southern California. (1997). *Family assessment form*. Washington, DC: CWLA Press.

Committee on Sexual Offences Against Children and Youths. (1984). *Sexual offences against children, Volume 1*. Ottawa: Minister of Supply and Services, Canada.

Costin, L. B. (1985). The historical context of child welfare. In J. Laird & A. Hartman (Eds.), *A handbook of child welfare: Context, knowledge, and practice* (pp. 34–60). New York: Free Press.

Costin, L. B., Karger, H. J., & Stoesz, D. (1996). *The politics of child abuse in America*. New York: Oxford University Press.

Crampton, D., & Riley-Behringer, M. (2012). What works in family support services. In P. A. Curtis & G. Alexander (Eds.), *What works in child welfare* (pp. 3–10). Washington: CWLA Press.

Department of Education. (2011). *The Munro review of child protection: Final report – A child-centred system*. London, UK: Her Majesty's Stationery Office.

Fournier, S., & Crey, E. (1997). *Stolen from our embrace: The abduction of First Nations children and the restoration of Aboriginal communities*. Vancouver: Douglas & McIntyre.

Fox-Harding, L. (1997). *Perspectives in child care policy* (2nd Ed.). London: Longman Publishers.

Gardiner, S., & Hachkowski, A. (2011). Outcome based service delivery: Launching, learning and looking forward. *Journal for Services to Children and Families, 4*, 16–21.

Gove, T. J. (1995a). *Report of the Gove inquiry into child protection in British Columbia: Mathew's story – volume 1*. Victoria: British Columbia Ministry of Services to Children and Families.

Gove, T. J. (1995b). *Report of the Gove inquiry into child protection in British Columbia: Mathew's legacy – volume 2*. Victoria: British Columbia Ministry of Services to Children and Families.

Government of Alberta. (2004). *Alberta response model: Transforming outcomes for children and families*. Edmonton: Alberta Children's Services.

Hodges, K. (1989). *Child and adolescent functional assessment scale*. Ypsilanti, MI: Eastern Michigan University, Department of Psychology.

Hodges, K. (1994). *The preschool and early childhood functional assessment scale (PECFAS) interview*. Ypsilanti, MI: Eastern Michigan University, Department of Psychology.

Jones, A., & Rutman, L. (1981). *In the children's aid: J. J. Kelso and child welfare in Ontario*. Toronto: University of Toronto Press.

Jordan, T. E. (1998). *Victorian child savers and their culture*. Lewiston: Edwin Mellen Press.

Kempe, C., Silverman, F., Steele, B., Droegemueller, W., & Silver, H. (1962). The battered child syndrome. *Journal of the American Medical Association (JAMA), 181*, 17–24.

Knitel, F. (2003). *Child protection: Trends and issues in Alberta*. Lethbridge: University of Lethbridge.

Lamothe, M. (2011). Redesigning the hollow state: A study of Florida child welfare service reform through the lens of principal-agent theory. *International Journal of Public Administration, 34*, 497–515.

Lonne, B., Parton, N., Thomson, J., & Harries, M. (2009). *Reforming child protection*. New York: Routledge.

MacLaurin, B., Trocmé, N., Fallon, B., McCormack, M., Pitman, L., Forest, N., ...Perrault, E. (2006). *Alberta incidence study of reported child abuse and neglect - 2003 (AIS-2003): Major findings report*. Calgary, AB: Faculty of Social Work, University of Calgary.

MacLaurin, B., (2005). A biography of J. J. Kelso and the Toronto children's aid society. In J. Herrick & P. Stuart (Eds.), *Encyclopedia of social welfare history* (pp. 207–208). Thousand Oaks, CA: Sage Publications.

MacLaurin, B., & Bala, N. (2004). Children in care. In N. Bala, M. K. Zapf, R. J. Williams, R. Vogl, & J. P. Hornick (Eds.), *Canadian child welfare law* (pp. 111–138). Toronto: Thompson Educational Publishing Inc.

Maluccio, A. N., Fein, E., & Olmstead, K. A. (1986). *Permanency planning for children: Concepts and methods*. New York: Tavistock Publications.

McKenzie, B. (2011). Differential response in child welfare: A new early intervention model. In K. Kufeldt & B. McKenzie (Eds.), *Child welfare: Connecting research, policy and practice* (pp. 101–115) (2nd Ed.). Waterloo, ON: Wilfred Laurier Press.

Milloy, J. S. (1999). *A national crime: The Canadian government and the residential school system, 1879–1986*. Winnipeg: University of Manitoba Press.

Morton, E. S., & Grigsby, R. K. (Eds.). (1993). *Advancing family preservation practice*. Newbury Park, CA.: Sage Publications, Ltd.

Ontario Government. (1996). Child and Family Services Act. Toronto: Queen's Printer of Ontario.

Ontario Government. (2000). Child and Family Services Act. Toronto: Queen's Printer of Ontario.

Provincial and Territorial Directors of Child Welfare & Rogers, J. (2003). New directions in child welfare. In N. Trocmé, D. Knoke, & C. Roy (Eds.), *Community collaboration and differential response: Canadian and international research and emerging models of practice* (pp. 1–13). Toronto: Centres of Excellence in Child Welfare.

Reichwein, B. P. (2002). *Benchmarks in Alberta's public welfare services: History rooted in benevolence, harshness, punitiveness, and stinginess*. Edmonton, AB: Alberta College of Social Workers.

Rosen, M. (1998). Child saving in America. In M. Rosen (Ed.), *Treating children in out-of-home placements* (pp. 1–18). New York: Haworth Press.

Sinha, V., Trocmé, N., Fallon, B., MacLaurin, B., Fast, E., Thomas Prokop, S., ...Richard, K. (2011). *Kiskisik awasisak: Remember the children. Understanding the overrepresentation of First Nations children in the child welfare system*. Ontario: Assembly of First Nations.

Squires, J., Potter, L., & Bricker, D. (1999). *The ASQ user's guide* (2nd Ed.). Baltimore, MD: Brookes.

Thomlison, R. J. (1984). *Case management review of northwest region, Department of Social Services and Community Health*. Calgary: University of Calgary.

Trocmé, N. (1997). Staying on track while the pendulum swings: Commentary on Canadian child welfare policy trends. *OACAS Newsmagazine*, (Winter), 13–14.

Trocmé, N., Fallon, B., MacLaurin, B., & Neves, T. (2005). What is driving
    increased child welfare caseloads in Canada? Analysis of the 1993 and 1998
    Ontario incidence studies of reported child abuse and neglect. *Child Welfare,*
    84, 341–363.

Trocmé, N., Fallon, B., MacLaurin, B., Sinha, V., Black, T., Fast, E., ...Holroyd,
    J. (2010). Rates of maltreatment-related investigations in the CIS-1998, CIS-
    2003, and CIS-2008. In Public Health Agency of Canada (Ed.), *Canadian*
    incidence study of reported child abuse and neglect - 2008: Major findings.
    Ottawa: Public Health Agency of Canada.

Trocmé, N., Fallon, B., Nutter, B., MacLaurin, B., & Thompson, J. (1999).
    Outcomes for child welfare services in Ontario. Toronto: Ontario Ministry of
    Community and Social Services, Children's Services Branch.

Trocmé, N., MacLaurin, B., & Fallon, B. (2000). Canadian child welfare
    outcomes indicator matrix: An ecological approach to tracking service
    outcomes. *Journal of Aggression, Maltreatment, and Trauma, 4*, 165–190.

Trocmé, N., MacLaurin, B., Fallon, B., Shlonsky, A., Mulcahy, M., & Esposito, T.
    (2009). *National child welfare outcomes indicator matrix (NOM).* Montreal,
    QC: McGill University: Centre for Research on Children and Families.

Turnell, A., & Edwards, S. (1999). *Signs of safety: A solution and safety oriented*
    approach to child protection. New York: Norton and Company.

Turnell, A. (2010). *The signs of safety, A comprehensive briefing paper.*
    Resolutions Consultancy. Retrieved December 14, 2012 from http: www.
    signsofsafety.net

United Nations Committee on the Rights of the Child. (1990). *United Nations*
    convention on the rights of the child. Geneva: Office of the United Nations
    High Commissioner for Human Rights.

Waldfogel, J. (1998). *Future of child protection: How to break the cycle of abuse*
    and neglect. Cambridge: Harvard University Press.

Wells, K., & Biegel, D. E. (Eds.). (1991). *Family preservation services: Research*
    and evaluation. Newbury Park: Sage Publications.

Whittaker, J. K., Kinney, J., Tracy, E. M., & Booth, C. (Eds.). (1990). *Reaching*
    high risk families: Intensive family preservation in human services. New York:
    Aldine de Gruyter.

CHAPTER 9

The Voices of Youth with Fetal Alcohol Spectrum Disorder Transitioning from Care: What Child Welfare Agencies and Youth Practitioners Need to Know

Don Fuchs and Linda Burnside

Introduction

The numbers of youth in care with disabilities have been growing across Canada. In Manitoba in 2005, 30% of children in care had a diagnosed disability, 74% of which were cognitive disabilities. In addition, it was estimated in 2005 that 17% of youth in care in Manitoba were diagnosed with or suspected to have a fetal alcohol spectrum disorder (FASD). Further, given improved access to diagnostic and treatment resources, it is estimated that the current percentage is around 25% (Fuchs, Burnside, Marchenski, & Mudry, 2005 & 2007; Fuchs, Burnside, Reinink, & Marchenski, 2010). Since 2005 the number of children in care has doubled to approximately 10,000 (Child Advocate Manitoba, 2013).

Suggested Citation: Fuchs, D., & Burnside, L. (2014). The voices of youth with fetal alcohol spectrum disorder transitioning from care: What child welfare agencies and youth practitioners need to know. In D. Badry, D. Fuchs, H. Montgomery, & S. McKay (Eds.), *Reinvesting in Families: Strengthening Child Welfare Practice for a Brighter Future: Voices from the Prairies* (pp. 183–199). Regina, SK: University of Regina Press.

Consequently, it is highly likely that the number of children in care with FASD has increased significantly.

As a result of these increased numbers in recent years, much attention has been given to the issues confronting youth who age out of the child welfare system, and their negative outcomes have been well documented. There is a growing amount of research indicating that youth who are emancipated from the child welfare system are more likely than those who have never been in care to be undereducated, experience homelessness, become young parents, be unemployed or underemployed and if employed to have earnings below the poverty line, be on social assistance, be incarcerated or involved with the criminal justice system, have mental health issues, and be at high risk for substance abuse issues (Courtney, Dworsky, Lee, & Raap, 2010; Tweedle, 2005).

Youth with FASD face additional challenges as they age out of care (Fuchs, Burnside, Reinink, & Marchenski, 2010). This places significant demands on child welfare agencies acting *in loco parentis* to develop services targeted specifically at assisting youth with FASD to transition out of care. This chapter attempts to provide an important contribution to theoretical and research knowledge aimed at informing the development of the policy, programs, and practices of child welfare agencies across the Prairies and other jurisdictions relating to the growing numbers of youth with FASD transitioning out of care.

Specifically, this chapter will discuss the need to develop unique transitional services to facilitate emancipation for youth with FASD, including a reformation of traditional child welfare services for youth in care. To illustrate this need, this chapter will provide a brief overview of the salient results of a recent study on the experiences of youth with FASD as they transition to adulthood from child welfare care (Fuchs et al., 2010). In particular, it will address the mismatch between agencies' efforts to prepare youth for adult responsibilities, when they are developmentally unable to make use of these services until well into early adulthood. The authors argue that a better understanding of the needs and experiences of youth with FASD transitioning out of care is critical for the development of appropriate supports and services to meet their needs. To assist in the development of this improved understanding, this chapter presents a reconceptualization of adolescent transition to adulthood that should be used to guide policy and program development for youth with FASD who transition out of care.

The final section of this chapter will present recommendations for service reformation outlining the benefits for youth with FASD and the implications for child welfare service delivery. In addition, the final section of this paper will provide some direction for further research and development of effective policy for youth with FASD transitioning out of care.

Changing Perspectives on Adolescence to Adulthood for Youth with FASD

Our understanding of the transition from adolescence to adulthood has changed significantly in recent decades. Adolescence and adulthood have each been thought of as distinct life stages, with individuals transitioning from one to the next. Yet, increasingly, the transition itself is being recognized as a distinct stage of development. The transition to adulthood in North America has traditionally been marked by completing school, departing from the family home, starting a career, marriage, and parenthood (Clark, 2007, as cited in McGregor, 2009; Tanner, 2006; Magyar, 2006, pp. 591–592).

Arnett (2004) has developed a theory concerning this period of development, which he calls emerging adulthood, and identifies five main characteristics: "(1) it is the age of identity explorations, or trying out various possibilities, especially in love and work; (2) it is the age of instability; (3) it is the most self-focused age of life; (4) it is the age of feeling in-between, in transition, neither adolescent nor adult; and (5) it is the age of possibilities, when hopes flourish, when people have an unparalleled opportunity to transform their lives" (p. 8). However, it has been suggested that this period of transition and the chance to try a variety of paths is primarily available to advantaged youth (Bynner, 2005, as cited in McGregor, 2009). For youth in the child and family service system who are forced to take on all the responsibilities of adulthood at age 18, there is little opportunity for exploration. Canton and Kagan's (2007) research suggests that youth with disabilities may also experience an extended period of transition, but for different reasons. They found that activities such as completing post-secondary education and obtaining employment may be more challenging for young adults with moderate learning disabilities, thereby increasing the amount of time required to meet the traditional milestones.

Recent research on brain development also supports the idea of emerging adulthood as a distinct development phase. It was previously thought that brain development was completed during the adolescent years but, as explained by Magyar (2006), studies using magnetic resonance imaging (MRI) are showing that certain areas of the brain, especially the prefrontal cortex, continue to develop for several years after adolescence and into the twenties. The prefrontal cortex is the part of the brain that is necessary for wisdom, common sense, sound judgement, working memory, attention allocation, and response inhibition. It is also the part "involved in controlling impulses, planning, thinking abstractly, organizing concepts, and weighing the consequences of one's actions" (Magyar, 2006, p. 582). Magyar indicates that many scientists now believe that the age of "biological maturity" is older than 18, which remains the age at which individuals are legally considered adults in Canada (p. 583).

For vulnerable youth, the developmental process may be even further delayed. Experiencing abuse or neglect as a child can hamper normal brain development (Magyar, 2006). What this means for youth in foster care is that, although many will be required to live independently at age 18 or 19, they are even less likely than other young adults to be developmentally ready for this responsibility. According to Magyar (2006), "they may be even less likely than their peers to have the 'hardwiring' necessary to make and implement plans for their futures, to weigh benefits and risks, to reign [sic] in their impulses, and to organize their often very complicated lives" (p. 597). Moreover, these youth are less likely to be surrounded by positive role models and consistent supports to help guide them through the process.

Similarly, youth with FASD are likely to lag behind their peers in the development process. Due to the damage done to the brain before birth, individuals with FASD may be at a developmental level that is several years behind their actual age (Malbin, 2004). Although they are developmentally younger than their peers, adolescents with FASD, particularly those who do not exhibit the physical signs associated with the disability, often face the same expectations. These unrealistic expectations can result in frustration for those holding the expectations and for the youth who is expected to comply, leading to inappropriate responses and the development of secondary behaviours (Page, 2007). For youth with

FASD who are transitioning out of the child welfare system, the challenges can simply be too great to overcome without a strong support system in place.

Changes have occurred in our understanding of the biological and social development of adolescents during the transition to adulthood. However, the delivery of services to young people who have become wards of the state has not changed correspondingly. Generally, youth in care are bound by the clock (Fuchs et al., 2010). That is, their independence is determined by their birthdate rather than their readiness. The readiness of youth in care for emancipation may be further delayed by factors that have impacted their development. One such factor is brain damage that has occurred as a consequence of prenatal alcohol exposure.

It has been well documented that youth leaving the care of child and family services agencies face many challenges that affect their future adjustment and functioning as adults. Youth with FASD who are aging out of the child welfare system face even more difficulties at adulthood (Fuchs, Burnside, Marchenski, & Mudry, 2008). They experience the same challenges as all youth in care, compounded by a condition that impacts their ability to adapt to and overcome these challenges. With few supports and services available to adults with FASD, their prospects are often bleak.

For youth with FASD, growing up in the child welfare system presents its own set of unique challenges. Children are removed from their family home for a variety of reasons, some of which may have lasting negative impacts on the child's development. Being maltreated as a child can increase the likelihood of certain behaviours in adolescence, including increased delinquency and/or violent behaviour, increased substance use, and self-abusive and self-destructive behaviours. It can also result in poor school performance and reduced cognitive functioning, difficulty in creating attachments to caregivers that can lead to poor self-esteem, and mental health issues (National Research Council & Panel on Research on Child Abuse and Neglect, 1993). In addition to these negative consequences, children experience a sense of loss from being removed from their biological family, and former foster youth report receiving little support in dealing with this event. A similar sense of loss may be experienced after a foster placement breakdown.

Important New Knowledge from the Voices of
Youth with FASD Aging Out of Care

In our recent study of the perceptions of 20 youth as they age out of care, it was discovered that among the findings were insights into their need for relationships, the nature of the developmental trajectory for this population, their experience as children in care and with agency transition activities, and their understanding of their diagnosis (Fuchs et al., 2010).

The youth interviewed demonstrated a craving for meaningful relationships and a place to belong. They were acutely aware of the time-limited nature of foster care and had experienced both relationship and placement breakdowns. The ability to count on the adults in their lives to follow through on commitments was critical to developing a trusting relationship. They wanted reliability from social workers who would respond to them as unique individuals. There was also a strong desire for a connection with their biological families, even where those relationships had been problematic in the past.

This study found that the commitment to maintaining placements must be shared by agencies and their workers (Fuchs et al., 2010, p. 89). Crisis intervention, conflict resolution, advocacy, risk management, and relationship preservation should be among the skills of workers used to support the continuity of placement as long it remains in the child's best interest. In addition, supporting the establishment of natural mentors in the lives of youth in care should be an important task for child welfare agency workers to undertake. Finally, strategies should be developed to coordinate addictions treatment with child welfare services in an effort to facilitate the safe reunification of children with their parents, or in cases where the child has already become a permanent ward, to help the biological family be in a healthier position to re-engage with their children who have grown up in care.

In many respects, the findings from this study reflect what is reported in the literature concerning youth in care. The youth desire genuine relationships with people who will love them for who they are, not simply care for them because they are paid to do so. Yet their previous experiences — dysfunction in the family of origin, frequent moves, changes in foster parents and social workers, and the feeling that they are not in control of their own lives — have made it difficult for them to trust the adults in their lives, thereby hindering the development of meaningful relationships. They have difficulty planning for the future, and although they are generally aware of the skills that they will need to live independently, they have been given little opportunity to practice those skills. However, they also exhibit a confidence in their abilities that belies their lack of skills and concrete plans for the future. Consequently, planning for the transition to adulthood is fraught with disengagement and rejection of potential supports, despite policies intended to ensure that youth are supported through emancipation.

A major issue this study found in examining programs that address youth transition out of care was that timing of the process of engagement needed to be addressed. Although preparation for emancipation through training in life skills, building decision-making capacity, and engaging in transition planning is critical, the current pathway for addressing these tasks occurs at a time when youth are still developmentally unprepared to make the most of these opportunities. These challenges and strategies to respond to them are articulated in the next section.

The Vital Supporting Role of Foster Parents for Youth Transition Out of Care

Foster parents are indispensable supports in the life of a child in agency care. The research of Fuchs et al. (2007, 2008, & 2010) has demonstrated that children growing up in care from a young age direct their need for attachment to those who provide consistent care to them—their foster parents. Without opportunities to live with biological family, children in care seek bonding with their caregivers, yearn for genuine relationships, a real family, and a place to belong and call home. Principles of permanency planning are based on the premise that it is a basic developmental need of children, especially younger children, to be stabilized in a consistent, nurturing, permanent family environment. The potential therapeutic and reparative benefits of consistent care for children whose family bonds have been disrupted are also well known.

However, foster care is often defined as a temporary state, according to Davis and Ellis-MacLeod (1994), because of the child welfare system's focus on family reunification as a primary goal. Only after all efforts to successfully reunite children with their parents have been exhausted (balanced always with the prioritization of children's right to safety and permanency, and the limitations to temporary status of care under the law) will foster parents be approached about providing long-term care to children.

However, there are risks when caregivers approach foster care as a temporary role. (Jones, 2004). Such ambiguity can affect children's willingness to engage emotionally in relationships with their foster parents, especially when their life experience has been that relationships are unpredictable and vulnerable to termination. Foster parents may also feel unsure of their role and refrain from actively planning for the child's future, waiting to "see what happens" as a result of guardianship decisions and agency direction, further perpetuating a state of insecurity. Uncertainty in relationships with caregivers may contribute to misbehaviour in adolescence, adding strain to the fostering relationship and increasing the risk of placement breakdown. Consequently, roles that all parents need to undertake in relation to adolescents, such as monitoring adolescent behaviour while also promoting age-appropriate independence, identifying and responding to risk indicators (such as signs of depression or substance use), assisting youth to develop greater responsibility in decision-making, role-modelling skills in conflict resolution, and advocating on behalf of the youth with external systems including schools (Small & Eastman, 1991), may not be fully employed by caregivers. This often leaves youth without the structure and guidance they need while navigating the challenges of adolescence.

It is critical, therefore, to develop alternative ways to ensure relational and ecological permanence for children in long-term care, subsequent to ascertaining a permanent placement. Specialized training for foster parents who are making a commitment to parent a permanent ward of a child welfare agency should address issues of role clarity, decision-making, transitional planning, and relational continuity.

The Role of Child Welfare Agencies

The importance of agencies maintaining the stability for youth in care cannot be overemphasized; for youth with FASD, consistency is an essential element in managing the impact of the disability on functioning. Recent research suggests that the biggest issue facing foster children is not the fact that they are growing up in care (which often has protective benefits) but the impact of disruptions in their social networks when placements break down and youth move to new neighbourhoods and transition to new schools, leaving behind an established network of caregivers, foster siblings, peers, and community supports (Pecora et al., 2005; Perry, 2006). Given that disruptions to ecological permanence are more likely in early and middle adolescence, agencies should plan for their services to involve a good deal of crisis intervention, conflict resolution, strong advocacy, risk management, and relationship preservation. In short, any and all efforts should be employed to resolve crises that arise to maintain continuity of placement and school, as long as that continuity remains in the child's best interests. Agencies partnering with foster parents in these endeavours are critical given the daily contact caregivers have with their charges, but if placements break down, the agency and the social worker become the youth's main source of advocacy and support.

Despite proactive strategies to preserve foster home stability, placement breakdowns still may occur for a variety of reasons, and alternative strategies to maintaining relational bonds are necessary. One alternative described by Greeson, Usher, and Grinstein-Weiss (2010) is supporting the establishment of natural mentors for youth in care: a stable, caring adult who is already present in a youth's environment and who is willing to take on a committed role in assisting the youth throughout life, including the transition into adulthood. The authors demonstrated that a natural mentor, termed "one adult who is crazy about you" (p. 576), provided an opportunity for role modelling and social learning for youth in care, resulting in guidance and advice, emotional support, and practical help, and increasing the likelihood that the youth achieved concrete assets (e.g., bank account, vehicle) in adulthood. Perry (2006) cautions that if that one supportive relationship ends, the impact of that disruption of supports can be devastating for a vulnerable youth. Therefore, having multiple strong support networks is recommended.

Munson, Smalling, Spencer, Scott, and Tracy (2010) encouraged the creation of formal mentoring programs that help youth get connected to stable, caring adults with similar life experiences who will support youth as they transition out of care, noting that some youth may not have

natural mentors in their personal networks due to the numerous relationship disruptions they may have experienced in their lives.

Our findings indicated that having close relationships with youth in
care can contribute to a greater awareness of issues that may arise during
adolescence, such as mental health concerns, substance misuse, sexual
exploitation, gang involvement, or criminal activity (Fuchs et al., 2009).
A key function of child welfare workers is supporting youth through their
involvement with other systems when these issues surface, ensuring that
the adolescents' needs are met and they receive the services they most
require. Advocating on behalf of youth in care, as well as coordinating
services across systems and with the foster home, are other important
worker functions that are facilitated by a strong relationship between
workers and youth in care.

Re-establishing contact with biological family may also provide a
source of support into adulthood for youth who have grown up in care.
However, youth in our study reported that when they reconnected with
biological family in later adolescence or early adulthood, they often found
that family members were encumbered by a range of unresolved issues
that prevented natural family from being reliable sources of support to
them (Fuchs et al., 2010). The issues that had contributed to the child coming into care initially (issues that likely included parental substance abuse
given the child's later diagnosis of FASD) have often persisted after permanent guardianship was granted and agency involvement had ended.

Implications of Research for Policies and Programs
for Youth with FASD Aging Out of Care

The final section of this chapter examines the directions that have
emerged from the current research on youth with FASD aging out of care.
Policies and programs do exist that mitigate the impact of FASD and the
effect of growing up in alternative care and that assist youth with the
transition to adulthood. However, the current efforts do not appear to
be sufficiently meeting the needs of youth transitioning out of care. Our
study indicated that youth are not being invited to become involved in
their own transition planning and are not aware of the specific skills
they might require to manage the responsibilities of adulthood. Youth do

not want to disclose that they do not understand the process; their fears are hidden behind a façade of self-confidence and a flawed perception that they will figure it out once they are on their own (Fuchs et al., 2010). Only the older respondents, already into their early twenties, showed an appreciation of the challenges they faced and acknowledged a degree of fear about how they would manage without the support of biological family, foster family, or their child welfare agency.

One of the most striking outcomes of this research is the clear progression of insight that developed as youth matured in early adulthood, leading to the assertion presented earlier that there is a significant mismatch between the timing of transitional planning activities/independent living preparation and the developmental readiness of youth in care. At age 16, when transitional planning is to begin, youth are still struggling with behavioural issues, school disruption, placement breakdowns, criminal justice involvement, experimentation with drugs and alcohol, and other well-known troubles of an adolescence spent in care (Fuchs et al., 2008). Child welfare workers may expend considerable energy responding to crisis issues experienced by the youth, leaving them little time to focus on transitional planning. But more importantly, at this stage the youth themselves are not able to focus on the future. Initiating transitional planning measures when youth are still in middle adolescence and not yet developmentally prepared to take full advantage of these processes appears to be a disservice to youth in care.

The timing of transitional planning is "bound by the clock," and stipulated by policy that endeavours to provide at least two years of preparation for emancipation before the youth exits care at age of majority. Only formal extensions of care for those youth who are willing and eligible provide any opportunity for matching developmental maturity with the provision of transitional planning services. However, the periods of extension provided to many of the respondents in this study tended to be a few months in duration, and not long enough to reach a stage of more advanced maturity.

An obvious solution to address this mismatch is to ensure that more youth in care, especially those with FASD, are granted sufficiently long extensions of care to allow them to work through the developmental tasks of adolescence more thoroughly and become better prepared for emancipation.

More importantly, youth who are offered an extension of care are, for all legal purposes, adults. Extensions of care that are merely a continuation of the same kinds of services provided to adolescents prior to age of majority do not adequately recognize the legal status of young adults receiving care. Providing services intended for youth to an adult population perpetuates the mismatch between service provision and developmental need, even if those extended child welfare services include an emphasis on transitional planning and training in independent living skills.

An extensive reconceptualization of adolescence as experienced by youth in care with FASD is required, leading to the development of a robust range of services aimed at young adults who need additional support beyond age of majority to master the tasks of emancipation. The literature reviewed by the Fuchs et al. (2010) study and the youth interviewed in this study indicated that at age of majority most youth have not yet attained the developmental readiness to live successfully on their own but *are* at a stage where they can take advantage of services that prepare them for independent living. This would indicate that a program of transitional support services (including care) for young adults aged 18–21 is an ideal bridge between being a child/youth in care and being a fully emancipated adult. In addition to age, criteria for eligibility in transitional support services would include being a permanent ward or a child who has been in care consistently since age 14, a diagnosis of FASD (to the extent that a diagnosis can be made under accepted diagnostic standards), and the consent of the young adult. Features of a robust transitional support services program for young adults with FASD at age of majority would include

- Negotiation of a transitional support services contract between the youth and the agency, including any additional supports such as alternative caregivers, community programs, educational/training programs, etc., outlining the nature of services being provided, the rights and responsibilities of the young adult in accepting services, and the roles that each party to the contract will play;
- Development of a wide range of living options that approximate living on one's own, such as supported independent living, proctor arrangements, supported room and board, as well as

foster homes and group homes that place heavy emphasis on the
development of independent living skills, allowing youth more
choice in where/how they will live as they make the transition to
independence;

- Wherever possible, the opportunity to continue in one's current
foster home at age of majority, with redefined roles, rules, and
responsibilities of the youth and foster parent clearly articulated
to provide youth with an appropriate balance between
protection/ oversight and autonomy into adulthood;

- Training for caregivers in the instruction of life skills, with special
attention to adaptations required for teaching youth with FASD;

- Development and evaluation of formal independent living skills
programs for youth with FASD, including sufficient opportunity
to practice skills frequently and receive feedback and guidance;

- The availability of youth mentors and life skills coaches to assist
youth in the practical application of independent living skills
and independent decision-making;

- Vocational planning, including skills/interests assessment,
training in employment-readiness skills (e.g., being on time,
following directions, etc., including adaptations required as a
result of the impact of FASD), job placements, and job coaching;

- The right of the young adult to leave the transitional services
program at any time, but also to return to the program up to six
months prior to reaching age 21.

Serious consideration should be given to the merits and disadvantages
of offering transitional support services under the auspices of the child
welfare system. There is no easy answer here: the opportunity to maintain child welfare placements while youth move through the latter stages
of adolescence and transition to independence clearly supports investing
transitional support services in child welfare agencies. However, the goal
of normalizing transition and promoting adult independence favours a
stand-alone program structure that supports residential care (whether
foster placement, group home, or independent living) but exists separate
from the child welfare system.

While establishing a unique program of transitional support services for young adults leaving care may be the ideal goal, moving in that

direction may take time that youth with FASD currently in care cannot afford. In the interim, legal provisions for extensions of care in child welfare legislation currently offer a mechanism for making services into adulthood possible for permanent wards with FASD who have reached age of majority. A defined extension of care program can be developed by creating a comprehensive cluster of transitional services and supports, accompanied by policies that articulate a different working relationship between young adults with FASD and the agencies that serve them, and between young adults with FASD and the caregivers who provide them with support.

Summary and Conclusion

This chapter has examined some of the major issues faced by youth with FASD aging out of care. It has identified the importance of reconceptualizing the current approaches to youth transition to adulthood. It has built its focus on the perceptions of youth with FASD and described the lived experience of youth with FASD transitioning out of care in Manitoba. The life stories of adolescents and young adults with FASD shared in the study referred to in this chapter have clearly demonstrated the impact of both being a child in care and being a youth with FASD in the process of transition to adulthood.

The chapter has emphasized the importance of stability in placements and how the abilities of caregivers and service providers to recognize and manage this disability were identified as important ameliorating factors. It has further demonstrated the advantage of moving from a system that determines readiness for independence in a purely arbitrary fashion (i.e., "bound by the clock") to establish a practice that would recognize the adaptive skills of the individual leaving care and plan according to their needs. It was evident that current assumptions related to adolescent development are not helpful in understanding the lived experience of these youth. This chapter has demonstrated that a reconceptualization of the developmental model to include an emerging adult phase would recognize that period of young adulthood when those beyond the age of majority are continuing with some supports to master the tasks of emancipation. This work would also significantly inform the nature of programs and services intended to assist transitioning youth. Ideally, that would include recognizing the adult status of those who have reached the age of majority by increasing independence and choices without curtailing support or shutting the door on those who need more than one try at independence.

Further research is necessary to develop new and effective methods of engaging youth in successful transitioning processes that will address issues of being in care with a disability. How does the population of young adults with FASD leaving care fare over time? Our view of them has been limited to a very short period after they leave the child welfare system. A longitudinal study of at least five years duration that would follow child-in-care alumni as adults with FASD would provide extremely valuable information on the emerging strengths, needs, and challenges of that group. The economic impact of children with FASD has been described (Fuchs, Burnside, Marchenski, Mudry, & De Riviere, 2008; Fuchs et al., 2009). Further research is needed to determine how the greatest return for social investment may be achieved.

The current research demonstrated that many young adults with FASD quickly become parents. The cost in human and fiscal terms of emancipating unprepared young adults with FASD is, in itself, significant. The cost of the generation they will produce may well be staggering. Little is known about the children of those with FASD. This second generation would be a most vital area for further exploration. Are these children also affected by FASD? Do they routinely come into care? How can parents with FASD be supported? There is an urgent need to understand and then address the needs of this group. There is great need for more research on developing more effective policy and practice in this often neglected sector of child welfare practice.

References

Arnett, J. J. (2004). *Emerging adulthood: The winding road from the late teens through the twenties.* New York, NY: Oxford University Press.

Canton, S., & Kagan, C. (2007). Comparing transition experiences of young people with moderate learning disabilities with other vulnerable youth and with their non-disabled counterparts. *Disability and Society, 22*(5), 473–488.

Children's Advocate Manitoba. (2013). *Change through engagement: 2012–2012 Children's Advocate Annual Report.* Winnipeg: Manitoba, Office of the Children's Advocate.

Courtney, M. E., Dworsky, A., Lee, J. S., & Raap, M. (2010). *Midwest evaluation of the adult functioning of former foster youth: Outcomes at ages 23 and 24.* Chicago, IL: Chapin Hall Center for Children at University of Chicago. Retrieved from http://www.chapinhall.org/sites/default/files/Midwest_Study_Age_23_24.pdf

Davis, I., & Ellis-MacLeod, E. (1994). Temporary foster care: Separating and reunifying families. In J. Blacher (Ed.), *When there's no place like home: Options for children living apart from their natural families* (pp. 123–161). Baltimore, MD: Paul Brookes, Ltd.

Fuchs, D., Burnside, L., Marchenski, S., & Mudry, A. (2005). *Children with disabilities receiving services from child welfare agencies in Manitoba.* Retrieved from http://www.cecw-cepb.ca/sites/default/files/publications/en/DisabilitiesManitobaFinal.pdf

Fuchs, D., Burnside, L., Marchenski, S., & Mudry, A. (2007). *Children with FASD involved with the Manitoba child welfare system.* Retrieved from http://www.cecw-cepb.ca/sites/default/files/publications/en/FASD_Final_Report.pdf

Fuchs, D., Burnside, L., Marchenski, S., & Mudry, A. (2008). *Transition out-of-care: Issues for youth with FASD.* Retrieved from http://www.cecw-cepb.ca/

Fuchs, D., Burnside, L., Marchenski, S., Mudry, A., & De Riviere, L. (2008). *Economic impact of children in care with FASD, Phase 1: The cost of children in care with FASD in Manitoba.* Retrieved from http://www.cecw-cepb.ca/publications/590

Fuchs, D., Burnside, L., De Riviere, L., Brownell, M., Marchenski, S., Mudry, A., & Dahl, M. (2009). *The economic impact of children in care with FASD and parental alcohol issues, Phase 2: Costs and service utilization of health care, special education, and child care.* Retrieved from http://www.cecw-cepb.ca/publications/1146

Fuchs, D., Burnside, L., Reinink, A., & Marchenski, S. (2010). Bound by the clock: The voices of Manitoba youth leaving care. Retrieved from http://cwrp.ca/publications/2138

Greeson, J. K. P., Usher, L., & Grinstein-Weiss, M. (2010). One adult who is crazy about you: Can natural mentoring relationships increase assets among young adults with and without foster care experience? *Children and Youth Services Review, 32,* 565–577.

Jones, K. (2004). Successfully raising resilient foster children who have fetal alcohol syndrome: What works? *Envision: The Manitoba Journal of Child Welfare, 3*(1), 1–18.

Magyar, K. A. (2006). Betwixt and between but being booted nonetheless: A developmental perspective on aging out of foster care. *Temple Law Review, 79*, 557–605.

Malbin, D. V. (2004). Fetal alcohol spectrum disorder (FASD) and the role of family court judges in improving outcomes for children and families. *Juvenile and Family Court Journal, 55*(2), 53–63.

McGregor, D. L. (2009). *Never say never: Struggle and determination in the lives of young adults with FASD* (Doctoral dissertation). University of Calgary, Calgary, AB.

Munson, M. R., Smalling, S. E., Spencer, R., Scott, Jr., L. D., & Tracy, E. M. (2010). A steady presence in the midst of change: Non-kin natural mentors in the lives of older youth exiting foster care. *Children and Youth Services Review, 32*(4), 527–535.

National Research Council & Panel on Research on Child Abuse and Neglect. (1993). *Understanding child abuse & neglect*. Washington, DC: The National Academies Press. Retrieved from http://www.nap.edu/catalog. php?record_id=2117

Page, K. (2007). Adult neuropsychology of fetal alcohol spectrum disorders. In K. D. O'Malley (Ed.), *ADHD and fetal alcohol spectrum disorders (FASD)* (pp. 103–124). Hauppauge, NY: Nova Science Publishers, Inc.

Pecora, P., Kessler, R., Williams, J., O'Brien, K., Downs, A., English, D., & Holmes, K. (2005). *Improving family foster care: Findings from the Northwest Foster Care Alumni Study*. Seattle, WA: Casey Family Programs. Retrieved from http://www.casey.org/NR/rdonlyres/4E1E7C77-7624-4260-A253-892C5A6CB9E1/923/CaseyAlumniStudyupdated082006.pdf

Perry, B. L. (2006). Understanding social network disruption: The case of youth in foster care. *Social Problems, 53*(3), 371–391.

Small, S. A., & Eastman, G. (1991). Rearing adolescents in contemporary society: A conceptual framework for understanding the responsibilities and needs of parents. *Family Relations, 40*, 455–462.

Tanner, J. L. (2006). Recentering during emerging adulthood: A critical turning point in life span human development. In J. J. Arnett & J. L. Tanner (Eds.), *Emerging adults in America: Coming of age in the 21st century* (pp. 21–56). Washington, DC: American Psychological Association.

Tweedle, A. (2005). *Youth leaving care – How do they fare?* Briefing paper prepared for the Modernizing Income Security for Working Age Adults Project. Retrieved from http://www.torontoalliance.ca/tcsa_initiatives/income_security/pdf/MISWAAYouthLeavingCareReport.pdf

Community Networking for Social Change: A Promising Practice for Aboriginal Child Welfare

Judy Gillespie, Georgina Supernault, and Miriam Abel

Introduction

The overrepresentation of Aboriginal children and families in statutory child protection systems constitutes a complex social problem characterized by multiple, intersecting factors (Trocmé, Knoke, & Blackstock, 2004; Tilbury, 2009). For thousands of years Aboriginal child welfare was sustained through socio-cultural lifeworlds that placed a high degree of value on children and ensured traditions, identities, roles, and relations that nurtured children's physical, spiritual, social, emotional, and intellectual growth. European colonization attacked these lifeworlds through systems of power that included genocide, confinement on reserves, outlawing of cultural traditions, and enforced removal of children to residential schools (Blackstock & Trocmé, 2005; Hand, 2006).

Suggested Citation: Gillespie, J., Supernault, G., & Abel, M. (2014). Community networking for social change: A promising practice for Aboriginal child welfare. In D. Badry, D. Fuchs, H. Montgomery, & S. McKay (Eds.), *Reinvesting in Families: Strengthening Child Welfare Practice for a Brighter Future: Voices from the Prairies* (pp. 201–219). Regina, SK: University of Regina Press.

The disturbance of a people's lifeworld has profound impacts on individual and collective well-being, including disruption and loss of tradition and collective identity, of social roles and relations, and of individual identity, motivation, and self-pride. Alienation, interpersonal violence, depression, addictions, and suicide become common (Duran & Duran, 2000). While many Aboriginal people survived and resisted these assaults on their personal and collective well-being, for many others the consequences have been severe, and the overrepresentation of Aboriginal children within child protection systems is one of the more obvious. These consequences are further magnified by barriers to housing, employment, and education.

Thus, widespread criticisms towards individualistic and residual approaches to child welfare are particularly resonant within the Aboriginal community, for whom lack of attention to the broader issues that impact their well-being is deeply problematic (Stanley, Tomison, & Pocock, 2003). An approach is needed that addresses community and structural issues impacting Aboriginal family and child well-being while respecting the resilience embedded within Aboriginal ways of caring for children, families, and communities (Blackstock & Trocmé, 2005).

Multi-sector community networks facilitate such an approach. They are viewed as being more capable of addressing complex social issues—such as Aboriginal well-being—that cannot be fully addressed by single organizations. However, multi-sector collaborations are difficult to establish and even harder to sustain. This chapter showcases a multi-sector community network—the Aboriginal Interagency Committee (AIC)—that has operated for more than 15 years in the Peace River region of northwestern Alberta to promote the well-being of Aboriginal people in the area.

The chapter begins with a discussion of three concepts—promotion of social change, collective impact, and place-based intervention—that have particular relevance for Aboriginal child welfare and the work of the AIC. This is followed by a discussion of conditions seen as necessary for successful multi-sector collaboration, comparing these with factors identified as critical to the successful functioning of the AIC, including the role of spirituality and culture and the support and guidance of Elders. An example of the AIC's promotion of social change is provided through its Sisters in Spirit vigil—an initiative developed by the Native Women's Association of Canada. The chapter concludes by highlighting the need for further research and dialogue regarding multi-sector community networks as a promising practice for Aboriginal child welfare.

Promotion of Social Change

Child welfare policy frameworks typically focus on the deficits of individual children and families, with interventions geared to "fixing" these deficits. Even early intervention and prevention approaches maintain the focus on deficits ascribed to specific "at risk" individuals and groups, attempting to address these deficits without attending to broader contributing social relations and dynamics. Blackstock and Trocmé (2005) suggest the overrepresentation of Aboriginal children in child protection systems is unlikely to improve as long as problems continue to be defined within this narrow focus; an approach is needed that addresses larger community and structural issues impacting Aboriginal child welfare. Promotion of social change offers a conceptual framework for such an approach.

> *Promotion lends itself to an opening up of intervention possibilities that extend beyond the mere absence of problems.... Prevention goals often are constrained to be the absence of problems or deviations from prescribed norms, and these goals are achieved by moving individuals and settings toward predefined and presumed-superior states by countering their deviation from those states. These efforts not only run the risk of maintaining the status quo, but they can limit the possibilities for individuals and communities to exercise their potentials. (Tseng et al., 2002, pp. 404–405)*

Promotion of social change facilitates community approaches through interventions targeted at social systems within a specific locality. Of particular interest are increased social cohesion and social inclusion for marginalized groups (Gilchrist, 2009). While not denying the importance of prevention, early intervention, and protection, promotion of social change constitutes a "missing link" in a full spectrum of approaches needed to address Aboriginal child welfare.

The AIC's promotion of social change has been identified as embracing three aspects, all relevant to Aboriginal family and child well-being (Gillespie & Whitford, 2010): first, strengthening Aboriginal lifeworlds, including celebrating Aboriginal identity and cultural knowledge, participating in cultural traditions, and enhancing social relations between Aboriginal people, including respect for diverse Aboriginal nations and cultures residing within the community; second, strengthening relations between Aboriginal and non-Aboriginal community members, including fostering increased respect for Aboriginal identities and cultures and their rightful place within the community; and third, challenging the institutional racism embedded in formal community systems that impact Aboriginal inclusion. A few examples—Aboriginal Gathering and Pow-wow, Sisters in Spirit, Aboriginal Dance Arbour, and General Health and Social Planning/Advocacy—highlight social promotion efforts across these three areas.

Aboriginal Gathering and Pow-wow

The presence of cultural assets and the preservation of and participation in cultural traditions have been identified as important aspects in Aboriginal well-being, promoting bonding and fostering child and family resilience (Lalonde, 2005; Filbert & Flynn, 2010). In 2013 the AIC organized and hosted its 18th annual Aboriginal Gathering and 10th annual Pow-wow. The event brings together Aboriginal and non-Aboriginal individuals and groups across the region in organizing, volunteering, donating, and celebrating.

Sisters in Spirit

Interpersonal violence is one of the most common reasons for child protection referrals, and Aboriginal women in Canada are heavily over-represented as victims of interpersonal violence, with forms of violence significantly more likely to be the most severe and potentially life-threatening (Standing Committee on the Status of Women, 2011). The inter-generational cycle is a vicious one—children are traumatized by the victimization of mothers, grandmothers, sisters, and other female family members. Yet if this trauma remains unresolved and unattended to by the larger community, these children grow into adults who often perpetuate the cycle. Sisters in Spirit vigils were developed by the Native Women's

Association of Canada to draw attention to violence against Aboriginal women, to honour the lives of missing and murdered Aboriginal women and girls, and to support and assist in healing for families who have lost loved ones to violence (Native Women's Association of Canada, 2012). An AIC subcommittee has organized the annual Sisters in Spirit vigil since its inception (discussed in detail below).

Aboriginal Dance Arbour

The AIC has worked to secure land and funding that will result in an Aboriginal dance arbour. The arbour will provide a permanent facility at which to hold Aboriginal gatherings and pow-wows. The structure will raise the profile of Aboriginal people, providing a concrete asset that will communicate Aboriginal culture as an important part of the regional fabric.

General Health and Social Planning/Advocacy

Aboriginal people often encounter barriers to health care, housing, and other basic services, and are disproportionally impacted by cuts to these services; this, too, has been identified as an underlying factor in Aboriginal child protection (Trocmé et al., 2004). The AIC consistently identifies and engages in advocacy to address systemic issues at the local level.

Collective Impact and Place-Based Intervention

Concepts of "collective impact" (Kania & Kramer, 2011) and "place-based intervention" (Bradford, 2005) draw on research noting that complex social issues such as Aboriginal well-being cannot be effectively addressed by any community organization or government department working in isolation. Such issues result from the interplay of multiple factors and require multi-sector coordination of change efforts. "No single organization is responsible for any major social problem, nor can any single organization cure it" (Kania & Kramer, pp. 38–39). Moreover, collective efforts must be grounded in and sensitive to local place.

> With their inherent complexity, these problems are resistant to traditional sectoral interventions designed and delivered in a top-down fashion by individual government departments. Required

instead are....strategies constructed with knowledge of the partic-
ular circumstances in communities, and delivered through collab-
orations crossing functional boundaries and departmental silos.
(Bradford, 2005, p. 4)

Multi-sector initiatives require the inclusion of representatives of community-based agencies with awareness of the lived experiences of residents, as well as the "joined-up" efforts of local representatives of senior and municipal government departments to enable the co-oper-ation, coordination, and communication that are key to successful social change (Bradford, 2005; Gilchrist, 2009; Walker, 2008). The AIC has achieved and, more importantly, has managed to sustain this broad cross-sector participation in its social change efforts. Analysis of par-ticipation in AIC meetings shows long-term involvement of individuals, agencies, and organizations across most major community sectors (Abel & Gillespie, forthcoming). This includes representatives from communi-ty-based agencies and government departments across sectors of health, social services, education, and justice, municipal and Aboriginal leaders, as well as representatives from business, cultural, and spiritual organiza-tions (see Fig.1). The participation of these individuals and organizations facilitates the various change activities that the AIC undertakes.

Conditions for Success in Multi-Sector Collaboration

The long-term multi-sector collaboration the AIC has achieved is difficult to establish and even harder to sustain (Provan, Veazie, Staten, & Teufel-Shone, 2005). Successful multi-sector collaboration is linked to a number of conditions including:

- A common agenda grounded in a theory of change;
- Mutually reinforcing activities;
- Strong leadership;
- Continuous communication;
- Backbone support organizations;
- Ongoing financial support;and
- Shared measurement systems.

Figure 1. Participation in AIC meetings by community sector

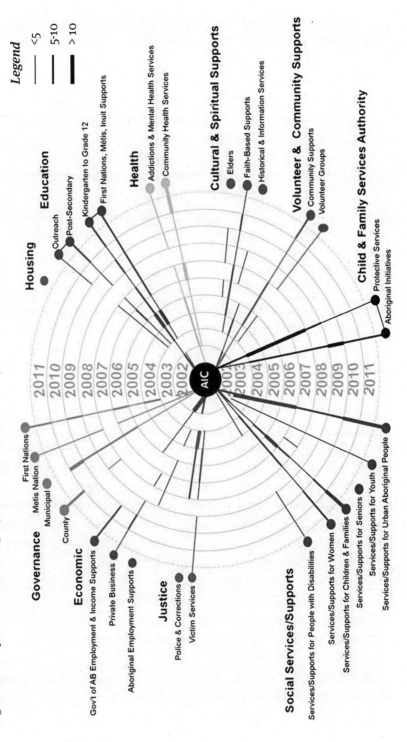

> *Collective impact requires all participants to have a shared vision*
> *for change, one that includes a common understanding of the*
> *problem and a joint approach to solving it through agreed upon*
> *actions....Every participant need not agree with every other par-*
> *ticipant on all dimensions of the problem.....All participants must*
> *agree, however, on the primary goals for the collective impact*
> *initiative as a whole. (Kania & Kramer, 2011, p. 39)*

Shared vision and collective goals must go beyond vague aspira-
tions; specificity is needed regarding what is to be achieved, as well as
how, and this should include clarity regarding roles of the various participants (Auspos & Kubisch, 2012). A well-articulated theory of change
can assist in achieving this specificity. "Theories of change illuminate
what is worth doing, shed light on promising ways to sequence change
efforts, can suggest what is not worth doing, and help participants
inject 'intentionality' and purpose into their activities" (Schorr,1997,
p. 364, cited in Torjman & Leviton-Reid, 2003, p. 14). Torjman and
Leviton-Reid also note that generating and maintaining momentum for
multi-sector coordination requires striking a balance between collective planning and collective action using workable "points of entry" to
achieve social change.

The work of the AIC is grounded in a collective vision, mission, and
values that have been developed by its members. These are periodically
reviewed to ensure their continuing relevance, and members identify this
as key to the work of the AIC. Goals and strategic activities linked to the
above are developed by the members on a regular (annual or biennial)
basis. Differences and disagreements are part of the process and are handled through dialogue, listening to one another and trying to arrive at a
high degree of consensus (Gillespie & Whitford, 2010).

The importance of mutually reinforcing activities has also been identified in successful multi-sector initiatives (Kania & Kramer, 2011). Diverse
stakeholders support and coordinate their own activities with the actions
of others. This coordination and mutual reinforcement facilitates the
success of their combined efforts in achieving social change.

The activities of the AIC are identified through a collective planning process and coordinated through various subcommittees; members participate in subcommittees based on interest or the relevance

of subcommittee activities to their organizational mandate. These sub-committees may be long- or short-term depending on how quickly they achieve their intended outcomes. The AIC also uses an asset-based approach in its social change efforts, drawing on members' contacts and organizational resources and mobilizing a wide range of individuals and groups well beyond that of its immediate membership. In addition, the AIC serves as a venue through which the activities of member organizations can be disseminated and supported; members highlight their own organizational activities or initiatives and identify needed supports, such as volunteers, donations, or simply the spread of information. Other members look for ways in which they or their organization can provide this support.

Strong leadership is a third component identified in successful multi-sector change initiatives. Torjman and Leviton-Reid (2003) suggest that leadership may take the form of individual champions that initiate support for local efforts or maintain commitment during difficult times, or it may mean a team of leaders that can respond to the numerous challenges entailed in these initiatives. The importance of leadership development strategies is also noted; these encompass development and renewal of skills for established leaders, as well as support and training for emerging leaders.

Team leadership best describes the approach of the AIC. The committee itself is led by two co-chairs, while the various subcommittees are also led by chairs/co-chairs. Leadership is rotational based on members offering or being asked to take on leadership roles, and the use of co-chairs in committees and subcommittees allows more experienced leaders to support and mentor emerging leaders. While there is no formal requirement that committee or subcommittee chairs must be Aboriginal, the involvement of Aboriginal members in the leadership of the AIC has been identified by both Aboriginal and non-Aboriginal members as an important component in its success (Gillespie & Whitford, 2010).

Continuous communication is a fourth component identified in successful multi-sector coordination; this includes regular face-to-face meetings with structured agendas and expert facilitation, as well as communication between meetings. The AIC holds monthly meetings, while subcommittees also meet on a regular basis. Meetings enable planning, reflection, identification of new issues, networking, and information sharing. An email distribution list facilitates information-sharing between members, as well as with a wider audience of community and regional stakeholders. Monthly AIC meetings include a presentation from an invited guest or representative of an AIC member organization, and these may lead to identification of issues that become targets for social change. For example, the housing sector, previously absent from the community network as shown in Figure 1, is now included via representatives from North Peace Housing. A representative from the organization presented at a 2012 meeting; a housing subcommittee was formed immediately afterwards to address issues identified in the presentation.

Agendas emailed prior to meetings provide structure. AIC meetings and subcommittee meetings are facilitated primarily by committee chairs/co-chairs that move the committee through the various agenda items. The AIC uses an expert facilitator for meetings that involve review of the AIC's collective mission, vision, and values, as well as for meetings that involve setting annual goals and activities. This facilitation is provided through a community development officer whose participation in the AIC is supported by an organizational mandate to assist with community collaboration and capacity-building efforts.

A supporting infrastructure is a fifth component identified as critical for successful multi-sector social change efforts; lack of supporting infrastructure is one of the most frequent reasons why such initiatives fail. Kania and Kramer (2011) suggest that this requires a separate "backbone organization."

> *Creating and managing collective impact requires a separate organization and staff...to serve as the backbone for the entire initiative....The backbone organization requires a dedicated staff... that can plan, manage, and support the initiative through ongoing facilitation, technology and communications support, data collection and reporting, and handling the myriad logistical and administrative details needed for the initiative to function smoothly. (Kania & Kramer, 2011, p. 40)*

The AIC illustrates a unique approach to the issue of supporting infrastructure. Space for AIC committee and subcommittee meetings is provided by the Sagitawa Friendship Centre and other participating organizations. The Friendship Centre also plays the role of banker for funds that are collected and dispersed in support of various AIC activities. Committee and subcommittee chairs/co-chairs provide leadership and coordination, while expert facilitation at visioning and planning sessions is provided through the formal role of one of the AIC members. Technology and communications support, data collection and reporting, and the "myriad logistical and administrative details" are handled primarily through two positions within the Northwest Child and Family Service Authority: the senior manager of Aboriginal Services for the region, and his administrative assistant.

Related to the above, a sixth component identified as critical to multi-sector social change initiatives is financial support. This refers primarily to funding for the supporting infrastructure—the backbone support—as well as the time and effort contributed by representatives of participating organizations. This financial support is often the most challenging aspect of social change initiatives; funders are often willing to support specific, time-limited projects with clearly defined goals but are more reluctant to provide support for the infrastructure needed for coordination of ongoing multi-sector efforts (Torjman & Leviton-Reid, 2003).

> *Collective impact requires...that funders support a long-term process of social change without identifying any particular solution in advance. They must be willing to stay with an initiative for years, recognizing that social change can come from the gradual improvement of an entire system over time, not just from a single breakthrough by an individual organization... funders must help create and sustain the collective processes, measurement reporting systems, and community leadership that enable cross-sector coalitions to arise and thrive. (Kania & Kramer, 2011, p. 41)*

The success of the AIC is enabled through the backbone support noted above, as well as through organizations that support representative participation in the AIC, from municipal districts to community-based organizations, to government departments. And here again, the role of the Northwest Child and Family Service Authority (CFSA) is key. CFSA funds the two positions that have provided long-term critical administrative infrastructure to the initiative.

A seventh component identified in successful multi-sector social change initiatives is that of shared measurement systems. Kania and Kramer (2011) suggest that agreement on a common agenda is illusory without agreement on the ways success will be measured and reported. This requires collecting data and measuring results on indicators at the community level and across all participating organizations. They argue that shared measurement systems provide a form of action research that enables collective efforts to remain aligned, holding participants accountable to one another and facilitating processes of feedback on successes and failures within the various change strategies. However, it has been noted that defining and obtaining clear measures for social change initiatives is highly challenging (Auspos & Kubisch, 2012; Berkowitz, 2001; Torjman & Leviton-Reid, 2003). In part, this is because broad goals and visions for social change are long-term; strategies to work towards them require significant flexibility in response to constantly changing factors and dynamics within communities. In addition, change efforts are often impacted by factors outside community control. Key strategies appear to be the development of theories of change that can be broken into incremental, concrete goals and indicators of success that encompass both process and outcomes. As Torjman and Leviton-Reid (2003) note, balance is needed between long-term vision and short-term actions with measurable outcomes. "Without interim measures, the vision never will be achieved; without the vision, the immediate actions may serve little real purpose" (Torjman & Leviton-Reid, p. 16).

Annual or biennial goal-setting by the AIC facilitates identification of indicators of success; an example is shown below in the discussion of the 2011 Sisters in Spirit vigil. Moreover, the AIC regularly engages in reflection on its efforts and achievements. The nature of this reflection mirrors Torjman and Leviton-Reid's (2003) suggestions that the central questions for community change initiatives should be: *What are we learning from this work? What appears to have been successful and why? What did not appear to work effectively?* and *What could we have done differently?*

The Importance of Spiritual and Cultural Aspects

Two aspects not mentioned in other research on multi-sector coordination, but which were identified as critical to the success of the AIC, are the inclusion of cultural and spiritual aspects, and the guidance and support of Elders. AIC meetings open with a prayer and often include a smudging ceremony for those who wish to participate. Ceremonies are held at least annually for the AIC membership and have included traditional pipe ceremonies, feasts, and round dances. For many Aboriginal AIC members, these aspects are particularly important.

> I like that we open with a prayer, I really appreciate that. I like the way we have the Elder if she's there or he's there opening with a prayer...a traditional prayer. I like the respect that is there. (AIC member, cited in Gillespie & Whitford, 2010, p. 158)

While participation in cultural ceremonies is voluntary for all members, non-Aboriginal members of the AIC also identify the importance of cultural and spiritual aspects to the work of the committee. Moreover, in recognition of their resilience-promoting impacts, cultural and spiritual elements are embedded in many of the social change activities coordinated by the AIC.

> The more a person walks with First Nation, or among the people, we have discovered that they are a very spiritual people. It is woven into their culture. It is so a part of who they are that if we want to be an Aboriginal Interagency, then we need to walk that path too. (AIC member, cited in Gillespie & Whitford, 2010, p. 158)

The inclusion of cultural and spiritual traditions depends on the guidance and support of Elders. Elders offer wisdom that assists members in the articulation of their collective vision, mission, and values, and in thinking about specific goals and strategies. Elders also provide mentorship to AIC leaders, enabling them with greater skill and confidence.

Sisters in Spirit: An Example of Collective Impact

Through its Sisters in Spirit subcommittee, the AIC has coordinated Sisters in Spirit vigils every year since their inception by the Native Women's Association of Canada; in 2006 the community was one of only

11 across Canada to host a vigil. As noted above, the intention of the vigils is to honour missing and murdered Aboriginal women, promote healing for families, and broaden awareness of the issue of violence against
Aboriginal women.

The development of the Peace River Sisters in Spirit vigils, as shared
by Brenda Brochu, executive director of the Peace River Regional
Women's Shelter, illustrates the importance of local knowledge and
place-based policy approaches, as well as shared vision and collective
goals, a workable point of entry for their achievement, and common
measures of success.

> *I was keeping track of who the murdered and missing women were
> around Peace River...and they were overwhelmingly Aboriginal
> women. ...So when I heard about the Sisters in Spirit Campaign,
> sponsored by the Native Women's Association of Canada, I thought,
> that might resonate with people here. So I took a proposal to [the
> AIC] and I was just thrilled with the result! Two Aboriginal members
> quickly volunteered to be co-chairs of the organizing committee...
> and we had, I think in the very first year, 70 people or something...
> and it was because the Aboriginal Interagency was able to reach
> out and find people who had been affected by this tragedy and they
> came and told their stories. We read the names of 40 missing or
> murdered Aboriginal women, mostly women from northwestern
> Alberta, and we invited family members of four missing or murdered
> Aboriginal women to come and talk about what they remembered
> of their loved one. We chose the number four because of its sacred-
> ness to Aboriginal people. And that really was much more mean-
> ingful to people in this area. And [in 2007] we had over 200 people
> at the memorial, and while once again we invited family members
> of four different women to speak, many more showed up—relatives
> of at least eight different women and girls who had been murdered
> or gone missing spoke out. So that has really forwarded awareness
> of violence against women, and particularly Aboriginal women.*

Analysis of the 2011 Sisters in Spirit vigil (Abel & Gillespie, forthcoming) identified six key components: participants and attendees, speeches
from local officials, personal stories from family members who lost a

loved one, music and dance honouring the missing or murdered women or girls, cultural protocols, and food and beverage served at or after the vigil. Additional elements included the financial and material resources needed for the event, logistical considerations, and public promotion of the event. Achieving all of the above involved mobilization of individuals, groups, and organizations across the community and broader region and provides a profound demonstration of the value and power of multi-sector coordination combined with a community-asset approach.

Additional Considerations

In discussing place-based multi-sector collaboration, or "comprehensive community initiatives" (CCIs), Torjman and Leviton-Reid (2003) raise a number of questions. First, is community defined as a geographical area and, if so, how large a geographical area? Or can community refer to a group of people with common characteristics or interests? They also raise the issue of inclusivity; that is, which individuals, groups, or sectors should be at the table? Must all participants be engaged in every level of the work or are there critical activities and junctures for the involvement of the wider community as opposed to a more limited set of partners? What is the role of individual participants—are they there as individual citizens with specific kinds of knowledge and resources or are they there as official delegates of their specific organizations? Must they wear a particular hat? Can they wear more than one hat?

For AIC members the definition of community is clearly regional (as opposed to community defined in terms of town or neighbourhood), and this reflects a common characteristic of rural areas (Gillespie, 2009; Gillespie & Whitford, 2010). The Sisters in Spirit vigils, for example, bring together individuals, families, and groups from centres across northwestern Alberta. However, the definition of community also refers to a group of people with common characteristics—in this case all those who identify as Aboriginal. It is their well-being that is the goal, although it is understood that the well-being of Aboriginal people within the region cannot be separated from the well-being of the region as a whole.

In terms of inclusivity, as per its formal values and beliefs, membership in the AIC is open to all individuals regardless of "race, colour, and creed" as long as they come together in a respectful way. However, as has been noted, not every individual is involved in every aspect of the initiative—individuals and member organizations are able to target their participation to roles that they view as most relevant to their interests or mandates. Moreover, as noted in the example of Sisters in Spirit, the AIC takes an explicit community-asset approach, intentionally seeking many avenues and junctures for wider community involvement. And in terms of the "hats" that AIC members wear, certainly there may be more than one—in fact, another defining feature of rural areas is that individuals often wear multiple hats.

Partnerships involving a two-way process of learning between practitioners and academic researchers can facilitate theoretical development and shared measurement (Torjman & Leviton-Reid, 2003). The research this chapter is based on offers an example of such a process; it involved collaboration between Dr. Judy Gillespie of the University of British Columbia, her research assistants, and members of the AIC (Gillespie & Whitford, 2010; Abel & Gillespie, forthcoming). This research is, however, only a small beginning in identifying community networking as a promising practice for Aboriginal child and family well-being. Much more is needed to understand these linkages and their impacts; such research needs to be sensitive to Aboriginal ways of knowing (Ermine, 1995) and recognize that the complexity of community collaborations may render them beyond the reach of reductionist scientific methods (Berkowitz, 2001).

Conclusion

As Kania and Kramer note: "[S]ubstantially greater progress could be made in alleviating many of our most serious and complex social problems if non-profits, governments, businesses, and the public were brought together around a common agenda to create collective impact" (2011, p. 38). Child welfare certainly constitutes a serious and complex social problem; however, limited collaboration and isolated interventions remain the primary approaches. In part, this reflects resistance to abandoning traditional approaches of individualizing and partializing child welfare problems and then funding single-sector organizations to address one or two of the parts. It is also due to the tension between evidence-informed policy approaches and the challenges of measuring and evaluating the impacts of cross-sectoral community change efforts in relation to child welfare. But it is due as well to the challenges of enabling and sustaining such efforts, for they require a core infrastructure and long-term commitment.

This chapter has showcased a case study of a long-term multi-sector collaboration to address the well-being of Aboriginal people in north-western Alberta. The conditions that enable and sustain this community network have been discussed and an example of one of its activities has been offered as an illustration of the power of cross-sector collaboration to promote social change. The interactions and contributions of the various AIC members within this multi-sector collaboration represent a "promising practice" to promote Aboriginal child well-being and to reduce the overrepresentation of Aboriginal children and families in statutory child protection systems. However, in showcasing this initiative, we are mindful that it is based on a single case study situated within a specific geographical and socio-political context. We hope it offers inspiration and practical ideas that can be useful in other contexts; nonetheless, we emphasize the need for further dialogue and investigation.

Acknowledgements

The research this article is based upon was made possible through funding provided by the Social Sciences and Humanities Research Council of Canada.

References

Abel, M., & Gillespie, J. (Forthcoming). Network analysis in co-productive research with a multi-sector collaboration. *Community Development Journal.*

Auspos, P., & Kubisch, A. (2012). *Performance management in complex, place-based work: What it is, what it isn't, and why it matters.* Washington, DC: The Aspen Institute. Retrieved from http://www.aspeninstitute.org/sites/default/files/content/images/rcc/Aspen_Performance_Management.pdf

Berkowitz, B. (2001). Studying the outcomes of community based coalitions. *American Journal of Community Psychology, 29*, 213–227.

Blackstock, C., & Trocmé, N. (2005). Community-based child welfare for
   Aboriginal children: Supporting resilience through structural change. In
   M. Ungar (Ed.), *Handbook for working with children and youth: Pathways to
   resilience across cultures and contexts* (pp. 105–120). Thousand Oaks, CA:
   Sage.

Bradford, N. (2005). *Place-based public policy: Towards a new urban and
   community agenda for Canada.* Family Network Research Report F|5. Ottawa,
   ON: Canadian Policy Research Networks.

Duran, B., & Duran, E. (2000). Applied postcolonial clinical and research
   strategies. In M. Battiste (Ed.), *Reclaiming Indigenous Voice and Vision* (pp.
   86–100). Vancouver, BC: UBC Press.

Ermine, W. (1995). Aboriginal epistemology. In M. Battiste & J. Barman
   (Eds.), *First Nations education in Canada: The circle unfolds* (pp. 101–112).
   Vancouver, BC: UBC Press.

Filbert, K., & Flynn, R. (2010). Developmental and cultural assets and resilient
   outcomes in First Nations young people in care: An initial test of an
   explanatory model. *Children and Youth Services Review, 32*(4), 560–564.

Gilchrist, A. (2009). *The well-connected community: A networking approach to
   community development* (2nd Ed.). Bristol, UK: The Policy Press.

Gillespie, J. (2009). Family centers in rural communities: Lessons for policy,
   planning and practice. *Families in Society: The Journal of Contemporary
   Social Services, 90*(1), 96–102. doi: 10.1606/1044-3894.3850

Gillespie, J., & Whitford, D. (2010). Keeping the circle strong: Community
   networking to address off-reserve child welfare. In J. P. White & J. Bruhn
   (Eds.), *Aboriginal policy research: Exploring the urban landscape, Vol. 8*
   (pp.151–170). Toronto: Thompson.

Hand, C. (2006). An Ojibwe perspective on the welfare of children: Lessons of
   the past and visions for the future. *Children and Youth Services Review, 28*(1),
   20–46. doi:10.1016/j.childyouth.2005.01.007

Kania, J., & Kramer, M. (2011). Collective impact. *Stanford Social Innovation
   Review,* (Winter), 36–41. Retrieved from: http://www.ssireview.org/articles/
   entry/collective_impact

Lalonde, C. (2005). Identity formation and cultural resilience in Aboriginal
   communities. In R. Flynn, P. Dudding, & J. Barber (Eds.), *Promoting resilience
   in child welfare* (pp. 52–71). Ottawa, ON: University of Ottawa Press.

Native Women's Association of Canada. (2012). SIS vigils. Retrieved from http://
   www.nwac.ca/programs/sis-vigils

Provan, K., Veazie, M., Staten, L., & Teufel-Shone, N. (2005). The use of network
   analysis to strengthen community partnerships. *Public Administration
   Review, 65*(5), 603–613.

Standing Committee on the Status of Women. (2011). *Call into the night: An overview of violence against Aboriginal women.* Ottawa, ON: House of Commons Canada. Retrieved from http://www.parl.gc.ca/content/hoc/Committee/403/FEWO/Reports/RP5056509/feworp14/feworp14-e.pdf

Stanley, J., Tomison, A., & Pocock, J. (2003). Child abuse and neglect in Indigenous Australian communities. *Child Abuse Prevention Issues, 19*(Spring), unpaginated. Victoria, AU: National Child Protection Clearinghouse. Retrieved from http://www.aifs.gov.au/nch/pubs/newsletters.html

Tilbury, C. (2009). The over-representation of Indigenous children in the Australian child welfare system. *International Journal of Social Welfare, 18*(1), 57–64. doi: 10111/j.1468-2397.2008.00577.x

Torjman, S., & Leviton-Reid, E. (2003). *Comprehensive community initiatives.* Ottawa, ON: Caledon Institute of Social Policy.

Trocmé, N., Knoke, D., & Blackstock, C. (2004). Pathways to the overrepresentation of Aboriginal children in Canada's child welfare system. *Social Service Review, 78*(4), 577–600.

Tseng, V., Chesir-Teran, D., Becker-Klein, R., Chan, M., Duran, V., Roberts, A., & Bardoliwalla, N. (2002). Promotion of social change: A conceptual framework. *American Journal of Community Psychology, 30*(3), 401–27.

Walker, R. (2008). Improving the interface between urban municipalities and Aboriginal communities. *Canadian Journal of Urban Research, 17*(1) (Summer Supplement), 20–36.

CHAPTER 11

What Albertan Adults Know about Fetal Alcohol Spectrum Disorders (FASD)

Cecilia Bukutu, Tara Hanson, and Suzanne Tough

Drinking alcohol is a common social activity for many Canadian women of reproductive age (Walker, Al-Sahab, Islam, & Tamim, 2011). In the Canadian Addiction Survey (Ahmand, Flight, Singh, Poole, & Dell, 2008), 76.8% of the female respondents reported drinking alcohol in the past year. Many women also drink alcohol during pregnancy despite a vast body of evidence suggesting harm to the fetus (primary disabilities) and subsequent, serious lifelong health outcomes for the baby (secondary disabilities) (Rasmussen, Andrew, Zwaigenbaum, & Tough, 2008). Health Canada reports approximately one-seventh of pregnant Canadian women consume alcohol to some extent (Health Canada, 2006). In their Albertan study, Tough and colleagues (2006) found that 18% of women reported alcohol consumption after knowing they were pregnant (Tough et al., 2006). The Public Health Agency of Canada (2011, pp. 7–8) warns, "There is no safe amount or safe time to drink alcohol

Suggested Citation: Bukutu, C., Hanson, T., & Tough, S. (2014). What Albertan adults know about fetal alcohol spectrum disorders (FASD). In D. Badry, D. Fuchs, H. Montgomery, & S. McKay (Eds.), *Reinvesting in Families: Strengthening Child Welfare Practice for a Brighter Future: Voices from the Prairies* (pp. 221–242). Regina, SK: University of Regina Press.

during pregnancy." Similarly, other agencies worldwide, including the U.S. Department of Health and Human Services and U.S. Department of Agriculture (2000), recommend that women abstain from drinking alcohol during pregnancy.

Fetal alcohol spectrum disorder (FASD) is an umbrella term used to describe a range of disorders caused by prenatal exposure to alcohol (Clarke & Gibbard, 2003). This term includes other conditions associated with fetal alcohol exposure such as fetal alcohol effects (FAE), partial FAS (PFAS), alcohol-related birth defects (ARBD), and alcohol-related neurodevelopmental disorder (ARND) (Astley, 2004; Tough, Clarke, Hicks, & Clarren, 2005). Individuals with FASD may have health, physical, developmental, behavioural, and learning disabilities (Riley, Mattson, & Thomas, 2009; Thanh & Jonsson, 2009 & 2010).

As the leading cause of preventable developmental and cognitive disabilities among Canadian children (Canadian Paediatric Society, 1997; Health Canada, 1996), FASD is estimated at 10 in 1,000 live births (Canadian Paediatric Society, 2002; Stade et al., 2009). The incidence of FASD in some Aboriginal communities in Canada is estimated to be higher (Canadian Paediatric Society, 2002; Kowlessar, 1997), with some studies suggesting that in some isolated northern communities incidence rates could range from 25 to 200 per 1,000 live births (Masotti, Szala-Meneok, Selby, Ranford, & Van Koughnett, 2003). The incidence of FASD among other subpopulations of Canadians has not yet been researched (Canadian Centre on Substance Abuse, 2005).

Consumption of alcohol during pregnancy disrupts fetal brain development at any point in gestation (Clarke & Gibbard, 2003; Guerri, Bazinet, & Riley, 2009; Kellerman, 2008). After birth, secondary disabilities arise as a result of neurological deficits. Some common secondary disabilities include mental health disorders; disrupted school and employment experiences; involvement with the correctional system; and addictions (Clark, Lutke, Minnes, & Ouellette-Kuntz, 2004). The resource and cost burden of FASD is profound, as medical treatment, special education, and family supports are often needed for people with FASD (Thanh & Jonsson, 2009). Stade and colleagues took into consideration both direct (medical, social, and education services) and indirect costs (productivity loss), and estimated the cost to Canada of FASD annually from day of birth to 53 years old at CAD 5.3 billion (Stade et al., 2009). Thanh and

Jonsson (2009) estimated total annual cost for FASD in Alberta to be from CAD 48 to CAD 142 million, depending on whether a lower (three FASD cases per 1,000 births) or higher (nine FASD cases per 1,000 live births) incidence rate was used.

Initiatives meant to prevent the incidence of both primary and secondary disabilities associated with alcohol consumption during pregnancy are important. Accessing data on the public's knowledge, beliefs, and attitudes about FASD and alcohol consumption among pregnant woman is useful in helping program developers design targeted and effective FASD awareness and prevention programs.

Addressing FASD is a priority of the Alberta government (Thanh & Jonsson, 2009). The government supports prevention programs and supports individuals and families affected by FASD. In 2003, Alberta formed a Cross-Ministry Committee (FASD-CMC) with a mandate to be the primary driving force behind the delivery of FASD programs offered by the provincial government. In 2006, the FASD-CMC created the government of Alberta *FASD 10-Year Strategic Plan* that was signed by 10 partnering ministers and endorsed by the Standing Policy Committee on Health and Community Living. In 2007, the government of Alberta invested $4 million, and in 2008 a further $16.5 million, to support the implementation of the strategic plan. The plan provides a high-level overview for the provincial organization, planning, and delivery of FASD services throughout the lifespan in 12 FASD Service Networks in three areas including 1) awareness and prevention, 2) assessment and diagnosis, and 3) supports for individuals and caregivers. The 10-year plan also outlines four secondary action areas including 1) research and evaluation, 2) training and education, 3) strategic planning, and 4) stakeholder engagement. The plan requires a full evaluation of progress towards targets and outcomes in year five (2011/2012), with subsequent evaluations in years seven (2013/2014) and 10 (2016/2017).

The Alberta Centre for Child, Family and Community Research (The Centre) received a grant from Alberta Health and Wellness to develop, coordinate, and manage the implementation of the year five evaluation of the 10-Year Strategic Plan. The Centre is a public-sector, innovative resource for evidence that develops, supports, and integrates research across sectors and disciplines to provide a strong, evidence-based foundation for identifying and promoting effective public policy and service delivery to improve the well-being of children, families, and communities in Alberta, Canada, and internationally. The current study intended to provide measurement of the FASD-CMC's awareness and prevention efforts by providing results that would establish a baseline measure for Outcome 1a of the strategic plan: Albertans understand that alcohol use during pregnancy can lead to FASD, that FASD can be prevented, and that FASD is a shared responsibility.

The specific objectives of the study were to examine Albertan adults' knowledge and attitudes about FASD and social supports required for women to abstain from alcohol during pregnancy.

Method

Population and Sampling Strategy

Individuals were eligible to participate if they were 18 years of age or older at the time of the survey and living in an Albertan household that could be contacted by direct dialling. Random-digit dialling was used to recruit participants. Within each household, one person was randomly selected to complete an interview.

The survey aimed for a sample size of 1,200 households across the province of Alberta (population approximately three million), with respondents equally distributed among three regions, each with a population of approximately one million: Metropolitan Calgary, Metropolitan Edmonton, and the remainder of Alberta. The sampling technique ensured an equal selection of male and female participants.

Study Design and Questionnaire

The survey questionnaire had five components: Demographic information (e.g., age, gender); FASD general knowledge and prevention (four questions); Contact with FASD (two questions); FASD as a shared responsibility (two questions); and Behaviour (two questions). The study questionnaire was pretested with 20 randomly selected adult Albertans. The purpose of the pretest was to assess question wording, response categories, question order, interviewer instructions, and length of interview. The questionnaire was then modified to improve clarity and ease of use based on the responses.

Ethical Approval

The study protocol was reviewed and approved by the Arts, Science, and Law Research Ethics Board (ASL REB) at the University of Alberta.

Survey Administration/Data Collection and Data Analysis

Trained interviewers administered the survey using a Computer-Assisted Telephone Interviewing system (CATI). Before administering the questionnaire, respondents were asked to provide verbal consent to their voluntary participation in the survey. Data collection was between May 25 and June 22, 2011.

Data were downloaded from a password-protected CATI system, cleaned, and transferred into SAS® Software (version 9.1.3, SAS Institute, Cary, NC) for analysis. For all comparisons made across groups, a significance level (p value) of 0.05 or less was considered significant.

Analyses were based on all available data. Question item response percentages were calculated by dividing the number of respondents who indicated a specific response category divided by the total number of respondents who answered the question item.

Descriptive analysis and bivariate comparisons (χ^2) were completed to assess differences in knowledge between various groups based on demographic characteristics and their responses to FASD questions compared (e.g., by gender (male to female), age, place of residence, employment and marital status, etc.). Between-group comparisons of categorical variables used chi-squared tests.

Results

Demographics

The response rate for the survey, calculated as the number of completed interviews divided by the number of completed interviews, refusals, and incompletes was 27.0%. The demographic background of the 1,203 survey respondents is summarized in Table 1. Most respondents were Caucasian (88.3%), were born in Canada (81.4%), had a post-secondary education (73.2%), were employed (64.2%), were married or in a common-law relationship (69.1%), were Christians (67.0%), had an annual household income over CAD 80,000 (59.0%), and did not have children (64.4%).

Some demographic characteristics were comparable to Albertan population census information. For example, our study found that 11.7% of respondents were non-Caucasian, which is comparable to the census report that 13.9% of Albertans were non-Caucasian (Statistics Canada, 2010). Non-Caucasian respondents in this sample were a diverse group that consisted of individuals who self-identified as Aboriginal, Asian, Latin American, and Black. About 18.6% of respondents were born outside of Canada, which is consistent with the census report that 16.2% of Albertans were foreign-born (Statistics Canada, 2010). About 26.5% of the respondents reported having no religion, which is close to the most current census religion statistics (Statistics Canada, 2001) that almost 24% of Albertan residents identify with no religion.

Table 1. Characteristics of all survey respondents (N=1203)

Survey respondents characteristics	Overall sample (N)*	Overall sample (%)
Gender		
Male	600	50
Female	600	50
Region of residence		
Edmonton	401	33.3
Calgary	399	33.3
Rest of Alberta	402	33.4
Age		
18–24	66	5.6
25–34	159	13.6
35–44	213	18.2
45–54	244	20.9
55–64	260	22.2
65+	228	19.5
Ethnic background		
Caucasian	1048	88.3
Non-Caucasian	139	11.7

Highest educational attainment		
Less than high school	99	8.2
High school completed	222	18.5
Post-secondary	879	73.3
Employment		
Employed (Full/part-time)	768	64.2
Retired	234	19.6
Other (Unemployed, maternity, students, disabled)	193	16.2
Marital status		
Married/common-law relationship	829	69.1
Single never married, divorced, separated, widowed	371	30.9
Children in the home		
Yes	427	35.6
No	772	64.4
Country of Birth		
Canada	976	81.4
Other	224	18.6
Born in Alberta		
Yes	559	57.2
No	417	42.8
Income		
<$39,999	128	14.5
$40,000 -$79,999	235	26.5
>$80,000	522	59.0
Religion		
Christian	757	67.0
Other religion	73	6.5
No religion	300	26.5

Not all respondents answered all the questions; therefore the denominators are different and do not add up to 1203.

FASD General Knowledge/Awareness

Overall, 85.7% (n=1028) of Albertan adults who participated in the survey reported having heard of FASD, while 14.3% (n=172) had not heard of FASD. Respondents who had not heard about FASD were provided with information that described FASD and were not asked the remaining three questions in the general knowledge/awareness section. They were, however, asked other FASD-related questions from the other sections of the survey. The demographics of respondents who had not heard of FASD were different from those of respondents who had heard about FASD (Table 2). Compared to respondents who had heard about FASD, respondents who had not heard of FASD were more likely to be male (62.8%), to reside in Calgary (47.7%), to have been born outside Canada (47.1%), to be younger (aged between 18 and 44 years; 47.9%), to have children (42.4%), and to be non-Caucasian (36.3%).

Table 2. Characteristics of respondents who had and had NOT heard of FASD

Survey respondents characteristics	Respondents who had heard of FASD N=1028* n (%)	Respondents who had not heard of FASD N=172* n (%)	p≤ Chi Square value (0.05)
Gender			
Male	492 (47.9)	108 (62.8)	0.0003
Female	536 (52.1)	64 (37.2)	
Age			
18–44 years	357 (35.8)	81 (47.9)	0.0025
45 and older	641 (64.2)	88 (52.1)	
Region of residence			
Edmonton	352 (34.2)	48 (27.9)	
Calgary	317 (30.9)	82 (47.7)	0.0001
Rest of Alberta	359 (34.9)	42 (24.4)	
Ethnic background			
Caucasian	938 (92.4)	109 (63.7)	0.0001
Non-Caucasian	77 (7.6)	62 (36.3)	

Children in the home			
Yes	354 (34.5)	73 (42.4)	0.0433
No	673 (65.5)	99 (57.6)	
Religion			
Christian	654 (67.8)	103(62.4)	
Other religion	45 (4.7)	28 (17.0)	0.0001
No Religion	266 (27.6)	34 (20.6)	
Country of birth			
Canada	885 (86.1)	91 (52.9)	0.0001
Other	143 (13.9)	81 (47.1)	

* *Not all respondents answered all the questions; therefore the denominators are different.*

Of respondents who were aware of FASD, 99.0% knew that alcohol use during pregnancy causes FASD. The same percentage knew that FASD is preventable. When asked the best way to prevent FASD, 96.3% of respondents who were aware of FASD selected the best answer, which was *no alcohol use during pregnancy or while trying to become pregnant*, followed by 2.1% who selected *no alcohol use in the first 3 months of pregnancy*, 0.9% who selected *no alcohol use in the first 6 months of pregnancy*, and lastly 0.7% who selected *no alcohol use in the last 3 months of pregnancy*. Respondents (3.7%) who did not select the best answer were predominantly male (62.2%). Similarly, respondents who selected the answer *no alcohol use in the first 3 months* (2.1%) were predominantly (67.0%) male.

Contact with FASD

All respondents were given a description of FASD and its associated disabilities and then answered the questions regarding whether they had contact with anyone with FASD or who looked after someone with FASD. Of the respondents who had heard of FASD, 40.1% reported knowing anyone who might have FASD, the results of which can be found in Table 3. Slightly fewer respondents knew anyone who provided care for an individual who might have FASD (39.1%). Respondents who had not heard of FASD before were less likely to know anyone with FASD (7.1%) or anyone who cared for someone with FASD (6.5%).

Table 3. Comparison of responses to FASD questions between respondents that had and had not heard about FASD

	Respondents who had heard of FASD N=1028* n (%)	Respondents who had not heard of FASD N=172* n (%)	p≤ Chi Square value (0.05)
Agreed (yes) with the following:			
Contact with FASD			
Know anyone who might have FASD?	406 (40.1)	12 (7.1)	0.0001
Know anyone who provides care for someone who has or might have FASD?	398 (39.1)	11 (6.5)	0.0001
FASD Support			
A woman should be supported by others not to drink while pregnant?	1008 (98.6)	159 (95.2)	0.0024
Who should be involved in encouraging a woman not to drink alcohol during pregnancy?			
Healthcare provider	889 (88.2)	124 (77.9)	0.0004
Partner or spouse	941 (93.4)	140 (88.0)	0.0173
Woman's family	963 (95.5)	140 (88.1)	0.0001
Woman's friends	904 (89.7)	122 (76.7)	0.0001
The community	778 (77.2)	96 (60.4)	0.0001
The government	714 (70.8)	99 (62.2)	0.0289
Behaviour			
If I saw a pregnant woman I knew drinking alcohol, I would tell her that using alcohol during pregnancy might harm the baby	875 (88.9)	146 (88.5)	0.6261**
If I saw a pregnant woman I did not know drinking alcohol, I would tell her that using alcohol during pregnancy might harm the baby	458 (49.7)	82 (50.3)	0.8817**

* Not all respondents answered all the questions; therefore the denominators are different.
** not significant

Support

All respondents were asked questions to gauge their views regarding support for pregnant women not to drink (see Table 3). Most respondents believe that women should be supported by others not to drink while pregnant, regardless of whether they had heard of FASD (98.6%) or not (95.2%). Among respondents who had heard about FASD, the woman's family (95.5%), the woman's partner/spouse (93.4%), and friends (89.7%) were identified as the three main groups to be involved in encouraging a woman not to drink alcohol during pregnancy. The other groups were identified in the following order: health-care provider (88.2%), the community (77.2%), and government (70.8%). Among respondents who had not heard of FASD (n=172), a pregnant woman's family (88.1%), partner/spouse (88.0%), and health-care provider (77.9%) were the three main sources of support selected, followed by friends (76.7%), government (62.2%), and lastly community (60.4%).

Behaviour

Respondents were asked two questions regarding behavioural responses to witnessing a pregnant woman drinking. Among respondents who had heard about FASD, 88.9% said that if they saw a pregnant woman they knew drinking alcohol, they would tell her that using alcohol during pregnancy might harm the baby, and nearly half (49.7%) of these respondents would tell a woman they did not know of the potential harm to the baby. The findings among respondents who had not heard about FASD were similar, with 88.5% of respondents indicating that they would tell a woman they knew or did not know (50.3%) who was using alcohol during pregnancy that it might harm the baby (Table 3). There were no significant differences in responses related to behaviour between respondents who had heard and not heard of FASD.

Differences among Respondents who Knew about FASD

Responses to FASD contact questions from individuals who had heard about FASD were analyzed to see if there were demographic differences (e.g., gender, age, and employment status), the results of which are found in Table 4.

FASD Contact

The percentage of respondents who reported knowing anyone who might have FASD differed by age, region of residence, and educational attainment. Respondents in the age group 55 to 64 (26.2%) were more likely to know someone with FASD, and those residing in Calgary were least likely to know anyone who had FASD (24.7%). Across Alberta the percentage of respondents who knew someone who might have FASD differed, with the "rest of Alberta" having the highest (39.9%), followed by Edmonton (35.4%) and Calgary (24.7%).

Respondents who reported knowing anyone who cared for someone with FASD were more likely to be female (60.3%), 55 to 64 years of age (26.0%), to have post-secondary education (77.6%), to reside in the "rest of Alberta" (38.2%), to be Canadian-born (90.2%), and to be Albertan-born (61.0%).

Table 4. Demographic differences associated with responses to FASD contact questions (N=1028)

	Yes n (%)	No n (%)	p≤ Chi Square value (0.05)
Do you know anyone who you think might have FASD?			
Age			
18–24	18 (4.6)	27 (4.6)	
25–34	58 (14.8)	71(12.3)	
35–44	70 (17.8)	108 (18.3)	
45–54	87 (22.1)	125 (21.2)	0.0115
55–64	103 (26.2)	120 (20.3)	
65+	57 (14.5)	139 (23.6)	
Region of residence			
Edmonton	144 (35.4)	204 (33.6)	
Calgary	100 (24.7)	211 (34.8)	0.0014
Rest of Alberta	162 (39.9)	192 (31.6)	
Highest educational attainment			
Less than high school	12 (3.0)	62 (10.0)	
High school completed	65 (16.3)	127 (20.5)	0.0001 .
Post-secondary	321 (80.7)	431 (69.5)	

Do you know anyone who provides care for someone with FASD?

Gender

Male	158 (39.7)	327 (52.7)	0.0001
Female	240 (60.3)	293 (47.3)	

Age

18–24	16 (4.2)	30 (4.9)	
25–34	60 (15.7)	71 (11.7)	
35–44	72 (18.9)	105 (17.3)	
45–54	85 (22.3)	127 (20.9)	0.0004
55–64	99 (26.0)	125 (20.6)	
65+	49 (12.9)	149 (24.6)	

Region of residence

Edmonton	145 (36.4)	204 (32.9)	
Calgary	101 (25.4)	213 (34.5)	0.0001
Rest of Alberta	152 (38.2)	203 (32.7)	

Highest educational attainment

Less than high school	21 (5.2)	54 (8.9)	
High school completed	70 (17.2)	122 (20.1)	0.0297
Post-secondary	315 (77.6)	431 (71.0)	-

Country of birth

Canada	359 (90.2)	516 (83.2)	0.0018
Other	39 (9.8)	104 (16.8)	

Alberta born

Yes	219 (61.0)	275 (53.3)	0.0237
No	140 (39.0)	241 (46.7)	

Behaviour

The majority (over 80.0%) of respondents, regardless of age, were likely to tell a pregnant woman they knew who was drinking alcohol that using alcohol might harm the baby (Table 5). Respondents were more likely to do so if they were female (54.2%), aged 18–24 years (all respondents in this age group agreed they would) (5.3%) and 35–44 years (37.4%), had a post-secondary education (74.2%), and were Christians (68.0%; Table 5). Respondents least likely to tell a woman they knew of the dangers of alcohol were over 65 years of age (34.9%), indicated they had no religion (37.1%), or had educational background less than high school (15.6%).

When a respondent did not know the pregnant woman who was drinking, women were more likely than men to inform the pregnant woman of the potential harm to the baby (Table 5). Across Alberta the percentage of respondents who would tell a pregnant woman they didn't know who was drinking about the dangers of alcohol also differed, with Edmonton having the highest (37.6%), followed by the rest of Alberta (37.1%) and Calgary (25.3%). Respondents aged 45–54 years old (24.8%), retired (23.0%), earning more than CAD 80,000 (62.2%) were least likely to inform a pregnant women they didn't know who was drinking about the potential dangers of alcohol to the baby (Table 5).

Table 5. *Differences in characteristics of respondents regarding FASD behaviour questions (N=1028)*

	Yes n (%)	No n (%)	p≤ Chi Square value (0.05)
If I saw a pregnant woman I knew drinking alcohol, I would tell her that using alcohol during pregnancy might harm the baby.			
Gender			
Male	401 (45.8)	62 (56.9)	0.0293
Female	474 (54.2)	47 (43.1)	
Age			
18–24	45 (5.3)	0 (0.0)	0.0002
25–34	119 (14.0)	7 (6.8)	
35–44	155 (18.2)	19 (18.5)	
45–54	181(21.2)	21 (20.4)	
55–64	202 (23.7)	20 (19.4)	
65+	150 (17.6)	36 (34.9)	
Highest educational attainment			
Less than high school	55 (6.3)	17 (15.6)	0.0020
High school completed	171 (19.5)	19 (17.4)	
Post-secondary	649 (74.2)	73 (67.0)	

Religion			
Christian	562 (68.0)	60 (61.9)	
Other religion	43 (5.2)	1 (1.0)	
No religion	222 (26.8)	36 (37.1)	0.0313

If I saw a pregnant woman I did not know drinking alcohol, I would tell her that using alcohol during pregnancy might harm the baby

Gender			
Male	201 (43.9)	251 (54.1)	0.0019
Female	257 (56.1)	213 (45.9)	

Age			
18–24	28 (6.3)	14 (3.1)	
25–34	68 (15.2)	52 (11.6)	
35–44	78 (17.4)	74 (16.6)	0.0283
45–54	103 (23.0)	94 (21.1)	
55–64	96 (21.4)	111 (24.8)	
65+	75 (16.7)	102 (22.8)	

Region of residence			
Edmonton	172 (37.6)	145 (31.2)	
Calgary	116 (25.3)	172 (37.1)	0.0006
Rest of Alberta	170 (37.1)	147 (31.7)	

Income			
<$39,999	59 (17.2)	37 (10.6)	
$40,000 – $79,999	92 (26.8)	95 (27.2)	0.0375
>$80,000	192 (56.0)	217 (62.2)	

Employment			
Employed (Full/part-time)	297 (65.0)	291 (63.3)	
Retired	77 (16.8)	106 (23.0)	0.0249
Other (Unemployed, maternity, students, disabled)	83 (18.2)	63 (13.7)	

Discussion

The current survey provides contemporary data on Albertans' knowledge and attitudes about alcohol consumption in pregnancy and its effects on the fetus, including their understanding of FASD. In the survey 85.7% of respondents had heard about FASD, which is consistent with the 86.0% rate found in the 2006 Canadian nation-wide survey commissioned by the Public Health Agency of Canada (Environics Research Group, 2006). We found that more women than men had heard of FASD, which is similar to previous research (Environics Research Group, 2006).

Respondents who had not heard of FASD (14.3%) were more likely to be male, aged between 18 and 44 years of age, born outside of Canada, non-Caucasian, and to reside in Calgary. This shows that there are gaps in FASD knowledge that exist within Alberta and provides information that is useful in the strategic planning process of FASD programs aimed at increasing awareness and education within the province.

Of respondents who were aware of FASD, almost all (99.0%) knew that alcohol use during pregnancy causes FASD and that FASD was preventable (99.0%). There was a slightly lower level of knowledge regarding alcohol consumption at different stages of pregnancy, with 3.7% of respondents unable to select the best answer for the *no alcohol use during pregnancy or while trying to become pregnant* statement. These respondents were more likely to be male (62.2%), which is consistent with the literature. Chang and colleagues (2006) examined knowledge about healthy pregnancy habits among pregnant women and their male partners and found that men were less likely to agree that there is no universally safe level of prenatal alcohol use than their partners (64.9% vs. 79.9%). Research supporting the adverse effects of maternal alcohol consumption across all drinking levels remains somewhat inconsistent (Walker, Al-Sahab, Islam, & Tamim, 2011), with a few research findings suggesting that having a glass of wine a week ("light drinking") will not harm the fetus (Kelly et al., 2012; Robinson et al., 2010). The lack of consensus in this body of research may send mixed messages to the general population and may explain why some respondents did not select *no alcohol use during pregnancy* as the safest measure to reduce any and all potential threats to fetal development.

A relatively high proportion of respondents knew someone with FASD or knew someone who cared for an individual with FASD; there is an opportunity to better understand, through future research, if the needs of caregivers for information and support are being met.

Evidence shows that a woman's ability to create an environment conducive to a healthy pregnancy, such as changing her alcohol use,

is influenced by the availability of and access to adequate social supports and services, and by underlying factors such as poverty, violence
(Burgoyne, 2005; Health Canada, 2005), and presence of mental health
disorders (Astley, Bailey, Talbot, & Clarren, 2000; Bhuvaneswar, Chang,
Epstein, & Stern, 2007). A pregnant woman's ability to make healthy
choices can also be influenced by the actions of her partner (e.g., presence of a heavy drinking partner is associated with pregnant woman con-
suming alcohol) (Clarke & Gibbard, 2003) and family members.

In the current study, most respondents believed that women needed
to be supported by others not to drink while pregnant, which suggests
that Albertans recognize that collective efforts are required to support
women at risk of an alcohol-exposed pregnancy. The identification of
family and partners as the main supporters for pregnant woman not to
drink supports the inclusion of family and partners in prenatal education that focuses not only on abstinence from alcohol for the pregnant
woman, but also on ways to be supportive (Chang et al., 2006).

Health-care providers, the community, and government were also
identified as important sources of support in encouraging women not
to drink during pregnancy. Albertans in this study identify a shared
responsibility among government agencies, health-care providers, and
communities in mitigating the risk for FASD. This suggests there may
be willingness in the general population to receive appropriate assistance from these supports and that they should take a leading role in
the implementation of effective, accessible, and respectful supports for
women at risk. Additionally, those working in agencies and programs
with women at risk of drinking during pregnancy should be trained to
identify these women and be able to provide appropriate supports or
referrals.

Alcohol use can be influenced by social factors and the broader determinants of health, including social norms and expectations (Burgoyne,
2005; Roberts & Nanson, 2000). Multiple factors can influence alcohol
use before and during pregnancy, including access to resources (e.g.,
having limited prenatal care services, or unstable housing and living
conditions) and social norms and expectations (e.g., history of drug use/
smoking during pregnancy) (Burgoyne, 2005; Roberts & Nanson, 2000).
In the current study, in order to gauge the acceptable social norms in relation to alcohol use during pregnancy, respondents were asked whether

they would tell a pregnant woman using alcohol that alcohol might harm the baby. Of respondents who had heard about FASD, 88.9% indicated that if they saw a pregnant woman they knew drinking alcohol they would tell the woman about the potential harm of alcohol to the baby, compared to 49.7% where the respondents did not know the pregnant woman. This finding may reflect the care and concern Albertans have for those in their communities and may be further evidence that policy- and decision-makers can be reassured that actions taken to support women would be valued by Albertans.

Limitations

Our population-based sample, selected by random-digit dialing, has provided insights into the knowledge and attitudes about FASD of adult Albertans. However, determining FASD awareness among those under age 18 is also important, as this would provide information to further inform prevention strategies that reduce the likelihood of an alcohol-exposed pregnancy, as well as normalize alcohol abstinence among those who may become pregnant. Other limitations of the current research include exclusion of those who could not answer the questions in English and information on non-respondents/refusers. Exclusion of or lack of information on these individuals may have led to under-representation of key subpopulations (e.g., those with unstable housing or living conditions).

The incidence of FASD is estimated to be higher for Aboriginal populations in Canada, but the current survey was unable to investigate the level of awareness among these populations due to small numbers in the sample. Future research to determine knowledge and attitudes about FASD among Aboriginal populations would further guide prevention strategies. Furthermore, while those who responded to the survey represented the Alberta census data with respect to ethnicity, religious background, and being Canadian-born, there remains an opportunity to better understand alcohol awareness among women who may be most highly at risk (e.g., past experience in child welfare, poor educational attainment, exposure to abuse or violence, underemployed, women of childbearing age not using birth control) (Mills, Siever, Hicks, Badry, Tough, & Benzies, 2009).

Conclusion

These results can inform FASD literacy strategies and prevention programs as they shed light on social norms regarding alcohol use during pregnancy, show areas where FASD awareness is low among individuals (e.g., individuals born outside of Canada), and provide insights for design of interventions that would be most effective (e.g., interventions that involve partners/families and health-care providers).

Acknowledgements

This research, commissioned by the Alberta Centre for Child, Family and Community Research (ACCFCR), was funded by Alberta Health as one project that contributed to the five-year Evaluation of the government of Alberta's *FASD 10-Year Strategic Plan*. The authors acknowledge the professional services of the Population Research Laboratory (PRL), University of Alberta, for survey consultation and data collection.

References

Ahmand, N., Flight, J., Singh, V. A., Poole, N., & Dell, C. (2008). *Canadian Addiction Survey (CAS): Focus on gender* (Cat.: H128-1/07-519E). Ottawa, ON: Health Canada.

Astley, S. J. (2004). *Diagnostic guide for fetal alcohol spectrum disorders: The 4-digit diagnostic code.* Seattle: University of Washington.

Astley, S. J., Bailey, D., Talbot, C., & Clarren, S. K. (2000). Fetal alcohol syndrome (FAS) primary prevention through FAS diagnosis: II. A comprehensive profile of 80 birth mothers of children with FAS. *Alcohol and Alcoholism, 35*(5), 509–519.

Bhuvaneswar, C. G., Chang, G., Epstein, L. A., & Stern, T. A. (2007). Alcohol use during pregnancy: Prevalence and impact. *Care Companion Journal of Clinical Psychiatry, 9*(6), 455–460.

Burgoyne, W. (2005). *What we have learned: Key Canadian FASD awareness campaigns* (Cat. no.: HP10-6/2006E). Canada: Best Start Resource Centre, Public Health Agency of Canada.

Canadian Centre on Substance Abuse (CCSA). (2005). *Introduction to FASD overview.* Retrieved from http://www.ccsa.ca/index,asp?ID=17&menu=&page=89%full=yes

Canadian Paediatric Society. (1997). Prevention of fetal alcohol syndrome (FAS) and fetal alcohol effects (FAE) in Canada. *Paediatrics and Child Health,* 2(2),143–145.

Canadian Paediatric Society. (2002). Fetal alcohol syndrome. *Paediatrics and Child Health,* 7(3), 161–174.

Chang, G., McNamara, T. K., Orav, E. J., & Wilkins-Haug, L. (2006). Alcohol use by pregnant women: Partners, knowledge, and other predictors. *Journal of Studies on Alcohol,* 67, 245–251.

Clark, E., Lutke, J., Minnes, P., & Ouellette-Kuntz, H. (2004). Secondary disabilities among adults with fetal alcohol spectrum disorder in British Columbia. *Journal of FAS International,* 2, e13.

Clarke, D. E., & Gibbard, W. B. (2003). Overview of fetal alcohol spectrum disorders for mental health professionals. *The Canadian Child and Adolescent Psychiatry Review,* 12(3), 57–63.

Environics Research Group. (2006). *Alcohol use during pregnancy and awareness of fetal alcohol syndrome and fetal alcohol spectrum disorder: Results of a national survey.* Toronto: Public Health Agency of Canada.

Guerri, C., Bazinet, A., & Riley, E. (2009). Foetal alcohol spectrum disorders and alterations in brain and behavior. *Alcohol and Alcoholism,* 44, 108–114.

Health Canada. (1996). *Joint statement: Prevention of fetal alcohol syndrome (FAS), fetal alcohol effects (FAE) in Canada.* Ottawa: Health Canada.

Health Canada. (2006). *Research update — alcohol use and pregnancy: An important Canadian public health and social issue.* Ottawa: Health Canada Publications.

Kellerman, T. (2008) *Prenatal alcohol exposure and the brain.* Bethesda, MD: National Institute on Alcohol Abuse and Alcoholism. Retrieved from http://www.come-over.to/FAS/FASbrain.htm

Kelly, Y. J., Sacker, A., Gray, R., Kelly, J., Wolke, D., Head, J., & Quigley, M. A. (2012). Light drinking during pregnancy: Still no increased risk for socioemotional difficulties or cognitive deficits at 5 years of age? *Journal of Epidemiology and Community Health,* 66(1), 41–48. doi: 10.1136/jech.2009.103002

Kowlessar, D. L. (1997). *An examination of the effects of prenatal alcohol exposure on school-age children in a Manitoba First Nation community. A study of fetal alcohol syndrome prevalence and dysmorphology.* Winnipeg, MB: University of Manitoba.

Masotti, P., Szala-Meneok, K., Selby, P., Ranford, J., & Van Koughnett, A. (2003). Urban FASD interventions: Bridging the cultural gap between Aboriginal women and primary care physicians. *Journal of FAS International,* 1, e17.

Mills, R. M. T., Siever, J. E., Hicks, M., Badry, D., Tough, S. C., & Benzies, K. (2009). Child guardianship in a Canadian home visitation program for women who use substances in the perinatal period. *Journal of Clinical Pharmacology, 16*(1), e126–139.

Public Health Agency of Canada. (2011). *The sensible guide to a healthy pregnancy.* Retrieved from www.phac-aspc.gc.ca/hp-gs/pdf/hpguide-eng.pdf

Rasmussen, C., Andrew, G., Zwaigenbaum, L., & Tough, S. (2008). Neurobehavioral outcomes of children with fetal alcohol spectrum disorders: A Canadian perspective. *Journal of Paediatric and Child Health, 13*(3), 185–191.

Riley, E., Mattson, S., & Thomas, J. (2009). Fetal alcohol syndrome. In L. Squire (Ed.), *Encyclopedia of neuroscience, Vol. 4* (pp. 213–220). Oxford: Academic Press.

Roberts, G., & Nanson, J. (2000). *Best practices: Fetal alcohol syndrome/Fetal alcohol effects and the effects of other substance use during pregnancy.* Ottawa, ON: Health Canada.

Robinson, M., Oddy, W. H., McLean, N. J., Jacoby, P., Pennell, C. E, de Klerk, N. H., ... Newnham, J. P. (2010). Low-moderate prenatal alcohol exposure and risk to child behavioural development: A prospective cohort study. *International Journal of Obstetrics & Gynaecology,* Aug, *117*(9), 1139-1150. doi: 10.1111/j.1471-0528.2010.02596.x

Stade, B., Ali, A., Bennett, D., Campbell, D., Johnston, M., Lens, C., ...Koren, G. (2009). The burden of prenatal exposure to alcohol: Revised measurement of cost. *The Canadian Journal of Clinical Pharmacology, 16*(1), e91–e102.

Statistics Canada. (2010). *Selected trend data for Alberta, 1996, 2001 and 2006 censuses.* Retrieved January 30, 2013, from http://www12.statcan.ca/census-recensement/2006/dp-pd/92-596/P1-2. cfm?Lang=eng&T=PR&GEOCODE=48&PRCODE=48&TID=0.

Statistics Canada. (2001). *Selected Religions, for Canada, Provinces and Territories – 20% Sample Data.* Retrieved January 7, 2013, from http://www12.statcan.ca/english/census01/products/highlight/Religion/Page. cfm?Lang=E&Geo=PR&View=1a&Code=48&Table=1&StartRec=1&Sort=2&B1= 48&B2=All

Thanh, N. X., & Jonsson, E. (2009). Costs of fetal alcohol spectrum disorder in Alberta, Canada. *Canadian Journal of Clinical Pharmacology, 16*(1), e80–e90.

Thanh, N. X., & Jonsson, E. (2010). Drinking alcohol during pregnancy: Evidence from Canadian community health survey 2007/2008. *Journal of Population Therapeutics and Clinical Pharmacology, 17*(2), e302–e307.

Tough, S., Clarke, M., Hicks, M., & Clarren, S. (2005). Attitudes and approaches of Canadian providers to preconception counseling and the prevention of fetal alcohol spectrum disorders (FASDs), *Journal of FAS International, 3,* e3.

Tough, S., Tofflemire, K., Clarke, M., & Newburn-Cook, C. (2006). Do women change their drinking behaviors while trying to conceive? An opportunity for preconception counseling. *Clinical Medicine & Research, 4,* 97–105. doi: 10.3121/cmr.4.2.97

US Department of Health and Human Services, & US Department of Agriculture. (2000). *Nutrition and your health: Dietary guidelines for Americans* (5th ed.). Washington: Authors.

Walker, M. J., Al-Sahab, B., Islam, F., & Tamim, H. (2011). The epidemiology of alcohol utilization during pregnancy: An analysis of the Canadian Maternity Experiences Survey (MES). *BMC Pregnancy and Childbirth, 11,* 52. doi:10.1186/1471-2393-11-52

Collaboration or Competition? Generalist or Specialized? Challenges Facing Social Work Education and Child Welfare

William Pelech, Rick Enns, and Don Fuchs

Over the past 20 years, the delivery of social work distance education has experienced a profound technological transformation. It has moved from paper- and telephone-based correspondence courses to courses offered via interactive television and the Internet. Demand for distance education and, in particular, online courses continues to grow. The 2010 Sloan Survey of Online Learning in the United States revealed that nearly 30% of students had taken at least one online course in their degree programs, with enrollment rising by almost one million students to 5.6 million students from a year earlier—the largest ever year-to-year increase in the number of students studying online (Allen & Seaman, 2010).

Such transformations will demand structural changes, potentially offering further incentives to enter into new collaborative relationships. One exemplar of just such a collaborative initiative is the Prairie Child Welfare Consortium and its e-learning committee, which has promoted

Suggested Citation: Pelech, W., Enns, R., & Fuchs, D. (2014). Collaboration or competition? Generalist or specialized? Challenges facing social work education and child welfare. In D. Badry, D. Fuchs, H. Montgomery, & S. McKay (Eds.), *Reinvesting in Families: Strengthening Child Welfare Practice for a Brighter Future: Voices from the Prairies* (pp. 243–262). Regina, SK: University of Regina Press.

collaboration among three major western Canadian universities. This paper will briefly describe the global transformation occurring in post-secondary education, the merits and challenges of collaboration between educational institutions, and the implications of the expansion of e-learning options and interinstitutional collaborations for our traditional undergraduate generalist curriculum; and it will describe the process of development and delivery of interuniversity online option courses in child welfare practice. Finally, future plans for collaborative development of child welfare related courses will be outlined. In this way, this paper will offer a model for a more responsive and sustainable model for social work education.

The Transformation in Social Work Education

For some, the idea of being educated in anything but a traditional face-to-face instructional milieu seems to conflict with the purpose of social work education. As Vernon, Vakalahi, Pierce, Pittman-Munke, and Adkins (2009) noted, "Social work educators and practitioners often describe themselves as 'people persons' who value human encounters. This is an understandable ethos given the nature of our profession" (p. 269); however, such a position limits the scope and creativity that may be brought to the project of social work education. For if we can only teach social work in a conventional classroom environment, only those who have access to the classroom can participate. Moreover, the notion that social work education can only be conducted in a traditional classroom may also be taking on an increasingly mythical status.

In a recent American survey of 137 social work programs, the Commission on Accreditation (COA) of the Council on Social Work Education (CSWE) found that "more than a third of the BSW programs and a quarter of the MSW programs surveyed did not require a face-to-face experience as an integral component of coursework. Instead, these programs offered courses that were entirely online, without direct human contact" (Vernon et al., 2009, p. 269). Sixty-one percent of BSW programs and 83% of MSW programs were currently delivering, developing, or contemplating distance education and were "open" to using technology to provide courses for their students (p. 267). As the authors of the CSWE survey report noted, "it is readily apparent that distance education has expanded exponentially in only a decade" (p. 274).

Two factors, in addition to technological change, may be driving this transformation. First, there is student demand. Students are voting with their feet or, perhaps more accurately, with their browsers. The aforementioned 2010 Sloan Survey of Online Learning in the United States (Allen & Seaman, 2010) leads one to ask if this increase arises from greater accessibility offered by online courses or from student preference or both. The second factor that may be driving the transformation is institutional pressure. According to Vernon et al. (2009) nearly two-thirds of social work program respondents reported being pressured from within institutions to develop online courses. There may be several reasons for such pressure, not the least of which are the substantial investments in distance education infrastructure and technology, and the perceived profits associated with online classes (Vernon et al., 2009).

Increasing demand and the opportunities afforded by technological developments have prompted some to argue that our educational institutions are outmoded and are unable to respond to these challenges. For example, Siemmens (2008) argued that institutional barriers and the relatively slow adoption of new technologies have led to a slow response to burgeoning global need. Day (2005) added that this imbalance between global supply and demand for access "makes the imperative of providing a decent education for all one of the greatest moral challenges of our age" (p. 186).

Collaboration or Competition?

The possibility of offering courses outside of the physical classroom has also monetized courses that can be offered online and, with the potential profits to be made, we have witnessed a dramatic increase in the number of education service providers and increased competition for students (Yang, 2008). Service providers in the United Kingdom and the United States have dominated the distance education market, and institutions in these countries have dramatically increased the value of their educational service exports, even as costs have increased over the past 20 years (e.g., UK institutions have increased the value of all their educational exports by over 500% from 2.2 billion to 11.1 billion; US institutions have increased their exports by 250% from 4.6 to 11.5 billion). Likewise, Australia has increased its educational service exports from 584 million to 2.1 billion for an increase of 367%. (OECD, 2004). One of the implications of an increasingly globalized post-secondary regime and expanded programming is increasing competition through the removal of geographical barriers to the delivery of programming. For example, while the University of Calgary has been given a "provincial mandate" for undergraduate and graduate social work education across Alberta, with increasing competition of programs from other domestic and international institutions this "mandate" may be more of an illusion than a reality.

In addition to the demand for courses and competition, the American Distance Education Consortium (2006) listed a number of other challenges faced by most post-secondary institutions, including constrained resources, increasingly diverse learners, increased demand for student access, and overcoming institutional inertia. Davies (2001) added that universities need to realize their own limitations in terms of in-house expertise in non-traditional teaching and learning, including course development. Many (Beaudoin, 2009; Davies, 2001; Fain, Blumenstyk, & Sander, 2009; Konrad & Small, 1989; Xu & Morris, 2009) have commented on the need for post-secondary institutions to examine the potential commercial possibilities and value-added dimension afforded by carefully constituted alliances. Indeed, co-operation rather than competition may be a more prudent course for small and medium institutions. Commenting on the increasingly competitive nature of post-secondary education, Joseph E. Aoun, the president of Northeastern University in Boston, observed that co-operation helps colleges better leverage their resources, stating that "You cannot go at it by thinking that the world stops at this campus....No university is self-sufficient" (cited by Fain et al., 2009, A20).

One such strategic response is the formation of educational consortia. Consortia can be viewed as somewhat diverse alliances. Beaudoin (2009) has defined an educational consortium as

a partnership among a number of educational institutions or other similar entities that have joined together to collaboratively provide instruction and other services to students that they might not otherwise be adequately equipped or inclined to do independently. These collaborations are designed and intended, at least in theory if not always in practice, to offer a broader range of courses and other products to consumers through the combined resources and expertise of their affiliate members. (p. 113)

As Beaudoin has noted, some consortia reflect a shared programmatic focus, others are created on the basis of a common organizational affiliation, while some are formed on the basis of territorial considerations, around a common philosophy, audience, delivery mode, or other shared attributes or activities. Regional consortia may include institutions from several provinces, and are thus able to market offerings in volume over a large area via a shared network.

The notion of an educational consortium is not a new concept. A number have been formed to serve various needs, regions, and specialized populations. Long before e-learning became a reality, Konrad and Small (1989) observed that in order for consortia to develop, institutions must move from their individualistic stance and commit to interdependence and co-operation. In addition to shared values and aims, each party must contribute something that is needed by other members. As Beaudoin (2009) has noted, some of the other benefits of forming consortia include reduced costs, reduced duplication, and, perhaps most relevant to our discussion here, expanded options for increasingly diverse learners. More recently, one successful initiative in the area of distance education is the Canadian Virtual University. Formed in 2000, the CVU is a consortium of 13 Canadian universities offering online and distance-education courses. In an interview with Vicky Busch, executive director of the Canadian Virtual University, Johnson (2008) reported that CVU registrations have increased by 10% each year since the consortium's inception, reaching some 150,000 course registrations in 2006.

However, if in the current context of increasing demand and competition consortia offer a sensible response, one may ask why we do not see more of such strategic alliances. Konrad and Small (cited by Beaudoin, 2009) identify several barriers to educational consortia including institutional autonomy, academic credibility, lack of trust, fiscal constraints, and structural arrangements. As Beaudoin (2009) observed, these obstacles can be overcome provided there is "forceful leadership" present in participating institutions:

> *Ultimately, however, such forward movement is likely to be realized only with the presence and perseverance of forceful leadership in those institutions, who recognize the potential of [distance education], who are willing to take certain risks, and who engage in transformative leadership that not only changes their respective institutions, but also reforms education practice, and thus moves a bit closer to improving access to education for more of its citizens. Certainly, this effort and its potential outcomes are far too important not to succeed! (p. 125)*

With leadership, some of the key elements required for successful consortia can emerge. Perhaps the most important of these elements is a formal agreement (Beaudoin, 2009; Davies, 2001; Hough, 1992; Xu & Morris, 2009). An agreement is essential in order to bring the necessary qualities of mutual expectations, scope, trust, and commitment to an institutional partnership (Davies, 2001). Such an agreement would specify financial and resource-sharing arrangements, transfer agreements, and dispute resolution processes. It would delineate a management structure and outline a requisite series of academic procedures and responsibilities (Beaudoin, 2009) and understandings relating to intellectual property (Davies, 2001), as well as an evaluative strategy that may serve to ascertain the extent to which the consortia benefits its membership (Xu & Morris, 2009). In addition to an agreement, consortia will also need to engage in strategic planning to guide and focus their activities (Xu & Morris, 2009):

> *It is patently clear that considerable effort and political judgment and commitment are needed in order to move a traditional university into purposeful alliances — but they are essential if movement into non-traditional domains is to be accomplished. (Davies, 2001, p. 510)*

Indeed, such consortia may be better able to respond to niche markets, where student interest in one location may not support program specialization; however, when the pool of available students is expanded across several partnering institutions, the development of collaborative specializations becomes much more viable.

Generalist or Specialist?

Traditional social work education has been offered throughout North America in similar fashion across the past 100 years or so, since its inception as a legitimate discipline and field of practice. Social work education at the first-degree level has, for the most part, followed a model of teaching generalist practice that offers a broad range of core and optional courses and topics to students. From a generalist practice lens, social work education "maintains a broad-based view of human functioning and explores processes for activating resources in people and their environments...it specifically focuses on the nature of the helping relationship itself as a resource for both workers and clients. Collaboration is the heart of this empowering approach" (Miley, O'Melia, & DuBois, 2004, p. xvii). The intent and focus of a generalist education is that bachelor of social work (BSW) graduates will leave the university prepared for employment as social workers throughout different agencies and institutions serving diverse populations.

Traditionally, graduate education in social work, such as master of social work (MSW) programs, has been perceived to provide an opportunity for more focused or specialized skill development through research and case studies. Although this approach has served the social work profession well in many ways, the sands in social work education are shifting as national societies become more diverse and globalization results in greater interdependence even as it produces greater inequities and disparities between and within countries. As a consequence, both the scope and field of social work practice have changed dramatically over the past decades. Greene (2005) clearly identified the climate of change faced by social workers and the need for a critical examination of the social work curriculum. Social work education should be shaped by the times and the critical issues faced within modern society.

There is an unspoken expectation that BSW students will leave post-secondary institutions prepared to work in the field. Through course offerings and practicum experience, there is an increasing awareness that students are not as technically prepared for the functions of their role, in contrast to such expectations. While recognizing that social work agencies and employers offer additional training specific to the needs of populations they serve, the question of how social work education can respond to the complexity of a postmodern social world looms. How can social work education improve and address the particular niche concerns of social work practice? Is there a way to embed social work education into a curriculum that considers these complexities? One approach posited by Goodyer (2007) discussed a qualifying degree in social work that offers a balance of education combined with training and direct work methods, while focusing on critical skill development for working in a particular area of practice, such as working with children.

While appreciating the history from which a model of generalist practice has developed, in response to educating social work students, it is a critical time to re-evaluate the efficacy of this model. It is also time to think about and evaluate the utility and value of differential means of delivering social work education in the current era. The Canadian Association for Social Work Education (CASWE) has a primary focus on the accreditation of social work education programs offered by universities in Canada. The 2011 CASWE report on accreditation included a set of principles to ensure that the quality of social work education appreciates the diverse needs of communities across Canada. A key point to note is that CASWE has recently indicated that new approaches to social work education must embrace a theory of change approach, whose focus is to link education and practice while integrating knowledge, skills, and values that contribute to competency in social work (CASWE Accreditation Task Force, 2011).

The very technology that contributes to the complexity of social work practice and suggests limitations in current models of social work education also offers a venue to develop some solutions—provided that the curriculum offered supports ready-to-work graduates, and virtual social work education has shown promise for responding to some of these concerns. Moreover, with the development of initiatives in social work education that can reach out to students across the nation and the globe, perhaps some of the assumptions underpinning our commitment to generalist education may come into further question. Our steadfast commitment to generalist education has been based on geographical limitations associated with campus-based delivery, which meant that our undergraduate programs must prepare students from a limited population base to work in a variety of settings. Under such a regime, faculty members must also teach a variety of courses. However, when we expand our student base, then these assumptions may no longer hold. Undergraduate programs can, and increasingly do, respond to niche interests, often associated with major fields of practice (e.g., child welfare, addictions, mental health, domestic violence, poverty). Social work programs, and their faculty members, may then teach to their strengths and further integrate their research and teaching activities.

Given its prominence in social work practice, and the demand for child welfare practitioners, it comes as no surprise that one such educational niche is child welfare practice. While there is very limited evaluative research available relating to the distance delivery of child welfare courses (Bellefeuille, 2006; Hollister & McGee, 2000), the findings of these studies are in keeping with general trends reported in the literature concerning distance education courses. For example, Hollister and McGee (2000) noted comparable levels of academic performance between distance (i.e., interactive television) and traditional delivery formats in a child welfare course. Bellefeuille (2006), utilizing focus groups, reported positive student experiences relating to the effectiveness and value of an online child welfare course. Given the demand for child welfare workers, and the challenges in responding to this need in a generalist undergraduate program, the Prairie Child Welfare Consortium has come forward to offer an innovative program of child welfare related courses.

Prairie Child Welfare Consortium

The story of the early beginnings of the Prairie Child Welfare Consortium (PCWC) is located in the first book published by the group (McKay, 2007). A key factor stimulating the initial bringing together of representatives of the four schools of social work (University of Calgary, University of Regina, University of Manitoba, and the First Nations University of Canada) was the desire to explore options for collaboration on child welfare course delivery among the four institutions.

Paralleling this interest, representatives of the three provincial government departments serving children and families expressed a desire to
explore options for working together on training material relevant to
child welfare service delivery.

In 2005, the PCWC steering committee established a subcommittee to
look at the development of a project that would lead to a sustainable
web-based portal, which would provide a means for effective ongoing
sharing of information relating to prairie child welfare. Specifically,
the subcommittee was set up to explore the use of web-based technology to foster communication, sharing of training materials, and collaborative research. The subcommittee worked through most of 2006 and
2007 to develop a detailed proposal and search out sources of funding
to assist the PCWC to accomplish its mission by using web-based information technology. The final proposal outlined a comprehensive strategy to foster communication amongst PCWC members using information
technology.

As the subcommittee continued its work on the proposal and course
development, it became apparent that the emerging web-based communication and information technology was evolving very rapidly. The
range of applications of the newly emerging technologies far exceeded
the knowledge base of the committee members. Consequently, the subcommittee organized a face-to-face meeting in June 2007 to consult with
informational technology (IT) experts from the three prairie universities
on the potential applications of emerging web-based IT to the mission
and goals of the PCWC.

This consultation greatly assisted the committee members in understanding the range of IT applications currently available through the
prairie universities. During this meeting it was determined that the PCWC
was interested in creating an e-learning community in child welfare
across the Prairies, consistent with our mission, to promote excellence
and innovation in education, training, practice, policy, and research. The
PCWC steering committee reaffirmed that IT would serve as a means to
create the e-learning community, but not be an end in itself.

The primary constituents/stakeholders of the e-learning community
were identified as students (BSW, MSW, doctorate), faculty (instructors, researchers), agency staff (front-line workers, supervisors, managers), trainers, universities, government, children and families, and

community-based organizations. The benefits to students would be more relevant knowledge and skill development, a space within which to have dialogue, inter/intra-provincial placements, access to more field sites/ instruction, better work opportunities, more opportunities for graduate research, stronger links between field and school, and innovative opportunities (such as paid internships). The benefits to the prairie universities would be enhancing innovative capacity and availability, providing cutting-edge leadership, enhancing students' engagement by offering diverse experiences for learning, enhancing opportunities for faculty collaboration on research, developing an effective model for interuniversity collaboration, increasing potential to attract more students, increasing relevance and social responsibility, and expanding potential to attract new research dollars. The committee identified the following benefits to faculty: mentoring for new faculty; increased research opportunities; collaboration on common issues; collaboration on course development and delivery, sharing resources and expertise; building relevant prairie-based resources and knowledge development;setting standards for leadership in child welfare policy, practice, education, and research; knowledge transfer and mobilization; meaningful community/government partnerships; and strengthening knowledge and skills in child welfare with First Nations/Métis/Inuit communities.

Also, at the June 2007 meeting, the committee identified four key areas to focus on for the ongoing development of the community: course delivery (e.g., introduction to child welfare, assessment and intervention planning, supervision in child welfare); sharing information (links to sites); online discussion; and development of training modules (offered concurrently to the on-campus course). Out of this meeting the portal development committee became a standing committee of the PCWC, known as the e-learning committee, that reported to the PCWC steering committee with the aim of becoming a virtual space for training and education, information-sharing, and collectively working together.

After the June 2007 meeting, the PCWC e-learning committee reworked its earlier portal proposal to reflect its new priorities. The University of Calgary, Faculty of Social Work, worked with the e-learning committee to seek funding for the broad-based portal proposal. However, the committee was not successful in acquiring funding for the proposal after several attempts. So, having been unable to secure funding and losing the phone lines previously made available through the Centre of Excellence in Child Welfare (due to the disbandment of the CECW), the committee shifted its focus to developing the educational focus of the e-learning initiative.

Development of PCWC Collaborative Course Offerings

In 2007, the e-learning subcommittee established a task group to work on the delivery of the first web-based course across the three Prairie provinces and four prairie faculties of social work. The first course was offered in spring of 2009 in conjunction with the Faculties of Social Work at the Universities of Calgary, Manitoba, and Regina. The course, entitled Residential Schools and Child Welfare, examined the history of Indian residential schools across the three Prairie provinces of western Canada. The course examines the federal policies that established and maintained the church-run residential school system across western Canada and the role of the social work profession, particularly following the Second World War, in the delivery of child welfare services to First Nations children and families. The course has also examined recent efforts at reconciliation and the effects of federal attempts to direct formal reconciliation efforts.

This course was selected as the e-learning course offered through the PCWC and member universities, since variations of the course had already been offered as an elective within the Faculty of Social Work at the University of Calgary. Beyond the convenience of offering a course that had been designed as an online elective, the course provided a forum for students in all three institutions and across all three faculties to examine the role of the social work profession in the residential school system and in child welfare practices that are, in many ways, closely tied to the federal and denominational initiatives of the early to mid-twentieth century. The course has been offered in the spring session since 2009 and has always been able to combine students from at least two of the three universities involved. Recently, efforts were made to include social work professionals employed in child welfare and related settings, and students not currently registered in any of the faculties. Although it has not been possible to broaden the offering in this way to date, this remains an important objective for the course and for the e-learning initiative of the PCWC. The course has been hosted using the Blackboard Learning System, either through the University of Calgary or through the corporate Blackboard portal.

As currently configured, the course is divided into three modules extending over the six or seven weeks allocated for spring courses at the three universities. Required and supplementary readings are provided for each module, and video clips and other online resources are also incorporated. Students are organized into small groups for the duration of the course and are given time to complete readings and review other material before engaging in asynchronous online discussions for each module. Students are also asked to maintain an individual journal to record their experiences throughout the course, and each group prepares a group assignment that is posted for all students in the class to view during the final week of the course. For the presentation, students are asked to imagine that they have been asked to speak to their colleagues, or at a social work conference, and to identify key learning from the course for their imaginary colleagues, who are presumed to have little knowledge of the residential school system and the practice of apprehension and removal that has characterized relationships between the Canadian state and First Nations families. Students have commented on the value of discussing often difficult material in small group settings and on the levels of trust and support that typically emerge as they interact with fellow students from other universities—a significant number of whom know former students of, or have family members who attended, residential schools. Students also welcome the opportunity to review and comment on the group presentations and the opportunity to consider the insights and perspectives of classmates who were not in their small group discussions. These feelings align with strong statements from students about the importance of learning about residential schools, and the need to examine other aspects of the relationship between First Nations and the Canadian state, and appreciation for the opportunity to learn in an online environment and with students from other universities and other provincial jurisdictions.

Many of the tasks associated with offering an online course take on added significance in this case. Since the University of Calgary is the only university in this collaboration that was using Blackboard for online courses, students from the Universities of Regina and Manitoba required additional assistance in order to become familiar with the online environment. Strategies to facilitate this can also enhance student engagement in the course. Students are welcomed to the course three to four weeks ahead of the start of class and are encouraged to establish accounts or log on to the course in order to become familiar with the structure of the site and the design of the course. Students are also encouraged to introduce themselves to the entire class through a forum set up for introductions, and to navigate to various sites and other resources that provide context for the material discussed in class. These activities are monitored by the instructor to ensure that students are successfully navigating the site, and are able to post material to the appropriate discussion forums, and to identify and encourage students who may be unable or reluctant to initiate Blackboard activity. Similar levels of oversight, including close tracking of online discussions and prompts for groups or students who may be slow to begin discussions, prompt assessment and grading of forum postings, and quick turnaround on all email questions are essential to address frustrations that may arise more quickly when students are using online platforms that they are not familiar with.

Moving Forward

In light of several successful offerings of the residential schools course, the e-learning committee decided to move forward with expanding the number of collaborative course offerings. Accordingly, in early 2011, the e-learning committee decided that it needed to develop a multi-year plan to offer education and training courses that would assist in clearly identifying and coordinating collaborative courses. In addition, it was decided that only courses that were offered minimally in two or more provinces would be included in the planning for PCWC courses. In this multi-year plan, the committee identified a small number of courses to enable the committee to work through the logistics and mechanics of regularly offering online courses across the three Prairie provinces. The committee has representation from those individuals who were interested in, and to some degree responsible for, distance delivery at each Faculty of Social work, as well as interested academics. In addition, it was felt at some point that the committee should engage associate deans responsible for online education in the work of the committee. It was also noted that the PCWC offerings should not take away from, or interfere with, scheduled courses for regular program students at each faculty. Courses should be targeted for students requiring flexible options (e.g., remote location and for practitioners wanting ongoing professional development or interested in exploring further courses of study).

A Two-Year Plan

The committee discussed a wide range of course options for delivery over the next two years. It was suggested that the course offerings could look at providing elective options to students across the Prairies to enhance the core program offerings. A tentative course sequence for course development and delivery was generated, including the following:

Table 1. Two-Year Plan of Courses Offerings

Spring 2011 and 2012	Residential Schools and Child Welfare
Summer 2012	FASD and Child Welfare Practice
Fall 2012	Addictions and Child and Family Service Practice
Fall 2012	Indigenous Approaches to Child and Family Service Practices
Winter 2013	Crisis Intervention in Child and Family Service Practice
Summer 2013	FASD and Child Welfare Practice
Fall 2013	Addictions and Child and Family Service Practice
Fall 2013	Child Welfare with Immigrants and Refugees

The committee agreed to regularize an equal distribution of students across the three universities. In the first instance, with the residential schools course, this number was set at eight to nine per student's institution, with an invitation to the School of Indian Social Work, First Nations University of Canada program for four to six students to participate (FNUC is a founding member of the PCWC, currently inactive). Each faculty would develop recruitment approaches to existing students and to agencies and government trainers to meet the enrollment numbers for each course. A liaison person at each institution would serve to assist with brokering the practical implementation of each course. Also discussed was the need to use a consistent platform for the delivery of courses. It was agreed that members would share information as each institution went forward with the development of a new platform and that in developing new courses for online learning they should be developed in modularized formats that could be used with different platforms. Committee members agreed to share course descriptions and outlines with the liaisons at the three sites to assist with the approval and marketing of the courses for summer session. The host institution for each course offering would be responsible for all costs associated with their course, with the other consortia members responsible for paying for tuition fees for each of their registrants.

Principles of Designated PCWC Courses

In later meetings, the committee approved principles as the guidelines for the vetting of new PCWC course offerings. These principles included

- Non-competition with core academic programs—courses offered are specialized;
- Collaboration and participation: working together to bring us together, share information, and build collaborative courses / curriculum;
- Accessibility for students, ministry, and/or agency staff;
- Seats available to at least two institutions;
- Offered for credit;
- Evaluative component built in that will be shared by the consortium;
- Aboriginal/Indigenous populations lens; Marginalized populations lens; Culturally inclusive;
- Practitioner lens incorporated/direct input as far as possible where offerings must be practitioner relevant;
- Fully online;
- Tech support offered by host institution;
- Library resources and required texts accessible to students from their home institution;

- Modularized course design;
- Geographic focus consistent with PCWC mandate.

Meeting Challenges

As the consortium, through the e-learning committee, has moved forward with additional course offerings, a number of academic, administrative, and logistical challenges have also emerged. The academic challenges include different grading schemes and spring session calendar dates across universities, as well as the challenges of offering courses that combine students and social work professionals from all university and government partners in equal numbers in one online classroom. Administrative challenges include the complexities of registering students for credit across universities and managing elective offerings across faculties. Other challenges include licensing restrictions for student access to course management systems; determining how teaching consortium offerings factors into faculty workload calculations; challenges with setting quotas for students who are not members of the university community; financial impacts arising from tuition fees not covering the full cost of each course offering; developing effective mechanisms to recruit and register students; and the need for clearer delineation of responsibilities within and between universities.

With the resolution of some of the aforementioned administrative challenges and greater student awareness about these course offerings, there has been broader participation by students from three universities (i.e., Calgary, Regina, Manitoba). For example, in spring 2012, the residential schools course was offered to 33 students. A second course, FASD and Child Welfare, was delivered in summer 2012 to 23 students, primarily from the University of Calgary. In spring 2013, the residential schools course included 30 students from all three universities, and FASD and Child Welfare included 13 University of Calgary students and 13 University of Manitoba students.

Accumulated experiences in this course show that the consortium's commitment to bring students together from across western Canada is possible, and welcomed by the students. As noted above, effective leadership is needed to sustain such collaborative arrangements, especially when there are financial constraints. On a positive note, the deans from each faculty have recently recommitted their support to this innovative and mutually beneficial initiative. As is customary with all new programs, we have now reached a stage where formalization is needed to support continued development. To this end, committee members are working on developing a written agreement that will address the specifics of the course offerings and the various responsibilities of each participating university.

Implications for Social Work Education

This initiative may offer a view of the future, when we may see that each school of social work will attract students not solely based upon their proximity, but based upon what it has to offer that is of value to its prospective students. From this perspective, if we limit ourselves to geographically delimited generalist programs, it is likely that competition with schools offering online programs will continue to erode the pool of available students for local programs. Specialized program offerings that speak to the needs and interests of students may become increasingly prominent factors in each student's enrollment choices. Consequently, on the horizon may be a reorganization of program delivery from geographically based structures to programmatically oriented ones. While we have traditionally adopted a generalist approach to teaching at the undergraduate level, if students had the option of a wide variety of program offerings, we might see the development of specializations at the undergraduate level in a variety of practice areas, including child welfare. Program organization could bring together instructors from various "universities" who have interests and expertise in each area. Indeed, a "university" may no longer be a place where one program is entirely situated.

Such a transformation will demand structural changes and the creation of new collaborative relationships. One exemplar of just such a collaborative initiative is the Prairie Child Welfare Consortium and its e-learning committee, which has promoted collaboration among three major western Canadian universities. Just as economic globalization predicated upon a Darwinist ethos of competition has wrought ecological calamity, so too might our cleaving to territorial domains limit our ability to respond and adapt to our changing global community of learners. Rather than competing for a limited pool of students, schools must increasingly adopt an ecological stance recognizing their interdependence with other institutions.

References

Allen, I. E., & Seaman, J. (2010). *Class differences: Online education in the United States, 2010*. Wellesley, MA: Babson College.

American Distance Education Consortium. (2006). *ADEC strategic plan*. Retrieved May 7, 2012, from http://www.adec.edu

Beaudoin, M. F. (2009). Consortia—A viable model and medium for distance education in developing countries? *Open Learning, 24*(2), 113–126.

Bellefeuille, G. L. (2006). Rethinking reflective practice education in social work education: A blended constructivist and objectivist instructional design strategy for a web-based child welfare practice course. *Journal of Social Work Education, 42*(1), 85–104.

Canadian Association for Social Work Education. (2011). *Accreditation Task Force Report, 2011*. Retrieved from http://www.caswe-acfts.ca/vm/newvisual/attachments/866/Media/FinalReportATFApril282o112.pdf

Davies, J. L. (2001). A revolution in teaching and learning in higher education: The challenges and implications for the relatively traditional university. *Higher Education in Europe, 26*(4), 501–514.

Day, B. (2005). ICT-enhanced open and distance learning. In Y. Visser, L. Visser, M. Simonson, & R. Amirault (Eds.), *Trends and issues in distance education* (pp. 183–204). Greenwich, CO: Information Age Publishing.

Fain, P., Blumenstyk, G., & Sander, L. (2009). Sharing ideas: Tough times encourage colleges to collaborate. *Chronicle of Higher Education, 55*(23), A20.

Goodyer, A. (2007). Ideas in action: Teaching qualifying social workers skills for direct work with children. *Social Work Education, 26*(7), 737–740.

Greene, R. (2005). Redefining social work for the new millennium: Setting a context. *Journal of Human Behavior in the Social Environment, 11*(1), 37–54. Retrieved from http://www.haworthpress.com/web/JHBSE

Hollister, C. D., & McGee, G. (2000). Delivering substance abuse and child welfare content through interactive television. *Research on Social Work Practice, 10*(4), 417–427.

Hough, P. (1992). *The impact of distance education on the organization of schools and school systems in Alberta* (Unpublished doctoral dissertation). University of Alberta, Edmonton, AB.

Johnson, T. (2008). Learning long distance. *University Affairs*. Retrieved from http://www.universityaffairs.ca/learning-long-distance.aspx

Konrad, A., & Small, J. (1989). Collaboration in distance education. In R. Sweet
(Ed.), *Postsecondary distance education in Canada: Policies, practices and
priorities* (pp. 197–203). Athabasca, AB: Athabasca University.

McKay, S. (2007). Development of the Prairie Child Welfare Consortium and
this book. In I. Brown, F. Chaze., D. Fuchs, J. Lafrance, S. McKay, & S.
Thomas Prokop (Eds.), *Putting a human face on child welfare: Voices from the
Prairies* (pp. xv–xxxvi). Regina: Prairie Child Welfare Consortium / Centre of
Excellence for Child Welfare.

Miley, K., O'Melia, M., & DuBois, B. (2004). *Generalist social work practice: An
empowering approach* (4th ed.). Toronto, ON: Pearson.

OECD (Organization for Economic Cooperation and Development). (2004).
*Internationalisation and trade in higher education: Opportunities and
challenges*. Paris, France: OECD Publishing.

Siemmens, G. (2008). *Learning and knowing in networks: Changing roles for
educators and designers*. Paper presented at the University of Georgia IT
Forum. Retrieved from http://it.coe.uga.edu/itforum/Paper105/Siemens.pdf

Vernon, R., Vakalahi, H., Pierce, D., Pittman-Munke, P., & Adkins, L. F. (2009).
Distance education programs in social work: Current and emerging trends.
Journal of Social Work Education, 45(2), 263–275.

Xu, H., & Morris, L. V. (2009). A Comparative case study of state-level virtual
universities. *New Directions for Higher Education* (146), 45–54.

Yang, R. (2008). Transnational higher education in China: Contexts,
characteristics and concerns. *Australian Journal of Education, 52*(3), 272–286.

Epilogue

Although many generations of social workers have undergone extensive training to prepare us to work collaboratively regardless of our ranks or places of employment within the helping professions, the dominant discourses that have come to be routinely transmitted to incoming employees across the child welfare domain are more typically framed within expressions of collegial distrust, interdisciplinary disbelief, institutional denial, and interpersonal disrespect, rather than the opposite manifestations of these relational dimensions. We need only to point to the omnipresence of high levels of staff turnover, stress-leave taking, union-management disputes, and the multitude of high profile practice audits and case reviews that have occurred over the past several decades to realize that the outcomes of failing to share information and/or developing mutually beneficial working relationships takes a toll on the lives of those whom our employers have been charged with "helping"—their employees and clientele alike.

Suggested Citation: Montgomery, H. (2014). Epilogue. In D. Badry, D. Fuchs, H. Montgomery, & S. McKay (Eds.), *Reinvesting in Families: Strengthening Child Welfare Practice for a Brighter Future: Voices from the Prairies* (pp. 263–265). Regina, SK: University of Regina Press.

It has not always been easy to point to many examples of intradisci-plinary collaboration that might serve to contradict entrenched narra-tives that keep some helping professionals from collaborating with each other. Often, the urgency of externally imposed deadlines, the interper-sonal crises of service users and colleagues, and the chronic underde-velopment of social capital in local communities create demands that may occlude our eyes from perceiving opportunities for collaboration, even when there is low-hanging fruit dangling nearby; collaborative relationships are often within easy reach, but sometimes it just seems as if it would simply take too much hard labour to manifest the condi-tions necessary to catalyze opportunities into actions. Although it may be most patently voiced through the feedback loops of media outlets and organizational client complaints mechanisms, the need to transform the organizational cultures of the helping professions is haltingly acknowl-edged—especially as this relates to the explicit and tacit messages given to new employees who have received professional training in, or have been recruited to work in, the organizations scattered across northern and western Canada. Unfortunately, too often it seems that if collabo-ration is not explicitly stated in job descriptions, it can simply become more convenient to reply, "Maybe next year" when reflecting upon half-hearted personal and professional resolutions to initiate better intrapro-fessional and interdisciplinary working relationships.

Fortunately, the Prairie Child Welfare Consortium stands as a testa-ment to collaboration across Canada's Prairie provinces. Rather than emphasizing differences, denying regional variability, encouraging com-petitiveness, or insisting that everyone must slavishly adhere to one uni-versal approach to resolving common issues, the members of the PCWC have managed to work together across our jurisdictional borders to build capacity for mutually beneficial collaboration. One need only look to the success of the initiatives that consortium members have been able to deliver upon—e.g., biennial symposia, transprovincial professional educational programs, and scholarly knowledge dissemination through peer-reviewed books—to see that collaboration can pay off through goodwill and sharing.

This book is the fourth in a series of publications that have emerged out of the collaborative partnership that is the Prairie Child Welfare Consortium. The commitment of the various editorial groups and the authors who have contributed to this series demonstrates a viable model of complementary partnership—between government and academia, practitioners and policy-makers, trainers and researchers, Aboriginal peoples and settler populations—all of whom have a common interest in improving the quality of services being delivered to children and families across Canada's Prairie provinces. As with all collaborations, however, this could not have happened without a substantial degree of give-and-take among those who contributed to the production of this book. Author groups collaborated among themselves to generate first and subsequent drafts of their submissions. Peer reviewers generously collaborated with assigned editors to ensure the submissions reflected community relevance and scholarly rigour. The co-editorial team collaborated across four provinces and three time zones to coordinate the efforts of everyone involved within tight production deadlines. Finally, the Alberta Centre for Child, Family and Community Research generously contributed proceeds of the 2012 PCWC Symposium in the form of a dedicated Publication Assistance Grant that enabled the PCWC to sustain our ongoing and long-term scholarly collaboration with the University of Regina Press.

This book is a physical manifestation of the applied collaborative efforts of many people who contributed their individual resources and their collective goodwill towards an achievable initiative. As such, this book does demonstrate that collaboration is possible, worthwhile, and within reach. While transforming organizational cultures and outdated practice modalities will need to draw upon substantial additional resources and the concerted efforts of many more actors, it is the co-editorial team's belief that all of these efforts will be worth the cost and should not be tabled indefinitely as a project to be initiated sometime in the indefinite future or perhaps by the next generation of helping professionals. Policies can be easily changed, but effective collaboration requires nurturance, commitment, mutuality, and patience. However, it is only through collaborative scholarship, policy-making, and practice that our collective actions will be noted as successes by future generations.

H. Monty Montgomery

Abstracts

The PCWC Story: A Remarkable Collaborative Effort across Provincial, Jurisdictional, and Cultural Boundaries
Sharon McKay

This chapter will focus on the development and evolution of the Prairie Child Welfare Consortium (PCWC) since its inception in 2001. This chapter will highlight the relationships and partnerships within and between provinces, the inner workings of a consortium through the dedicated work of child welfare agencies, First Nations communities, academics from the Prairie provinces of Manitoba, Saskatchewan, and Alberta. The PCWC has been instrumental in the establishment of post-secondary courses related to child welfare for online delivery to university students, primarily those studying social work; the biennial PCWC symposium; the publication of four books based on conference presentations and relevant research; and maintaining connections between the three provinces in the interest of supporting best practice in child welfare.

The FASD Community of Practice Project: Promising Practices for Children in Care with Fetal Alcohol Spectrum Disorder: A Model for Casework Practice
Dorothy Badry, William Pelech, and Denise Milne

Casework practice for children in care who live with a fetal alcohol spectrum disorder (FASD) requires complex case management tailored to their particular needs. It takes a team to meet the needs of children who have high needs in care, particularly those with a lifelong disability. The FASD Community of Practice is grounded in key research that took place in the province of Alberta from 2003 to 2005 and from 2009 to 2011. This project has demonstrated that the utilization of promising practices that offer more intensive case management are effective in supporting children and youth in their foster care homes. This work is grounded in its approach in several major areas: intensive training on FASD, increased hours for case management for caseworkers, increased contact with children and foster parents, and the provision of negotiated respite resources. This research focused on outcomes of the promising practices and indeed discovered that such practices were of benefit to children and youth, caseworkers, and foster parents. One of the strongest areas of benefit was placement stability, which showed a marked increase during the project period. Additionally, it was discovered that structures around casework, supervision, training, and resource management were important features and functions in the overall response to caring for children and youth with FASD in care. This chapter will address case management and practice issues that are perceived as beneficial to effectively responding to care needs.

The Edmonton Model for Improving Delivery of Health-care Services for Children and Families in Care through Pediatric Case Management
Tami Masterson

This chapter describes the health burden of children in care and the extreme difficulty I experience caring for them from a pediatrician's perspective, focusing upon the creation of the Edmonton Model of Pediatrics for Kids in Care (E-PKIC). E-PKIC has the primary objective of providing comprehensive medical assessments for children in care. We strive to ensure the medical plan, based on our assessment, is carried out to completion. We partner with other health-care providers, Children's Services workers (CSW), foster parents, and biological parents. We have identified and are starting to overcome many barriers to health-care delivery: incomplete history at time of contact with health services; global lack of recognition of the need for consistent high quality health care; lack of communication about movement within the Child and Family Services (CFSA) system; obstruction of medical recommendation; health-care professionals, CSWs, and caregivers who lack knowledge about the health burden of children in care; health-care professionals and caregivers who lack knowledge about children's services; and health-care policies that disadvantage children in care. Through continued team building and practice change we hope to improve the health outcomes for children in care in Edmonton.

Hearing their Voices: The Experiences of Women with High-risk Substance Misuse Involved with Mentoring Programs to Prevent FASD
Linda Burnside

Fetal alcohol spectrum disorder (FASD) is a condition caused by prenatal exposure to alcohol and is considered to be a condition that can be prevented. The Parent Child Assistance Program (PCAP) was developed in Seattle in the 1990s to provide women with a mentoring relationship that would reduce the risk of prenatal alcohol exposure. PCAP evaluations demonstrate that mentoring is an effective intervention to assist women with high-risk alcohol misuse issues in altering the life circumstances that create risk to themselves and to their children, who are vulnerable to being born with FASD. Mentoring programs have been established in many communities in northwestern Canada in response to the need to engage women more effectively in recognizing the dangers of alcohol use during pregnancy. Manitoba initiated two programs based on the PCAP model in 1998, and Alberta's first PCAP programs began in 1999. These two provinces have been the leaders in Canada in the provision of PCAP-modelled mentoring programs. This chapter will describe the results of interviews with women who had completed a PCAP mentoring program in Alberta or Manitoba conducted by a research team of the Canada FASD Research Network (CanFASD), a group of formally and informally connected professionals from a range of research sciences across Canada.

Determinants of Mental Health Difficulties among Young Aboriginal Children Living Off-reserve
Christine Werk, Xinjie Cui, and Suzanne Tough

Mental health difficulties (high emotional or behavioural symptoms) were assessed in young (age 2 to 5) Aboriginal children living off-reserve in Canada using Statistic Canada's 2006 Aboriginal Children's Survey. Health and mental health indicators including health status, visits to a psychologist or psychiatrist, and/or diagnosis of a cognitive or mental health condition were strongly associated with mental health difficulties. Young off-reserve Aboriginal children were less likely to have mental health difficulties if they lived in environments that included any or all of the following: low moves, living in a home that was owned, smaller household size, higher maternal education, no regular smoke in the home, and food security. In addition, off-reserve Aboriginal children who had older parents or who lived with biological parents were less likely to have mental health difficulties compared to children living with younger parents or foster or single parents. Children whose caregivers reported that they explained things to the child on a daily basis had higher rates of mental health difficulties, and lower rates of mental health difficulties were found among off-reserve Aboriginal children who were given the opportunity to watch and learn from their caregivers and/or who had caregivers that told stories to them on a daily basis. On the other hand, children who had high daily screen time were more likely to have mental health difficulties. Addressing these health and environmental influences in early childhood could improve the mental well-being of young off-reserve Aboriginal children across the developmental spectrum.

Research *with*, not *on*: Community-based Aboriginal Health Research through the "Voices and PHACES" Study

Amrita Roy, Wilfreda Thurston, Lynden (Lindsay) Crowshoe,
David Turner, and Bonnie Healy

Aboriginal communities have historically suffered harm from academic research done "on" them by external researchers. There is now growing recognition of the need for community-based approaches and academic-community partnerships to yield research that is valid and meaningful. The First Nations principles of OCAP (ownership, control, access and possession) mandate that research involving Aboriginal communities must be respectful, participatory, and community-driven and that dissemination of results must be done in a way that brings benefit to the communities. Guidelines for respectful research with Aboriginal communities are also offered in the Tri-Council Policy Statement: Ethical Conduct for Research Involving Humans. While the benefits of community-based research are unquestionable, its execution can often be challenging. This chapter reflects on the community-based approach and academic-community partnerships involved in "Voices and PHACES," an ongoing study, which is seeking to understand the determinants of depression in pregnant Aboriginal women. Academic researchers at the University of Calgary are engaging with stakeholders and community members to conduct the study. Five community organizations in Calgary are partners, and representatives from each of them serve on the research team alongside the academic members. Furthermore, there is a separate Oversight Committee consisting of four Aboriginal community members (including two Elders), and a representative from the Government of Alberta's Ministry of Human Services. The study's governance process includes regular meetings to consult with the community partners and the Oversight Committee members on all aspects of the study, ranging from the design and methods, data analysis and interpretation, and dissemination of findings. The latter includes translation of research results into recommendations for policy and practice, for broad dissemination to stakeholders. The community-based nature of the study has introduced certain challenges into the research process. However, we are finding that these challenges can be overcome with mutual respect, cooperation and compromise, patience and flexibility, and clear and open communication.

The Youth Restorative Action Project: Evaluating Effectiveness as a Youth-run Program

Elly Park and Katie Gutteridge

As an internationally recognized youth justice committee, Youth Restorative Action Project (YRAP) is a youth justice committee recognized in Alberta and across Canada as a program ripe with passion, innovation, and mostly notably, good common sense. This chapter describes the findings of a program evaluation, along with the unique perspectives of a group of YRAP volunteers based on the results of this current evaluation. A program evaluation of YRAP was completed in September 2012, and provided YRAP members an opportunity to reflect on the program itself as well as ongoing changes within this community organization. This evaluation discovered some unexpected and intriguing findings as we acknowledged how much of our program to date had been based on intuition, urgency, and immediacy. This chapter shares the process and outcomes of the program evaluation, and provides specific examples of collaborative insight, giving readers the opportunity to better understand YRAP in terms of what we do, why and how we do it, and what we believe.

Outcomes-based Service Delivery (OBSD): The Process and Outcomes of Collaboration

Susan Gardiner, Jon Reeves, and Bruce MacLaurin

Since the late 1990s, provinces and territories have collaborated on the development of a common framework for tracking child welfare outcomes, resulting in the National Child Welfare Outcomes Indicator Matrix (NOM) (Trocme, MacLaurin, et al., 2009). Alberta's Ministry of Human Services used this framework as a foundation for Outcomes-based Service Delivery (OBSD) in Alberta, a collaborative effort involving a lead agency model. At this point, OBSD sites are being piloted in most regions of Alberta. Recent publications reporting on the implementation of OBSD have documented the value and purpose of this policy shift designed to better meet the needs of vulnerable children and families in Alberta (Brodziak, 2010; Gardiner & Hachkowski, 2011). This chapter will provide a brief review of the recent developments in Canadian child welfare legislation and policy with a specific focus on the development of the Alberta Response Model legislation and Casework Practice Model in Alberta. The shift to an outcomes orientation to services for children and families at risk in Alberta has gained momentum, and the authors will provide an overview of how this policy and practice change occurred in this province as well as a review of the literature on related initiatives in North America. Wood's Homes was selected as the lead agency for OBSD for the Calgary Forest Lawn region. A case study of this initiative will examine the key elements of the tender and contract processes, considerations for building systems and partnerships with a lead agency, and challenges in establishing consistent data collection and outcome definitions.

The Voices of Youth with Fetal Alcohol Spectrum Disorder Transitioning from Care: What Child Welfare Agencies and Youth Practitioners Need to Know
Don Fuchs and Linda Burnside

This chapter will provide an overview of the results of a recent study on the experiences of youth with FASD as they transition to adulthood from child welfare care. It will discuss the unique research design and sampling approach used to access youth who have transitioned or were transitioning out of care. The youth shared poignant information about their lives, their hopes and fears for the future, and what they need to transition to adulthood successfully. In particular, youth demonstrated that there is a mismatch between agencies' efforts to prepare them for adult responsibilities when they are developmentally unable to make use of these services until well into early adulthood. A better understanding of the experiences of youth with FASD transitioning out of care is critical for the development of appropriate supports and services to meet their needs. This chapter will address the need to develop unique transitional services to facilitate emancipation for these vulnerable youth, including a reformation of traditional child welfare services. Recommendations for service reformation will be identified, outlining the benefits for youth with FASD and the implications for child welfare service delivery. Finally, the chapter will examine how this research can inform policy development and service delivery, as well as set the stage for future research.

Community Networking for Social Change: A Promising Practice for Aboriginal Child Welfare

Judy Gillespie, Georgina Supernault, and Miriam Abel

Addressing the overrepresentation of Aboriginal children and families within statutory child protection systems appears to require approaches targeting the larger community and structural issues impacting Aboriginal child welfare, while respecting the resiliency embedded within Aboriginal ways of caring for children, families, and communities (Blackstock & Trocmé, 2005). Interorganizational and multi-organizational networks are viewed as being more capable of addressing social issues that cannot be fully addressed by single organizations — including child welfare (Smith & Herbert, 1997). However, they are difficult to establish and often struggle to survive and grow. This chapter of "Voices from the Prairies" will showcase findings from community-based participatory research with a community network that has operated for more than 12 years in the Peace River region of northwestern Alberta to strengthen Aboriginal well-being. The presentation illustrates the use of network analysis as a method to assist communities in developing and sustaining partnerships to address Aboriginal child welfare, including understanding of membership, roles, and relations within the network, and the nature and flow of resources in relation to Aboriginal child welfare.

What Albertan Adults Know about Fetal Alcohol Spectrum Disorders (FASD)

Cecilia Bukutu, Tara Hanson, and Suzanne Tough

The objective of this study was to conduct a survey examining knowledge and attitudes about fetal alcohol spectrum disorder (FASD) and social support required for women not to use alcohol during pregnancy. The survey, commissioned by the Alberta Centre for Child, Family and Community Research (ACCFCR), is an initiative that falls under the Government of Alberta's *FASD 10-Year Strategic Plan* (2008). A population-based sample of 1,203 Albertans over 18 years of age participated in a random digit dialing telephone survey. Data was collected May 25 to June 22, 2011. The results of this research can inform FASD literacy strategies and prevention programs as they shed light on social norms regarding alcohol use during pregnancy, show FASD awareness is low among individuals born outside of Canada and in certain regions of Alberta, and suggest that interventions involving family/friends and/or health-care providers would be most effective.

Collaboration or Competition? Generalist or Specialized? Challenges Facing Social Work Education and Child Welfare
William Pelech, Rick Enns, and Don Fuchs

This chapter will briefly highlight the global transformation occurring in e-learning and assess the development of online social work education in Canada and describe the development of the Prairie Child Welfare Consortium and its e-learning committee as well as explain the process of development and delivery of interuniversity online option courses in child welfare practice. While the triumphant project of globalization has continued unabated by economic downturns, many have come to realize that this planet is becoming increasing local. Indeed, what is arising in our collective consciousness is a more profound sense of economic and ecological interdependence. However, as George Siemmens (2008) has noted, it is not the institutions of knowledge that are primarily driving this transformation; rather it is technology and generational preferences that are pushing post-secondary institutions to shift our approaches to designing and delivering education. This chapter will examine the implications for social work education generally, and specifically the field of child welfare. While we have traditionally adopted a generalist approach to teaching at the undergraduate level, if students had the option of a wide variety of program content, we may see the development of specializations at the undergraduate level in a variety of practice areas including child welfare. Program organization could bring together instructors from various "universities" who have interests and expertise in each area. Indeed, "universities" may no longer be places where one program is entirely situated. One exemplar of just such a collaborative initiative is the Prairie Child Welfare Consortium and its e-learning committee, which has promoted collaboration among three major western Canadian universities.

Contributors

Miriam Abel is a registered social worker in Alberta. She holds a B.A. Honours and received her Master of Social Work from the University of Calgary while working as a graduate research assistant on this research. Her practice interests include multi-sector collaboration, social justice, and child and family well-being. She provides intensive intervention with families involved with child welfare and is an active member of Edmonton's Young Parent Network.

Dorothy Badry is an associate professor in the Faculty of Social Work, University of Calgary. She has long-standing research interests in FASD and child welfare practice, developmental disability, women's health issues in relation to addictions and FASD prevention and is an active member of the Canada FASD Research Network Action Team on Prevention. She joined the FSW in 2002 after a 16-year career working in child welfare in Alberta. Since 2010, Dorothy has been engaged in FASD prevention work using Photovoice from a women's health perspective in the Northwest Territories and currently in Alberta, Manitoba, and New Brunswick with research grants from the First Nations and Inuit Health Branch. She has also received grants from the Public Health Agency of Canada and the Alberta Centre for Child, Family and

Community Research, focusing on a number of projects related to FASD and child welfare practice. She has been a member of the PCWC Steering Committee since 2007.

Erik Bisanz was instrumental in building and maintaining the success of the Youth Restorative Action Project (YRAP) as program coordinator for the past five years. One of the key characteristics of YRAP is that it is run by youth and young adults, and it provides a mentorship program to support youth in working on their goals. Erik's roles included advocacy, training, support, and bridging to resources. His passion for YRAP and its core beliefs has made a lasting impact on the organization and all the young people who come to YRAP for support. In 2011, Erik received an award for outstanding leadership by the Edmonton Restorative Justice Network.

Auralia Brooke is a graduate student in the University of Alberta's Department of Educational Policy Studies. She is a facilitator with Humanities 101, a program that offers university-level education to those with significant barriers to school participation, and works as Student Engagement Coordinator for Alumni Relations. For the past few years, Auralia has been working with non-profit organizations to design experiential learning projects for university syllabi. Her research uses digital media and storytelling to examine non-formal learning within public school environments.

Cecilia Bukutu is a senior partnership/process manager and research scientist at the Alberta Centre for Child, Family and Community Research (ACCFCR) in the Child and Youth Data Laboratory (CYDL). Her research at the CYDL centres on using linked administrative data to study issues, policies, and practices affecting Alberta's children. Her research focus is on child care and on children receiving child intervention services as a result of maltreatment. Cecilia is an adjunct professor in the Faculty of Social Work, University of Calgary.

Linda Burnside is a social worker whose career has focused on the needs of children, youth, and families involved with the child welfare system. A specific area of interest is children with FASD involved in child welfare. This interest led to numerous research projects with Don Fuchs from the Faculty of Social Work, University of Manitoba, on the experiences of children with FASD in child welfare care. After more than 25 years of employment with the provincial child welfare system in Manitoba, she now works in private practice with her company, Avocation: Counselling, Consulting, Research and Training. She continues to conduct research with Dr. Fuchs on children in care with FASD. She also has worked with the Canada FASD Research Network as co-lead of the research team examining the role of mentoring in the lives of women with high risk substance misuse.

Lynden (Lindsay) Crowshoe is a member of the Peigan First Nation. He is a family physician and associate professor in the Department of Family Medicine at the University of Calgary. His roles include primary care physician, primary health service developer, primary health service administrative lead, researcher, and educator. He provides care to the urban Aboriginal population of Calgary from the Elbow River Healing Lodge, a primary health-care service that he developed. He is also the director of the Undergraduate Medical Education Aboriginal Health Program, which is mandated to train all medical students and faculty regarding Aboriginal health and to recruit, support, and train Aboriginal students as physicians. Dr. Crowshoe's research interests include the connections between inequity and chronic disease within Aboriginal populations.

Xinjie Cui has a strong background in research relevant to health and social policy using administrative data and data centre development and management. She is the inaugural director of Child and Youth Data Lab (CYDL) at the Alberta Centre for Child, Family and Community Research and was instrumental in the establishment of CYDL. She also has an adjunct appointment with the School of Public Health at the University of Alberta. Dr. Cui leads the CYDL team and works closely with multiple provincial partnering ministries in linking administrative data from a variety sources and conducting research projects that are relevant to provincial policy priorities. Dr. Cui earned her bachelor's degree in medicine from China. She also has a Ph.D. in psychology and an M.B.A. from the University of Alberta. Xinjie was involved in analysis planning and editing the manuscript of Chapter 5.

Rick Enns is associate dean in the Central and Northern Alberta Region of the Faculty of Social Work at the University of Calgary. His research interests include the negotiation of the 1870 numbered treaties and the establishment of industrial and residential schools across western Canada. He has taught courses examining the link between residential schools and early child welfare practices and recent efforts by the federal government to shape the discourse of reconciliation through the federal apology to survivors of the residential school system. His research has highlighted the complicity of the federal government in the high mortality rates and neglect that characterized the industrial and residential school systems since the 1880s.

Don Fuchs is a full professor in the Faculty of Social Work at the University of Manitoba. He has conducted extensive research on FASD and children in care in the province of Manitoba. Don is a founding member of the Prairie Child Welfare Consortium and has co-edited all four books emerging from the biennial conferences held in Alberta, Saskatchewan, and Manitoba. His current program of research focuses on establishing the prevalence of children with disabilities in care and examining the determinants that result in children with disabilities (particularly FASD) coming into care and their experiences while in care. Don supported development of the First International Awareness, Prevention and Research Conference on Fetal Alcohol Spectrum Disorder (FASD) in Ghana in 2013. Don has extensive experience in international social development work in Russia for the past twelve years as part of CIDA-funded projects. Don's research focus on child welfare and children with disabilities and FASD has resulted in bringing national attention to the needs of vulnerable populations in child welfare care.

Susan Gardiner is a registered psychologist and director of Programs at Wood's Homes in Calgary, Alberta. She has been responsible for the development of Outcomes Based Services related to programs in Calgary and Lethbridge. Susan has over 25 years of experience in clinical practice, management, program development, and collaborative partnerships. Her interest in evidence-based practice and outcome-measurement systems stems from the belief that we can do better in applying knowledge to our practice.

Judy Gillespie is an associate professor in the School of Social Work at the University of British Columbia's Okanagan campus. She holds a Ph.D. in urban planning and a master's degree in Social Work. Prior to obtaining her Ph.D. she worked for many years in Children's Services in Northwestern Alberta. Her research and teaching interests are in theories of child welfare, with a focus on the role of communities and their social, physical, and political infrastructures.

Kate Gutteridge is the former program coordinator of the Youth Restorative Action Project (YRAP), a youth-run non-profit that provides mentorship and support to youth involved in the criminal justice system. YRAP works with youth on issues and challenges that they are facing, especially in areas of education, employment, housing, and addictions. She is currently a student at University of Victoria's School of Social Work.

Tara Hanson is director of Knowledge and Partnership Development with the Alberta Centre for Child, Family and Community Research. She leads provincial research, evaluation, and knowledge mobilization strategies in collaboration with academic, government, and community stakeholders. Much of her work focuses on priorities relevant to vulnerable populations. Tara led the Year 5 evaluation of the Government of Alberta's FASD 10-Year Strategic Plan.

Bonnie (Aapooyaki) Healy is a Blackfoot woman of the Blood Tribe. She has worked for 20 years as a registered nurse, including in Vancouver's Downtown Eastside and in various First Nations communities. She is involved in the Aboriginal Health Human Resource Initiative, and in the development of the National Stand Alone Entity (First Nations Information Governance Centre) and the Regional Centre (Alberta First Nations Information Governance Centre). She was one of the Inaugural Board Members of First Nations Information Governance Centre as the Alberta representative, and held the position of treasurer. She served as the Alberta Region's Regional Health Survey research coordinator through Treaty 7 Management Corporation. She is currently operations manager of The Alberta First Nations Information Governance Centre.

Margaret Kovach is of Plains Cree and Saulteaux ancestry. She holds an interdisciplinary Ph.D. in Education and Social Work. She is currently an associate professor in the Department of Educational Foundations, College of Education, University of Saskatchewan.

Bruce MacLaurin is an assistant professor at the Faculty of Social Work, University of Calgary, and a senior researcher at Wood's Homes. He has been a co-investigator on the three cycles of the Canadian Incidence Study of Reported Child Abuse and Neglect, as well as the principal investigator for provincial/territorial studies in British Columbia, Alberta, Saskatchewan, and Northwest Territories. His research and publishing has focused on child maltreatment, child welfare service delivery and outcomes, youth at risk, and street-involved youth. He has more than fifteen years of front-line and management experience in non-profit children's services in Alberta and Ontario.

Tami Masterson is a pediatrician with PKIC (Pediatric Kids in Care) and through this program provides specialized, comprehensive, and consistent medical care to socially vulnerable children. PKIC works directly with the Child and Family Services Authority in Edmonton. PKIC focuses on the health of the entire family and understands that the health of the child's family affects the health and well-being of the child. Dr. Masterson presented the work of the PKIC program at the 2013 Alberta FASD Conference. Her interests include children's social determinants of health and family-centred care.

Sharon McKay is professor emerita, Faculty of Social Work, University of Regina. Prior to beginning her teaching career at Lakehead University (1975–90), she worked in the fields of child and family services and mental health. She served as dean of Social Work at the University of Regina (1990–2000) and is a founding member of the Prairie Child Welfare Consortium, serving as steering committee chair from 1999–2001. She served as president of the Canadian Association of Schools of Social Work (2002–2004) and served as president of the Ontario Association of Professional Social Workers (now the OASW) from 1985–87. Now retired, she continues to be active in the community and in the PCWC in a variety of capacities.

Denise Milne is currently the CEO of CASA, Child Adolescent and Family Mental Health, in Edmonton, Alberta. Until 2013, Denise was a Senior Manager on Alberta Human Services and her current portfolio is lead of the Provincial FASD Initiative. Denise has master's degrees in Clinical Social Work, Health Care Administration, and Counseling Psychology and bachelor's degrees in Social Work and Criminology, Sociology and Law. Denise is currently working on her dissertation for her Ph.D. in Psychology. Denise is an advanced clinical social worker and registered provisional psychologist. Denise has taught at the Faculty of Social Work, University of Calgary, and conducts investigations for the Alberta College of Social Workers. She also has been in private practice for the past 25 years, in which she sees individuals, couples, and families. Her research interests focus on FASD and adoptive families as well as FASD and child welfare practice.

H. Monty Montgomery (Monty) is of Irish Canadian and Mi'kmaq ancestry from the Eastern Shore of Nova Scotia, although he has resided in Western Canada for most of his life.

Over the past 25 years, Monty has worked in the field of child and family services with provincial and First Nations governments and non-profit Aboriginal organizations in British Columbia and Saskatchewan. He has completed undergraduate and graduate degrees in Social Work and he achieved a Ph.D. in Educational Administration in 2012. He currently holds an assistant professorship with the University of Regina, Faculty of Social Work, in Saskatoon, Saskatchewan. Monty's major areas of scholarly interest are social science research with Indigenous peoples, distance education, and First Nations child welfare.

Elly Park is a Ph.D. candidate at the University of Alberta. Her research interests include youth and young adults involved the criminal justice system, social justice, and restorative justice practices. Her doctoral work focuses on using a narrative inquiry approach to understand experiences of young women with learning difficulties involved in the Canadian criminal justice system. She has volunteered for different community organizations that work with marginalized populations, including the Youth Restorative Action Project (YRAP) for the past few years, and she hopes to bridge her research with social policies and community initiatives.

William Pelech is associate dean (Academic) and professor in the Faculty of Social Work at the University of Calgary. He has been a member of the Prairie Child Welfare Consortium's e-Learning Committee and was a member of a research team on a Public Health Agency of Canada, which has developed a FASD Child Welfare Interprovincial Community of Practice. His practice focus has included FASD, e-learning and distance education as well as group work, and practice in Aboriginal communities. He was awarded a Killam Award in Educational Innovation for his work in the development and leadership of the BSW Virtual Learning Circle. Dr. Pelech has research interests in FASD, group work, diversity, and Aboriginal issues. Dr. Pelech has also received research grants from Canadian Institutes of Health Research, Social Sciences and Humanities Research Council, and the Alberta Centre for Child, Family and Community Research.

Jon Reeves is the chief executive officer for the Calgary and Area Child and Family Services – Ministry of Human Services. Jon brings a wealth of experience to the Calgary and Area Child and Family Services Authority, and has dedicated his career to serving and improving the lives of vulnerable children and families. Jon has spent 25 years in the social work field as a child welfare worker, manager, and CEO and is focused on improving practices in the field. He believes services and supports for children and families can be enhanced through evidence-based practice and collaborative and innovative approaches.

Amrita Roy is presently an MD-Ph.D. candidate in the Leaders in Medicine joint-degree program of the University of Calgary's Faculty of Medicine. Her Ph.D. studies are in the Population and Public Health program of the University of Calgary's Department of Community Health Sciences. She is particularly interested in social inequities and health, and has been involved in numerous academic and community projects related to Aboriginal populations, immigrant and refugee populations, women, youth, and global health. Her dissertation takes a mixed-methods approach to examining the determinants of depression in pregnant Aboriginal women. In the future, she hopes to continue to work in collaboration with Aboriginal communities, both as a population health researcher and as a physician.

Georgina Supernault is the program administrator for the Manning Community Resource Centre. The Centre focuses on family literacy, prevention, and early intervention programs. She also has extensive experience in community organizing and advocacy. Georgina has been a longstanding member of, and currently co-chairs, the Peace River Aboriginal Interagency Committee.

Wilfreda (Billie) Thurston has a B.A. in Psychology from Acadia University, a master's degree in Community Medicine from Memorial University of Newfoundland, and a doctorate in health research and social epidemiology from the University of Calgary. She worked in family services and addictions, and was director of a shelter for women escaping abusive relationships before entering academia. She is a professor, Department of Community Health Sciences, Faculty of Medicine and Department of Ecosystem and Public Health, Faculty of Veterinary Medicine; adjunct professor, Faculty of Nursing; and member of the Institute for Public Health and the IPH Group for Research with Aboriginal Peoples on Health. Her program of research and training includes the development and evaluation of population health promotion programs that address social inequities. Particular foci include the interplay of gender, culture, and socioeconomics as determinants of health; gender-based interpersonal violence; and participation as a key tenet of population health promotion.

Suzanne Tough is a professor in the Faculty of Medicine at the University of Calgary and a Health Scholar supported by Alberta Innovates–Health Solutions. She is also the scientific director of the Alberta Centre for Child, Family and Community Research. As principal investigator of the All Our Babies Study, her research program focuses on improving health and well-being of women during pregnancy to achieve optimal maternal, birth, and early childhood outcomes.

David Turner is a non-status Indian of Saulteaux (Fairford Band, Manitoba) and African American descent. He holds a diploma in social work. He is currently vice president, Western Canada, of the First Peoples Group. David's experience includes initiatives in health, social services, management, and policy development, concerning both urban and First

Nations programs. He has facilitated complex government contracts and public/stakeholder relations with Aboriginal communities across Canada, including facilitation between northern First Nations and Métis settlements and the oil and gas industry. David has advocated on Aboriginal homelessness through previous roles at Inn from the Cold, the Aboriginal Friendship Centre of Calgary, and the Homelessness Partnering Strategy (HPS), and served as Aboriginal health research coordinator in the Faculty of Medicine at the University of Calgary. He works with many organizations to facilitate cultural awareness and partnerships.

Christine Werk joined the Alberta Centre for Child, Family and Community Research (ACCFCR) in 2008 and is currently a research scientist in the Child and Youth Data Laboratory (CYDL) at the ACCFCR. Her research is focused on linkage of cross-ministry administrative data to inform policy. Christine's research focus includes the health and mental health of Alberta's children and youth, as well as the correctional involvement of youth. Christine is an adjunct faculty member at the School of Public Health at the University of Alberta and teaches child and adolescent development courses on a sessional basis for the Department of Psychology.

Subject Index

A

Aboriginal children: in care
placements, 3-5, 54, 175; and child
welfare, xxiv, 3, 6, 158, 201-3, 202-
3, 217; determinants of mental
health, 87-88, 95-102

Aboriginal Children's Survey (ACS)
(2006), xxii, 88-90, 94, 100-1, 103

Aboriginal communities, 55, 88, 112,
116-17, 258; child welfare in, xxi,
12, 14-15, 205, 253; and FASD, 222,
238; and involvement in research,
113-14, 124; wellbeing of, 202,
204-5, 215-17. See also colonialism;
residential schools

Aboriginal Dance Arbour, 204-5

Aboriginal Gathering and Pow-wow,
204

Aboriginal Interagency Committee
(AIC), xxiii, 205, 215; multi-sector
collaboration in, 202, 206-9, 212;

as promoting social change, 202,
204, 210-13, 217; See also multi-
sector collaboration

Aboriginal sharing circle, 5

Aboriginal storytelling, 101

Aboriginal women: and
intergenerational trauma, 116,
204; and prenatal depression, 111,
115-16, 120; as victims of violence,
204-5, 214. See also pregnancy

Act for the Prevention of Cruelty to
and Better Protection of Children,
157

Act for the Protection and
Reformation of Neglected
Children, 157

Addictions and Child and Family
Services Practice course, 10, 257

adjusted mental health difficulties
model: and mental health
predictors, 94, 96-103

Adult Aboriginal Mental Health
    Program, 119
Ages and Stages Questionnaires,
    173-74
Alberta, University of, 239
Alberta Centre for Child, Family and
    Community Research (ACCFCR),
    xxiii, 38, 40, 88, 115, 129, 223, 239,
    265; mental health study, 101-3
Alberta Children's Services, 11
Alberta First Nations Information
    Governance, 120
Alberta Health, 239
Alberta Health and Wellness, 223
Alberta Health Services, 119
Alberta Incidence Study of Reported
    Child Abuse and Neglect, 170
Alberta Innovates-Health Solutions
    (AIHS), 129
Alberta Ministry of Children and
    Youth Services, 115
Alberta Ministry of Children's
    Services, 7
Alberta Ministry of Human Services,
    40, 115, 120, 164
Alberta Response Model (ARM), xxii,
    160-62
alcohol: consumption during
    pregnancy, 28, 46, 64, 83, 222-
    24, 235, 237, 239. See also fetal
    alcohol spectrum disorder (FASD);
    pregnancy; substance abuse
alcohol-related birth defects (ARBD),
    222
alcohol-related neurodevelopment
    disorder (ARND), 222
American Pediatric Society, 102
Anderson, Jordan Rivers, 3
Aoun, Joseph E., 246
Arts, Science, and Law Research
    Ethics Board (ASL REB), 225

Awakening the Spirit: Moving Forward
    in Child Welfare symposium, 10
Awo Taan Healing Lodge, 119

B
battered child syndrome, 157
Blood Reserve, 7
British Columbia, University of, 216
Brochu, Brenda, 214
Burton, Brenda, 40
Busch, Vicky, 247

C
Calgary, University of, 10-11, 117, 119-
    20, 122, 130, 255, 259; Faculty of
    Social Work, 2, 6-7, 27, 251, 253-54,
    256; and social work education,
    246
Calgary and Area Child and Family
    Services, 165-66, 178
Calgary Urban Projects Society
    (CUPS), 119
Canada FASD Research Network
    (CanFASD), 64
Canadian Addiction Survey, 221
Canadian Association for Social Work
    Education (CASWE), 250
Canadian Association of Social
    Workers, 14
Canadian Child Welfare League, 2
Canadian Incidence Study of Reported
    Child Abuse and Neglect, 172
Canadian Institutes of Health
    Research (CIHR), 129
Canadian Virtual University, 247
Cardinal, Richard, 158
caregivers: of at-risk children, 49,
    56-57; and child mental health,
    100-3; and training in FASD, 31;
    for youth in care, 189-90, 195-96.
    See also foster parents

care placements. *See* placements, care

Casework Practice Model (CWPM), 161, 163, 165, 171-72

caseworkers: of children with FASD, 21-25, 29, 49; needs of, 25-26; perspectives of, 32-35, 38; roles of, 37, 39-40, 57; and training in FASD, 30, 35-36; and youth transition planning, 193. *See also* social workers

Centre of Excellence for Child Welfare (CECW), 2, 7, 9, 13, 17, 254

Child, Youth and Family Enhancement Act, 162-63, 172, 175

child abuse. *See* child maltreatment

Child and Adolescent Functional Assessment Scale (CAFAS), 173-74

Child and Family Service Authorities (CFSA) in Alberta, xxi, 24-25, 46

Child and Youth and Family Enhancement Act (CYFEA), 161

child care placements: and Aboriginal children, 175

Child & Family Services Transformation: Research, Policy and Best Practices symposium, 9

child intervention services, 160, 164-65, 172. *See also* child protection

child maltreatment, 47, 157-58, 167, 187

child protection, xxiv, 14, 31, 167, 169, 171, 174, 201, 204; *See also* children in care; foster care

child welfare: and children with FASD, 25, 28; legislation, xxii, 156-57, 160, 196; policy for, 12, 156, 160; child welfare practice, xx-xxiv, 1, 5-7, 12, 40, 117, 244, 251, 254

Child Welfare and Human resources Development Canada, 164

child welfare practitioners, 251. *See also* caseworkers

child welfare system, xxi-xxii, xxiv, 137, 141, 155, 157, 172, 189, 216-17, 263; and Aboriginal children, 158; and addictions treatment, 188; and children with FASD, 24; courses on, 1, 4, 12, 251; reform of, 167, 169; services of, 5, 156, 158; and transition services for youth, 194-95

child welfare workers. *See* caseworkers

children, at-risk, 49, 51-52, 56; effects of trauma on, 53, 59; health needs of, 45-46, 48, 54, 60. *See also* trauma

children, vulnerable. *See* children, at-risk

children in care, xx, 50-54, 56-57, 190; with FASD, xxiv, 21, 26, 28-30, 32, 37-38; placements, 30-31, 49, 52-53, 64, 74, 158, 170-71; *See also* foster care

Children with Disabilities Involved with the Child Welfare System (Manitoba): research project, 7, 9

Children and Family Services Authority (CFSA), 27, 47-49, 51, 54, 57-58, 60

children with FASD, 24, 26, 35-36, 95; *See also* fetal alcohol spectrum disorder (FASD)

Children's Protection Act, 157

colonialism: impact on Aboriginal people, xx, 4-5, 55, 112-14, 116, 129

Commission on Accreditation (COA), 244

community-based research (CBR), 113, 117-18, 120-23, 129; challenges of, 125, 127-28; involving Aboriginal peoples, 112, 114, 124, 128

comprehensive community initiatives
    (CCI), 215
Computer-Assisted Telephone
    Interviewing system (CATI), 225
Conjoint Health Research Ethics
    Board (CHREB), 120-21
Constitution Act (1867), 3
Council on Social Work Education
    (CSWE), 244
Covenant Health Organization, 60
Creating Conditions for Good Practice
    project, 14
criminal justice system, xxii, 133, 141,
    147, 151
Crisis Intervention in Child and
    Family Service Practice course,
    7, 257
Cross-Ministry Committee (FASD-
    CMC), 223
Cui, Xinjie, 88

D
Debolt, Donna, 25, 40
Department of Indian Affairs, 3
depression, 115, 117

E
Edinburgh Postnatal Depression
    Scale, 125
Edmonton-Pediatrics for Kids in Care
    (E-PKIC) program, xxi, 46-47,
    50-54, 56-60
educational consortium, 246-49,
    259-60
e-learning community in child
    welfare, 252-53
Elbow River Healing Lodge, 119

F
families, at-risk, 46, 50-51, 58-59;
    health needs of, 45, 47-49, 59

families, vulnerable. *See* families,
    at-risk
family, biological: in contact with
    children in care, 58, 188, 192
Family Assessment Form, 173-74
family of origin. *See* family, biological
family preservation, as policy, 159
family reunification, 188-89
Family Support Network, 171
FASD 10-Year Strategic Plan, 233, 239
FASD Community of Practice (FASD
    CoP), xxi, 22-24, 26-28, 31, 33-36,
    38-40
FASD Service Networks (Alberta), 223
Federation of Saskatchewan Indian
    Nations (FSIN), 2, 8, 11
fetal alcohol effects (FAE), 222, 237
fetal alcohol spectrum disorder
    (FASD), xx, xxii, 235; and adjusted
    mental health difficulties model,
    94-95; and alcohol use during
    pregnancy, 224, 236; and children/
    youth in care, xxiii-xxiv, 21-23,
    26, 28-29, 183; cost of, 222-23; and
    disabilities, 21, 30, 222; prevention
    of, 29, 40, 63, 223-24, 236-39.
    See also alcohol; pregnancy;
    substance abuse
Fetal Alcohol Spectrum Disorder
    (FASD) and Child Welfare Practice
    course, 6-7, 10, 257, 259
Fetal Alcohol Spectrum Disorder
    Practice Standards, 23-24, 26-28,
    31; Evaluation Project, 27
First Nations Child and Family Caring
    Society, 2-3, 17
First Nations University of Canada
    (FNUC), 2, 2n.1, 7-8, 11, 15-17, 251,
    257
Forest Lawn pilot site, 156, 165-66,
    169, 176

foster care, 99, 170, 186-87, 189-90;
    extensions of, 193-94, 196;
    stable placements in, 158, 187,
    190-91, 196; *See also* children
    in care
foster parents, 22-27, 38-40, 99-100,
    188-91, 268-69; and FASD, 21-25,
    29-31, 35-36; perspectives of, 32-35,
    37. *See also* caregivers

G
Gazzola, Larry, 40
General Health and Social Planning/
    Advocacy, 204
genocide, cultural, 55. *See also*
    trauma, intergenerational
Gillespie, Judy, 216
Gove Inquiry, 159
Group for Research with Aboriginal
    Peoples for Health (GRAPH), 120

H
Hanson, Tara, 40
Hickey, Jamie, 41
homelessness, xx, 47, 55; and youth,
    134, 184
Honoring the Voices symposium, 8

I
Identity, Community and Resilience:
    The Transmission of Values
    research project, 7, 9
Improving Outcomes for Children,
    Youth and Families forum, 164
Indian Act of 1867, 55
Indian Federated College
    (Saskatoon), 5
Indigenous Approaches to Child and
    Family Services Practice course,
    257
Inn from the Cold, 119

Institute of Health Economics, 39
Inuit communities: child welfare in,
    253
Izaak Killam Trusts, 129

J
Johnson, Dude, 41
Jordan's Principle, 3

K
Kelso, J.J., 156
knowledge translation, 117, 119
Konrad, A., 247
Kotkas, Darci, 40

L
Lead Agency Model, 165, 168
living skills programs: for youth with
    FASD, 195

M
Making Our Hearts Sing research
    project, 7, 9
Manitoba, University of, 8, 10-11, 255,
    259; Faculty of Social Work, 2, 6-7,
    251, 254, 256
Manitoba Family Services and
    Labour, 11
Mann, Julie, 41
maternal education: and mental
    health, 46, 100, 103
mental health, 88-90, 115;
    determinants of, 87-88, 95-102;
    diagnoses, 90-94; mental illness,
    3, 54, 95
mental health difficulties, 97-98, 103;
    and the adjusted mental health
    difficulties model, 90-94; and
    maternal education, 100
mentoring, youth. *See* youth
    mentoring

mentoring programs, 70-71, 82; for
    at-risk women, 64-68, 84; benefits
    of, 83-85; as supporting change,
    77, 81; for youth in transition, 191;
    for youth with FASD, 64, 83; *See
    also* youth mentoring
mentors: as providing support,
    69-72, 74-75, 77, 79, 82, 84; for
    youth in care, 192; *See also* youth
    mentoring
Métis communities: child welfare in,
    253
Métis Nation of Alberta Association
    (MNAA) (*also* Métis Nation of
    Alberta), 2, 2n.1, 9, 11, 15-16
Miller, Shawn, 41
Milne, Denise, 40
Mount Royal University, 122
multi-sector collaboration: for child
    welfare, xxiii, 202-3, 208, 211, 215

N
National Aboriginal Organizations,
    89
National Outcomes Matrix (NOM),
    163-64, 172, 175
Native Women's Association of
    Canada, 202, 204, 213
North Peace Housing, 210
Northeastern University, 246
Northwest Child and Family Service
    Authority (CFSA), 211

O
OCAP principles, xxii, 114, 117, 120,
    129
Outcomes-based Service Delivery
    (OBSD), xxii, 156, 161, 170, 174-78;
    as collaborative partnerships,
    xxiii, 164-67, 173

P
Parent-Child Assistance Program
    (PCAP), 63; mentoring program
    of, 64, 66
partial FAS (PFAS), 222
*Passion for Action in Child and Family
    Services* symposium, 9
Peace River Regional Women's
    Shelter, 214
permanence in care. *See* foster care;
    placements, care
placement breakdown (foster care),
    187-88, 190-91, 193
placements, care, 3-5, 49, 52-54, 64,
    74, 139, 158, 170-71, 187, 190; for
    children with FASD, 30-31, 188,
    191, 195-196
Population Research Laboratory
    (PRL), 239
postpartum depression, 114-15
poverty, 2, 47, 49, 55
Prairie Child Welfare Consortium
    (PCWC), xx-xxi, xxiii-xxiv, 13-14,
    265; as collaborative initiative,
    12, 243, 260, 264; course offerings
    of, 251, 257-59; e-learning
    committee, xxiii, 243, 252-53, 255-
    56, 256, 259-60; operations of, 1-8,
    10-12, 15-17; *See also* educational
    consortium
Prairie Child Welfare Consortium
    (PCWC) Conference, xix
pregnancy, 56, 115, 237; and alcohol
    consumption, 64, 83, 221, 223-24,
    235-37, 239. *See also* alcohol; fetal
    alcohol spectrum disorder (FASD)
Prenatal Alcohol Exposure (PAE), 187
prenatal depression, xxii, 111, 114-16
Prenatal Health in Aboriginal
    Communities and EnvironmentS
    (PHACES), xxii, 111

Preschool and Early Childhood
    Functional Assessment Scale
    (PECFAS), 173-74
Public Health Agency of Canada
    (PHAC), 7, 9, 13, 236
*Putting a Human Face on Child
    Welfare* symposium, 9

R
reactive attachment disorder (RAD),
    46, 56-57
*Reconciliation in Child Welfare:
    Touchstones of Hope for
    Indigenous Children, Youth and
    Families,* xix
Regina, University of, 8-11, 255;
    Faculty of Social Work, 2, 7, 251,
    254, 256
Region 10 Child and Family Services
    Authority, 7
Reinvesting in Families symposium,
    10
residential schools, 3, 5, 14, 55, 116,
    158, 201, 254-55
Residential Schools and Child
    Welfare course, 6, 10, 254-57, 259
restorative justice, 137, 144, 148-52
Rouine, Eoin, 40

S
Sagitawa Friendship Centre, 210-11
Samson, Tiara, 41
Saskatchewan Indian Federated
    College (SIFC), 8
Saskatchewan Social Services, 11
School of Indian Social Work, 2, 2n.1,
    7-8, 11, 15-17, 257
Signs of Safety approach, 171
Sisters in Spirit, xxiii, 216; vigils, 202,
    204-5, 212-15
Sixties Scoop, 3, 5, 158

Sloan Survey of Online Learning
    (2010), 243, 245
Small, J., 247
Social Sciences and Humanities
    Research Council of Canada
    (SSHRC), 217
social work education, 244, 246,
    249-50, 4-5, 7; on FASD, 24, 30;
    generalist programs, 244, 249,
    260; online, 244, 250; specialized
    programs, 249, 251, 260
social work profession: and role in
    Aboriginal oppression, 4, 254
social workers, xxiii, 188, 191; and
    collaborative relationships, 263-
    64. *See also* caseworkers; social
    work education
Standing Policy Committee on Health
    and Community Living, 223
Statistics of Canada Research Data
    Centre, 88
Stoddard, Sandra, 28
storytelling: and mental health of
    Aboriginal children, 101, 103
Streissguth, Ann, 27
Strengths and Difficulties
    Questionnaire (SDQ), 89-90, 94
Sturgeon Lake Cree Nation, 7
substance abuse, xx, xxii, 22-23, 25,
    29, 56, 116, 134, 184, 192. *See also*
    alcohol; fetal alcohol spectrum
    disorder (FASD)

T
Toronto Children's Aid Society, 157
Tough, Suzanne, 88
transitional support services for
    youth, 193-95
Transmission of Values project, 7, 9
trauma: causes of, 54-55; effects of,
    46, 54, 56-57, 59

trauma, intergenerational, 55-56, 111.
  See also genocide, cultural
*Tri-Council Policy Statement: Ethical
  Conduct for Research Involving
  Humans* (TCPS), 114, 117

U
UN Declaration of the Rights of the
  Child (1989), 2
United Nations Convention on the
  Rights of the Child, 160

V
Voices and PHACES study, 111-12, 116,
  118, 123-27, 129

W
Washington, University of, 27
Weninger, Mark, 40
Werk, Christine, 88
Woods' Homes, 165-68, 170-73, 177

Y
Yanchuk, Darla, 41
Youth Criminal Justice Act, 133, 140,
  150
youth in care: and readiness for
  adulthood, 186-89, 193; with
  disabilities, 183; placements, 139;
  support networks, 191-92
youth in care with FASD, 183, 190, 193;
  placements, 188, 191, 195-96; and
  transition to adulthood, 184-87,
  192, 194, 196
youth mentoring, 133-36, 139-40, 143-
  44, 148, 195
Youth Restorative Action Project
  (YRAP), xxii, 135-36, 141-42, 144-46,
  151; evaluation of, 134, 137, 139-40,
  143, 150; and restorative justice,
  137, 147-48, 152

Author Index

A

Abel, M., 206, 214, 216

Aboud, F., 98

Adkins, L.F., 244, 245

Agano Consulting, 146

Ahmand, N., 221

Al-Sahab, B., 221, 236

Albert, V., 158

Alberta Government, 160, 162, 175

Alberta Human Services, 160

Alexander, D., 98

Ali, A., 222

Allen, I.E., 243, 245

Altstein, H., 159, 160

American Academy of Pediatrics (AAP), 102

American Distance Education Consortium, 246

American Youth Policy Forum, 145

Anderson, J.M., 118

Andrew, G., 30, 221

Angel, C.M., 149

Angold, A., 98

Anselmo, S., 161

Armitage, A., 160

Arnett, J.J., 185

Aronson, M., 29

Astley, S., 22, 28, 40, 222, 237

Auinger, P., 96

Auspos, P., 208, 212

Autti-Ramo, I., 22

Avison, W.R., 99

B

Babinski, L.M., 87

Badry, D., 22, 24, 26, 32, 238

Baetz, M., 99

Bagley, C., 157

Bailey, D., 28, 237

Baker, W. L., 56, 57

Bala, N., 157, 158, 159, 160

Bao, A.M., 115

Baranowski, T., 102

Barbieri, M., 99

Bardoliwalla, N., 203

Bargen, C., 150

Barnett, T.A., 102

Barr, H.M., 22

Barth, R.P., 158

Bartonova, A., 96

Bastien, B., 7

Bayer, J.K., 101

Bazemore, G., 149

Bazinet, A., 222

Beaudoin, M.F., 246, 247, 248

Beck, C.T., 115

Becker-Klein, R., 203

Becker, A.B., 112, 126

Beecher, M.D., 98

Bellefeuille, G.L., 251

Bennett, D., 222

Bennett, M., 4, 115, 116

Bennett, S., 149

Benzies, K., 238

Berger, L.M., 101

Berkowitz, B., 212, 216

Bettiol, H., 99

Beyene, Y., 100

Bhuvaneswar, C.G., 237

Biegel, D.E., 159

Binder, V., 150

Birch, L.L., 98

Black, T., 155, 158, 172

Blackstock, C., x, xix, 4,
    14, 201, 202, 203, 205

Blaicley, T. L., 56, 57

Blumenstyk, G., 246

Bohjanen, S., 22

Boivin, M., 100

Bookstein, F.L., 22

Booth, C., 159

Bor, W., 96, 98

Bowen, A., 99, 111, 115

Boyle, J., 94

Boyle, M.H., 95, 98, 99

Bradford, N., 205, 206

Braithwaite, J., 147, 149

Brand, A.E., 99

Bricker, D., 173

Brinich, P.M., 99

British Columbia
    Government, 160

Brodziak, J., 156, 164

Brooks-Gunn, J., 99, 101

Brown, H., 114, 117, 124,
    125

Brown, I., x, xix, 4, 8,
    9, 10

Brownell, M., 192, 197

Buchanan, M.J., 114, 117,
    124, 125

Buck, M., 150

Bullen, J., 156, 157

Burakoff, A., 97, 98

Burd, L., 22

Burgoyne, W., 237

Burns, B.J., 98

Burnside, L., 7, 22, 38,
    183, 184, 187, 188,
    189, 192, 193, 194, 197

Butchart, A., 99

Byambaa, M., 99

C

Cabrera, N., 99

Cairney, J., 99

Calam, B., 114, 117, 124,
    125

Caley, L.M., 31

Callahan, K., 4

Callahan, M., 4, 22

Calvert, M., 145

Campbell, D., 222

Canadian Centre on
    Substance Abuse,
    222

Canadian Paediatric
    Society, 222

Canton, S., 185

Capen Reynolds, B., x

Cardinal, J.C., 88

Castellano, M.B., 113

CASWE Accreditation
    Task Force, 250

Chan, M., 203

Chang, G., 236, 237

Chaze, F., 8, 9

Chen, L., 98

Chesir-Teran, D., 203

Chiang, T.-L., 99, 100

Child Advocate
    Manitoba, 183

Child Welfare
    Information
    Gateway, 169

Children's Bureau of
    Southern California,
    173

Chinitz, S., 29

Cho, S.-C., 96

Christakis, D.A., 102

Churchill, W., 55

CIHR (Canadian
    Institutes for Health
    Research), 114

Clark, E., 222

Clarke, D.E., 222, 237

Clarke, M., 221, 222

Clarren, S., 27, 28, 39,
    40, 222, 237

Coles, C.D., 22

Collishaw, S., 101

Committee on Early
    Children, Adoption
    and Dependent Care,
    46, 47, 51, 53, 57

Committee on Sexual
    Offences Against
    Children and Youths,
    157

Costello, E.J., 98

Costin, L.B., 156

Coté, S.M., 100

Courtney, M., 158, 184

Couzens-Hoy, D., 150

Crampton, D., 171

Crey, E., 158

Cross, T., xix

D
da Silva, A., 99
Dahl, M., 192, 197
Daoust, G., 24, 32
Darley, J.M., 149
Davies, J.L., 246, 248
Davies, L., 99
Davis, I., 189
Day, B., 245
de Klerk, N.H., 236
De Riviere, L., 192, 197
De Wit, D., 96
De, R., 99
DeKlyen, M., 99
Dell, C., 221
Dennison, B.A., 102
Denzin, N., 32
Department of
    Education (UK), 171
Dhami, M.K., 151
Dietrich, K., 96
DiGiuseppe, D.L., 102
Dion Stout, M., 113
Dowden, C., 151
Downs, A., 191
Droegemueller, W., 157
DuBois, B., 249
Dubow, E., 102
Duerr-Berrick, J., 158
Duncan, L., 95
Duran, B., 202
Duran, E., 202
Duran, V., 203
DuRant, R.H., 102
Dutton, D.J., 113
Dworsky, A., 184

E
Eastman, G., 190
Edwards, S., 171
Elberling, H., 96, 99, 101

Elgen, I., 96
Ellis-MacLeod, E., 189
Emery, H.E., 113
English, D., 191
Environics Research
    Group, 236
Epstein, L.A., 237
Epstein, L.H., 98
Erb, T.A., 102
Erkanli, A., 98
Ermine, W., 216
Ernst, C.C., 64
Esposito, T., 159, 163,
    172, 175

F
Fagan, J., 99
Fain, P., 246
Fallon, B., 155, 157, 158,
    159, 163, 170, 172, 175
Fast, E., 155, 158, 172
Fein, E., 158
Field, B., 22
Filbert, K., 204
Findlay, L., 89
First Nations Centre,
    113, 114
First Nations Information
    Governance Centre,
    114
Fitzpatrick, C., 102
Flight, J., 221
Flynn, R., 204
Ford, T., 94, 101
Forest, N., 170
Formsma, J., xix
Fournier, S., 158
Fox-Harding, L., 159
Fuchs, D., x, 7, 8, 10, 22,
    38, 183, 184, 187, 188,
    189, 192, 193, 194, 197

G
Gardiner, S., 156
Garner, A., 48, 54
Gatward, R., 94
George, T., xix
Georgiades, K., 95
Gerritsen, S., 99
Gibbard, W.B., 222, 237
Gilchrist, A., 203, 206
Gillberg, C., 96
Gillespie, J., 204, 206,
    208, 209, 213, 214,
    215, 216
Gleason, M., 46, 56, 57
Gonzales, A., 95
Goodman, A., 89, 90
Goodman, P., 161
Goodman, R., 89, 90,
    94, 96, 99, 101
Goodyer, A., 250
Gove, T.J., 159
Government of Alberta,
    115, 161
Government of Alberta
    Fetal Alcohol
    Spectrum Disorder
    Cross-Ministry
    Committee, 64
Grant, T., 64
Gray, R., 236
Green, D.L., 149
Greene, R., 249
Greeson, J.K.P., 191
Grigsby, R.K., 159
Grinstein-Weiss, M., 191
Gromet, D.M., 149
Guerri, C., 222
Gutteridge, K., 134, 137,
    139, 140, 142, 143,
    144, 146, 147, 150, 152

H

Hachkowski, A., 156
Hacking, B., 98
Hale, L., 101
Hallam, D., 96, 98
Hamilton, S., 145
Hand, C., 201
Hanke, W, 96
Harkness, A., 94
Harries, M., 167, 171, 177
Harris, F., 94
Harris, M.K., 150
Hartsough, C.S., 87
Head, J., 236
Health Canada, 221, 222, 237
Health Link Alberta, 103
Healthy Child Manitoba, 64
Heimens Visser, J., 87
Henneveld, D., 64
Hepworth, H.P., 14
Herbert, M., 14
Hermansson, G., 96
Hicks, M., 222, 238
Hiscock, H., 101
Hodges, K., 173
Hogeveen, B., 141, 150
Hollister, C.D., 251
Holmes, K., 191
Holroyd, J., 155, 158, 172
Hong, S., 96
Hong, Y.-C., 96
Hornung, R., 96
Hough, P., 248
Huggins, J.E., 64
Huhndorf, S.M., 117
Humphrey, M., 22
Hurlburt, M., 46, 50, 51, 53, 56
Hysing, M., 96

Hyun, E., 134, 137, 139, 140, 142, 143, 144, 146, 147, 150, 152

I

Islam, F., 221, 236
Israel, B.A., 112, 126
Inkpen, N., 149

J

Jackson, S., 22
Jacoby, P., 236
Japel, C., 100
Jenkins, P.L., 102
Jirikowic, T., 22
Johansson, A., 96
Johnson, M., 102
Johnson, T., 247
Johnston, M., 222
Johnston, P., 3, 14
Jones, A., 157
Jones, K., 190
Jones, K.L., 22, 39
Jonsson, E., 39, 222, 223, 237
Jordan, T.E., 156
Joy, P., 151

K

Kagan, C., 185
Kalland, M., 22
Kania, J., 205, 208, 210, 211, 212, 216
Kanter, J., 22
Kaplan-Myrth, N., 113, 114
Kaplow, J.B., 99
Karger, H.J., 156
Kartin, D., 22
Kelleher, K., 46, 50, 51, 53, 56
Kellerman, T., 222

Kelly, J., 236
Kelly, Y.J., 236
Kelnar, C.J.H., 98
Kempe, C., 157
Kendall, G.E., 98
Kessler, R., 191
Khan, K.B., 118
Kim, B.-N., 96
Kim, H.-W., 96
Kim, J.-W., 96
King, G., 96
King, Martin Luther, Jr., xi
Kinney, J., 159
Kipling, G., 113
Klinger, D., 96
Knab, J., 99
Knitel, F., 157
Knoke, D., 14, 201, 205
Kogan, J., 22
Kohen, D., 89
Kokaua, J., 99
Konrad, A., 246, 247
Koot, H.M., 87
Koponen, A.M., 22
Koppe, J.G., 96
Koren, G., 222
Kowlessar, D.L., 222
Kozol, J., 145
Kramer, M., 205, 208, 210, 211, 212, 216
Kramer, M.S., 98
Kubisch, A., 208, 212
Kuhle, S., 98, 99
Kyhle Westermark, P., 52
Kyu, H.H., 95

L

Lafrance, J., 7, 9
Laing, L., 88
Lalonde, C., 204

Lambert, N.M., 87
Lamothe, M., 174, 177
Landsverk, J., 46, 50, 51, 53, 56
Lanphear, B.P., 96
LaPrairie, C., 149
Latimer, J., 151
Law, J., 94
LeBlanc, C., 102
LeBourgeois, M.K., 101
Lee, J.S., 184
Lee, Y., 99
Lens, C., 222
Leslie, L., 46, 50, 51, 53, 56
Leviton-Reid, E., 208, 209, 211, 212, 215, 216
Li, J., 98
Lin, S.-J., 99, 100
Lincoln, Y., 32
Linneberg, A., 96, 99, 101
Lipman, E.L., 98
Lipnowski, S., 102
Liu, Y.-H., 97, 98
Lombe, M., 113
Lonne, B., 167, 171, 177
Lu, H.-M., 98
Lucassen, P.J., 115
Ludvigsson, J., 96
Lundervold, A.J., 96
Lundquist, A., 22
Lung, F.-W., 99, 100
Lutke, J., 222

M
MacDougall, K., 100
MacKean, G., 112
MacLaurin, B., 155, 156, 158, 159, 163, 170, 172, 175
MacMillan, H.L., 95

Magyar, K.A., 185, 186
Malbin, D.V., 186
Maluccio, A.N., 158
Maracle, D.T., 55
Marchenski, S., 7, 22, 38, 183, 184, 187, 188, 189, 192, 193, 194, 197
Mariano, D.N., 31
Martin, K.L., 114
Maslach, C., 138
Masotti, P., 222
Mattson, S., 222
Matush, L., 98
McBride-Chang, C., 47
McCarty, C.A., 102
McCormack, M., 170
McDaniel, A.K., 145
McDougall, J., 96
McDowell, Z.C., 98
McFarlane, A., 64
McGee, G., 251
McGregor, D.L., 185
McIntosh, C., 89
McKay, S., x, 5, 7, 8, 10, 12, 251
McKenzie, B., 155
McLanahan, S., 99
McLean, N.J., 236
McNamara, T.K., 236, 237
McRoy, R., 159, 160
McShane, K., 113, 114
Meltzer, H., 94, 101
Mental Health Commission of Canada, 87
Menzies, P., 55
Methven, E., 98
Meyer, K., 96
Mikkonen, J., 55
Miley, K., 249
Miller, L., 96

Milloy, J.S., 158
Mills, R.M.T., 238
Minnes, P., 222
Mironova, E., 98
Mitchell, T.L., 55
Mohamed, I., 145
Morris, L.V., 246, 248
Morrison, K.B., 88
Morrissette, P.J., 55
Morton, E.S., 159
Mudry, A., 7, 22, 183, 187, 189, 192, 193, 197
Muhajarine, N., 99, 111, 115
Muise, D., 151
Mulcahy, M., 159, 163, 172, 175
Munson, M.R., 191

N
Nachtigall, R.D., 100
Nagin, D.S., 100
Najman, J., 96, 98
Nanson, J., 237
National Collaborating Centre for Mental Health, 51
National Research Council & Panel on Research on Child Abuse and Neglect, 187
National Scientific Council on the Developing Child, 54, 56
Native Women's Association of Canada, 205
Neves, T., 157, 158
Newburn-Cook, C., 221

Newbury-Birch, D., 149
Newman, V., 114, 117, 124, 125
Newnham, J.P., 236
Norman, D., 26
Norman, R.E., 99
NSERC (National Sciences and Engineering Research Council of Canada), 114
Nutter, B., 158, 159
Nye, C., 94

O

O'Brien, K., 191
O'Callaghan, M., 96, 98
O'Connor, M., 22, 30
O'Donnell, V., 89, 94
O'Hagan, K.P., 47
O'Malley, K., 22
O'Melia, M., 249
Oddy, W.H., 98, 236
OECD, 246
Offord, D.R., 96, 99
Oliver, L., 89
Olmstead, K.A., 158
Olsen, E.M., 96, 99, 101
Olson, H.C., 22
Ontario Government, 160
Orav, E.J., 236, 237
Ory, N., 30
Ouellette-Kuntz, H., 222

P

Pagani, L.S., 102
Page, K., 186
Paley, B., 22, 30
Palkovitz, R., 99
Paluch, R.A., 98

Parker, E.A., 112, 126
Parton, N., 167, 171, 177
Pavlich, G.C., 150, 151
Pecora, P., 191
Pedersen, J.Y., 64
Pelech, W., 22, 24, 26, 32
Pennell, C.E., 236
Perrault, E., 170
Perry, B.D., 56, 57
Perry, B.L., 191
PHAC, 111
Pickford, R., 161
Pierce, D., 244, 245
Pitman, L., 170
Pittman-Munke, P., 244, 245
Platt, R.W., 98
Pocock, J., 202
Polanska, K., 96
Pollard, R.A., 56, 57
Poole, N., 221
Potter, L., 173
Price, A., 101
Provan, K., 206
Provincial and Territorial Directors of Child Welfare, 156
Public Health Agency of Canada, 221

Q

Quigley, M.A., 236

R

Raap, M., 184
Racine, Y., 99
Raine, K., 98, 99
Ranford, J., 222
Raphael, D., 55
Rasmussen, C., 30, 221
Ratner, R., 150, 151

Reading, J., 113
Reichwein, B.P., 157
Reilly, J.J., 98
Reimer-Kirkham, S., 118
Reinink, A., 38, 183, 184, 187, 188, 189, 192, 193, 194
Richard, K., 158
Riley-Behringer, M., 171
Riley, E., 222
Ritas, C., 113
Roberts, A., 203
Roberts, G., 237
Robinson, M., 98, 236
Rodriquez, J., 99
Roemmich, J.N., 98
Rogers, J., 156
Rolls, J., 46, 50, 51, 53, 56
Rona, R., 99
Ronchetti, R., 96
Rosen, M., 156
Royal Commission on Aboriginal Peoples (RCAP), 113
Rutman, D., 22
Rutman, L., 157
Ryan, S., 22

S

Saab, H., 96
Sacker, A., 236
Sallnäs, M., 52
Salmon, A., 39
Sander, L., 246
Savan, B., 112, 118, 126
Schnarch, B., 114
Schopflocher, D.P., 88, 95
Schore, A., 47, 54, 56
Schultz, A.J., 112, 126
Scott, C.M., 112, 119

Scott, J., 99
Scott, L.D., Jr., 191
Seaman, J., 243, 245
Selby, P., 222
Sevcikova, L., 97, 98
Shapiro, S., 98
Sherman, L., 149
Sherraden, M., 113
Shin, M.-S., 96
Shlonsky, A., 159, 163, 172, 175
Shu, B.-C., 99, 100
Shulman, L., 29
Shuttlewood, G., 96, 98
Sider, D., 112, 118, 126
Siemmens, G., 245
Siever, J.E., 238
Silver, H., 157
Silverman, F., 157
Simmons, H., 94
Singh, V.A., 221
Sinha, V., 155, 158, 172
Skovgaard, A.M., 96, 99, 101
Small, J., 246, 247
Small, S.A., 190
Smalling, S.E., 191
Smith, D.W., 22, 39
Smolewski, M., 113
Smylie, J., 113, 114
Sobotova, L., 97, 98
Sotero, M., 116
Spady, D.W., 95
Spencer, R., 143, 191
Squires, J., 173
SSHRC (Social Sciences and Humanities Research Council of Canada), 114
Stade, B., 222
Stahlkopf, C., 149

Standing Committee on the Status of Women, 204
Stangl, D.K., 98
Stanley, F.J., 98
Stanley, J., 202
Stannard, D., 55
Stark, K., 64
Staten, L., 206
Statistics Canada, 89, 93
Steele, B., 157
Stern, T.A., 237
Stewart, L., 98
Stewart, N., 99
Stiegelbauer, S.M., 120, 128
Stoddard, S., 28, 31, 32
Stoesz, D., 156
Strang, H., 149
Streissguth, A.P., 22, 27, 64
Suzack, C., 117
Svenson, L.W., 88, 95
Swaab, D.F., 115
Szala-Meneok, K., 222

T

Talbot, T., 28, 237
Tamim, H., 221, 236
Tanner, J.L., 185
Templeton, R., 99
Teng, N.-C., 98
Teufel-Shone, N., 206
Thanh, N.X., 222, 223
Thomas Prokop, S., 7, 9, 158
Thomas, J., 222
Thomlison, R.J., 14, 158
Thompson, A.H., 95
Thompson, D.A., 102
Thompson, J., 158, 159

Thompson, W.O., 102
Thomson, J., 167, 171, 177
Thurston, W., 113, 119
Tilbury, C., 201
Timpson, J., 4, 5, 14
Tobias, M., 99
Tofflemire, K., 221
Tomison, A., 202
Tomporowski, B., 150
Topitzes, D., 145
Torjman, S., 208, 209, 211, 212, 215, 216
Tough, S., 30, 115, 221, 222, 238
Tracy, E.M., 159, 191
Tremblay, R.E., 100
Trickett, P.K., 47
Trocmé, N., 14, 155, 157, 158, 159, 160, 163, 170, 172, 175, 201, 202, 205
Trumper, R., 87
Tseng, V., 203
Tuhiwai Smith, L., 114, 124
Turnell, A., 171
Turpel-Lafond, M., x, 5
Tweed, D.L., 98
Tweedle, A., 184

U

Ukoumunne, O.C., 101
United Nations Committee on the Rights of the Child, 160
US Department of Agriculture, 222
US Department of Health and Human Services, 222
Usher, L., 191

V

Vakalahi, H., 244, 245
Van Der Ende, J., 87
Van Koughnett, A., 222
Van, D.H., 96
Vanilovich, I., 98
Varcoe, C., 114, 117, 124, 125
Veazie, M., 206
Verhulst, F.C., 87
Vernon, R., 244, 245
Veugelers, P., 98, 99
Vig, S., 29
Vigilante, D., 56, 57
Vinnerljung, B., 52
Vos, T., 99

W

Wahlqvist, M.L., 98
Wake, M., 101
Waldfogel, J., 155, 156
Walker, M.J., 221, 236
Walker, R., 206

Weitzman, M., 97, 98
Wells, K., 159
Wesley-Esquimaux, C.C., 113
Wheeler, W., 145
Whitford, D., 204, 208, 209, 213, 215, 216
Whitney, N., 64
Whittaker, J.K., 159
WHO (World Health Organization), 103, 112
Widom, C.S., 99
Wilkins-Haug, L., 236, 237
Williams, G., 96, 98
Williams, J., 191
Willows, N., 98, 99
Winkelman, M.S., 31
Wolke, D., 236
Wood, P., 46, 50, 51, 53, 56
Woods, D.J., 149

Woolford, A.J., 150, 151
Worthman, C.M., 98

X

Xu, H., 246, 248
Xu, Q., 100

Y

Yang, R., 245
Yolton, K., 96
Yoo, H.J., 96

Z

Zeanah, C., 46, 56, 57
Zehr, H., 148
Zeldin, S., 145
Zimmerman, F.J., 102
Zoccolillo, M., 100
Zubrick, S.R., 98
Zuurbier, M., 96
Zwaigenbaum, L., 30, 221